Mel Cobb

the CP/M handbook with mp/m

rodnay zaks

Notice

CP/M is a registered trademark of Digital Research.
MP/M is a trademark of Digital Research.

NAD, QSORT are registered trademarks of Structured Systems Group Inc.
WORDMASTER, WORDSTAR are trademarks of Micropro International Corporation.
MDS is a registered trademark of Intel Corporation.
Z8000, Z80 are registered trademarks of Zilog Inc.
TRS80 is a registered trademark of Tandy Corporation.
APPLE is a registered trademark of Apple Inc.
PET and CBM are registered trademarks of Commodore Inc.

Cover Design and Graphics by Daniel Le Noury

Technical Illustrations by J. Trujillo Smith

Every effort has been made to supply complete and accurate information. However, Sybex assumes no responsibility for its use, nor for any infringements of patents or other rights of third parties which would result.

Library of Congress Card Number: 80-51415
ISBN 0-89588-048-2
Printed in the United States of America
Printing 10 9 8 7 6 5 4 3 2 1

Acknowledgements

I would like to acknowledge the contributions of the many people who have provided valuable assistance and suggestions toward improving the completeness of this book. Tony Bove painstakingly checked program examples and wrote many of the initial command descriptions. David Haverty of the Computer Center in Berkeley made valuable comments for improvements. Dorothy Kildall of Digital Research continuously supported this effort by providing early information on new developments. Finally, all of the in-house users at Sybex determined the need for many of the practical explanations provided throughout the book. The author will be grateful for any further improvements suggested by CP/M users.

Contents

Illustrations

Preface

This book is intended to teach you how to use CP/M and its resources. No prior computer knowledge is assumed. What is assumed, however, is that you have access to a computer system equipped with CP/M.

CP/M has become a standard operating system for microcomputers. Most users of microcomputer-based systems will at some time utilize CP/M. Depending upon the application programs that they execute on the computer, they will use part or all of the resources provided by CP/M. For example, a data entry clerk typing data into an accounts receivable program will normally only need to know how to activate the required accounts receivable program, and how to recover from errors. On the other hand, an experienced programmer might want to install a new permanent program on the computer system or perform sophisticated editing functions on files. This book has been structured to satisfy this wide variety of needs.

Chapter 1 introduces you to CP/M. It takes you by the hand and shows you how to turn the computer on, and how to perform all the usual operations on files, including diskette duplication. After reading Chapter 1, you will know how to operate your CP/M-equipped computer system and how to perform the following functions: create a file, copy a file, handle diskettes, copy diskettes, as well as use several important commands operating on files. This knowledge will be sufficient to allow you to execute known application programs safely. In fact, you will probably be surprised by the short amount of time that it takes to become proficient at using the computer through CP/M.

After learning the basics of CP/M you will probably want to know more. Chapter 2 is a reference chapter on CP/M, to be read and then referred to as specific information is needed. It presents an overall, comprehensive description of all the CP/M commands, with the exception of PIP, which is described in Chapter 3. Although it is not necessary for most users to understand all of the options available on CP/M, a general knowledge will improve the effectiveness of any CP/M user.

A thorough understanding of the file transfer program PIP is indispensable to the experienced CP/M user. Chapter 3 describes PIP in complete detail and shows how to merge files, list multiple files on the printer, and use the numerous other facilities available.

Chapter 4 takes you through a sample session with the editor program, 'ED'. ED is a powerful text processing program that can be used to conveniently create or manipulate text files. Although ED is complex, it is relatively easy to learn.

By this point in the book, you will have learned about all of the capabilities of CP/M in detail, and you may now be interested in knowing how CP/M operates. Chapter 5 takes you inside CP/M and explains its internal operation. This knowledge is not necessary in order to use CP/M, but is required if you intend to modify it.

Chapter 6 uses a convenient format to summarize all of the commands and symbols used by CP/M (detailed in Chapter 2). Chapter 6 will be an essential reference for the user of CP/M.

Chapter 7 presents an important collection of practical hints. Once you have become familiar with CP/M, and are using the computer frequently, there are important guidelines that should be followed. Chapter 7 makes recommendations on how to handle as well as prevent practical problems that can arise when using CP/M. This chapter should be considered essential reading for everyone.

Finally, Chapter 8 presents a brief historical overview of CP/M and its future.

Many useful reference tables are presented in the Appendices. They should be consulted after you have read the book. These tables include the common binary codes, error messages, symbols and commands provided by CP/M, ED, and PIP.

CP/M was designed to make microcomputers easy to use. *CP/M Handbook With MP/M* should make CP/M easy for *you* to use.

This book covers CP/M and its various versions, including CP/M 1.4 and CP/M 2.2, and the new multi-user operating system called MP/M. It is also applicable to CP/M-compatible operating systems, such as Cromemco's CDOS.

1

INTRODUCTION TO CP/M AND MP/M

INTRODUCTION

The purpose of this chapter is to teach you how to perform basic operations on your computer system using CP/M. No prior knowledge of computers is required. You will first learn the vocabulary and the definitions related to the computer's operation. You will then learn how to turn the computer on, insert your *System Diskette,* and bring CP/M up. You will learn about *files*; how to create them, give them names, and make copies of a file or a complete diskette. You will learn to use the keyboard as well as the screen and the printer to manipulate, display or print the contents of a file. By the end of this chapter, you will have learned how to use all of the most important CP/M commands.

BASIC DEFINITIONS

A typical computer system is shown in Figure 1.1. This system includes the computer, the disk drives, the printer, and the CRT terminal. To use the computer you should sit at the terminal and type on the keyboard. Messages will then be displayed on the screen of the CRT terminal. By using the printer, you will also be able to print text, if you wish. The programs to be executed by the computer will be stored on diskettes inserted into one of the disk drives.

In this chapter you will learn, step-by-step, how to perform all of the operations requried to use your computer system.

THE COMPUTER SYSTEM

A computer system consists of *hardware* and *software* components. The hardware refers to the physical components of a system (bolts, nuts, wires, etc.). Software refers to the programs and the files.

Figure 1.1: A Typical Computer

The Hardware Elements

The hardware elements of a typical small computer (the computer, the keyboard and the CRT display, the printer and one or more disk drives) appear in Figure 1.1. Additional hardware elements, such as a tape recorder, and other devices (a microphone, a card reader, etc.) may also be added to a computer system.

The Computer

The computer itself is typically housed in a cabinet. Because most applications of CP/M usually require a large amount of memory (48K or 64K) and two disk drives, many manufacturers enclose the computer and the two disk drives in the same box. This is the case in Figure 1.1. With the TRS80, the Exidy, and the older SOL, the microcomputer is enclosed in the same box as the keyboard.

The computer's role is to manipulate information. Its operation is controlled by *programs* installed in the computer's *memory*. The purpose of the computer's memory is to store information, either programs, or data. Its size is measured in words (8-bit bytes for an 8-bit microcomputer), in multiples of 1K, where 1K = 1024. Typical sizes are 16K, 32K, 48K, and 64K.

With the present technology, most of the computer's memory is volatile, and its contents will disappear when the computer is turned off. In other words, every time a program is to be executed, it must be loaded from the disk into the computer's memory. This operation is performed automatically by CP/M.

The Disks

Because the computer's memory (called "RAM" for Random Access Memory) is volatile, i.e., it does not retain information once power is no longer applied, a permanent storage device is required for every computer. Disk drives, either floppy or hard, are used for that purpose on small computers. All information can be preserved on this medium, including programs, files (collections of text or data), and a copy of the CP/M program itself.

The CRT Terminal (Display and Keyboard)

The CRT terminal consists of a combination of a CRT display (a television-like screen) and a keyboard. It is the means by which a person can directly communicate with the computer system. The keyboard is used by the user to type characters that are interpreted by the program in execution on the computer. The CRT screen displays information to the user. Unfortunately, like the internal memory of the computer, the CRT is volatile, i.e., the information is displayed temporarily on the screen and then disappears.

In most business systems, a classic CRT terminal is used, which combines a keyboard with a CRT display. In cases where the keyboard is already incorporated into the computer's packaging, a separate (or integrated) video monitor is added.

The Printer

The printer is a *hard-copy* device. It is the printer's role to provide a permanent printout of any information requested by the user. The printer is used to list programs and documents.

Now that we have become familiar with the hardware components of a system, let us define the software components.

The Software Components

The term "software components" refers to the program (a sequence of instructions) and the data. To be more specific, a *program* is a sequence of instructions that, once installed into the computer's memory, will direct the computer to perform specific actions. *Data* are collections of characters or numbers manipulated by programs. Programs and data are logically called *files* once they have been assigned a name by the user. Later in this book you will learn how to use a variety of programs, and how to create or manipulate common types of files.

CP/M itself is a special program, or rather, collection of programs usually supplied on a diskette. The programs used in this book will be stored on diskettes.

There are two essential classes of software: system software and applications software. The *system software* is the software usually provided with the computer system which is required for its operation. It includes CP/M as well as a number of "utility" programs, such as PIP and ED, that will be described in detail later.

The *applications software* is the collection of programs that a user can use to perform specific tasks. Examples of applications software include a mailing list program, an inventory program, a general ledger program, or a word processing program.

Defining CP/M and MP/M

CP/M stands for *Control Program for Microprocessors.* MP/M stands for *Multiprogramming Control Program for Microprocessors.* CP/M and MP/M are both *operating systems.* The purpose of CP/M or any operating system is to execute user commands and allow the user to conveniently use all of the hardware resources provided by the computer. For example, it will send text to the printer, read and process information from the keyboard, and display information on the CRT (display screen). In addition, the CP/M operating system will perform internal chores, such as managing the disk space, or managing the computer's memory space.

Once installed in the computer's memory, CP/M becomes an integral part of the complete system, and is often referred to as "the system." (It should be noted that in computer jargon "the system" may also be used to describe the set of hardware components, i.e., the computer, the printer, the CRT and the disk drives.) In this text, when referring exclusively to programs, "the system" refers to CP/M — the operating system.

System Operation

The operation of the complete system will become clear as we use it. The essential function of the CP/M operating system is to allow the user to conveniently use the computer system's resources. As soon as the computer is turned on, the operating system is installed inside the computer's memory and starts monitoring the keyboard for commands. The user is then able to enter into dialogue with CP/M and to activate the desired applications program. Once an applications program terminates, CP/M takes over again and waits for the next command. CP/M could be viewed as an ever-present servant ready to obey commands and manage the computer's resources, as long as the user is not in the midst of executing an applications program. Specifically, once an applications program (e.g., a mailing list program) is executed, the applications program takes over the memory of the computer, and all further dialogue is with that program. However, when the applications program terminates, CP/M is activated again, and is ready to accept new commands.

In summary, CP/M is a collection of programs which reside on a diskette called the system diskette. The *resident monitor* or the *bootstrap loader* (present in every computer) will usually load it automatically from the diskette once the system is turned on. (Occasionally, manual intervention by the user is required.)

CP/M provides specific commands for transferring information between the devices connected to the computer system, executing programs and manipulating files conveniently. Like any good operating system, CP/M provides many additional features as well. The most important features will be described in this chapter and comprehensive descriptions of all of the features will be provided in following chapters.

CP/M, MP/M and Other Versions

CP/M and MP/M

A number of versions of CP/M have successively been released. This book first presents the standard features of CP/M up to version 1.4, and then points out the enhancements available with later versions, such as CP/M version 2.2 and MP/M version 2.1. Several other versions of CP/M have also been released by other manufacturers as "CP/M Enhancements." For example, Cromemco's CDOS is "CP/M-compatible" and provides added facilities. All of CP/M's features described in this book are applicable to these versions. In the case of Cromemco's CDOS, specific comments are presented in the relevant sections.

The essential difference between CP/M and MP/M is that CP/M has been designed as a single-user operating system. MP/M, on the other hand, is a multi-user operating sytem that allows several terminals to be used simultaneously on a computer system. MP/M provides all of CP/M's facilities and more. The additional facilities provided by MP/M will be described systematically in every chapter.

Cromemco's CDOS

Cromemco's CDOS is claimed to be compatible with CP/M version 1.3. In other words, CP/M version 1.3 commands are embedded into CDOS. However, the reverse is not true: programs relying on CDOS' facilities might not run under CP/M. In addition, CDOS provides a number of additional facilities when compared to CP/M. CDOS uses a file system that is identical to CP/M so any diskette which may be read by CP/M may also be read by CDOS. There are minor differences: the system prompt used by CDOS is a period instead of a > sign. Also, the special CONPROC (Console Processor) program must be present on all system diskettes as a file. In CDOS, another version of the PIP program is provided under the name XFER. It operates essentially like PIP with a few enhancements. However, PIP can also be executed under CDOS.

The primary practical difference is that some control characters that have no meaning to CP/M are interpreted by CDOS and may not be used by application programs written to run under CP/M. Typically, the program will still run, but it may not be possible to use some of the control characters.

Other Programs

Strictly speaking, the CP/M operating system includes only those programs required to dialogue with the computer and manage the file system. However, the standard version of CP/M also comes with several standard utility programs such as PIP and ED (described in detail in later chapters).

Naturally, every user of the computer system will execute a number of specific application programs. Several specific examples will be provided to demonstrate how such programs are executed under CP/M, and relevant definitions will be presented. Because most application programs assume a specific file system organization, it is important to remember that application programs intended to run on your system have to be CP/M-compatible. Also, if they are written in a specific language such as BASIC, they will require a *language interpreter* such as a BASIC interpreter (discussed later in this chapter).

We have now learned all of the basic definitions. Let us turn on our computer and communicate with CP/M.

BRINGING UP CP/M

Approaching the Computer

The best way to overcome a fear of computers is to learn how to turn them ON, and how to turn them OFF, without damaging anything. If you turn on the computer properly, the operating system takes over and waits for you to type a command (i.e., explain your presence and request something). If you fail to say anything coherent or give the wrong instructions, the operating system will ask you to repeat your request.

Try it, if your computer is already turned on. Type random words or letters and see what happens. If nothing happens, press 'return'. The system will probably repeat what you typed, followed by a question mark. It will then wait again for your next request. You cannot hurt the operating system by typing at the terminal. You might, however, erase files if you keep trying. So wait, and read on.

Turning On the System

In order to turn on the system and "bring up" CP/M, you must manipulate a diskette (unless your system is a hard disk-based system). A few words of caution about diskettes are therefore in order.

Diskettes

Two common types of disk storage are used: floppy disks and hard disks. *Floppy disks* are also referred to as *disks* or *diskettes*, and are available in two formats: 8 inch and 5¼ inch. These are shown in Figures 1.2 and 1.3. Diskettes (floppy disks) can be used to store a large amount of data at a low cost. However, floppy disks are relatively slow and despite their large capacity, they are still too small to store some files, (e.g., large business files). *Hard disks* solve this problem. They offer large capacity and high access speed, but at a higher cost. Most small computer systems are equipped with one or both of these disk types. Since floppy disks are by far the most frequently used, all our examples in this book will refer to them.

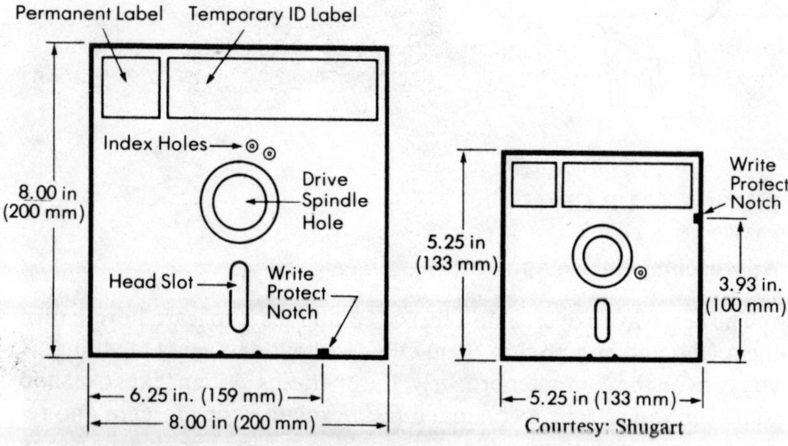

Figure 1.2: Mini-Floppy and Regular Floppy: Dimensions

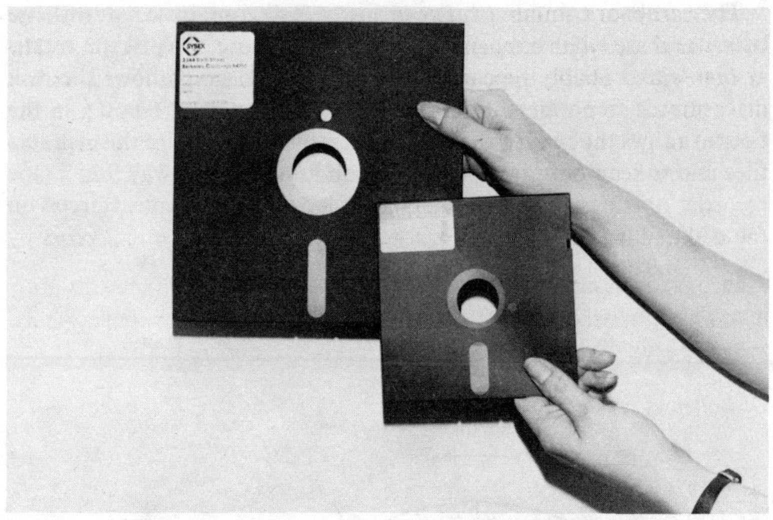

Figure 1.3: Comparing a Mini and a Regular Floppy

Diskettes are magnetic media and are physically fragile. They should be protected from magnetic influence, and treated gently. A diskette is shown in Figure 1.4.

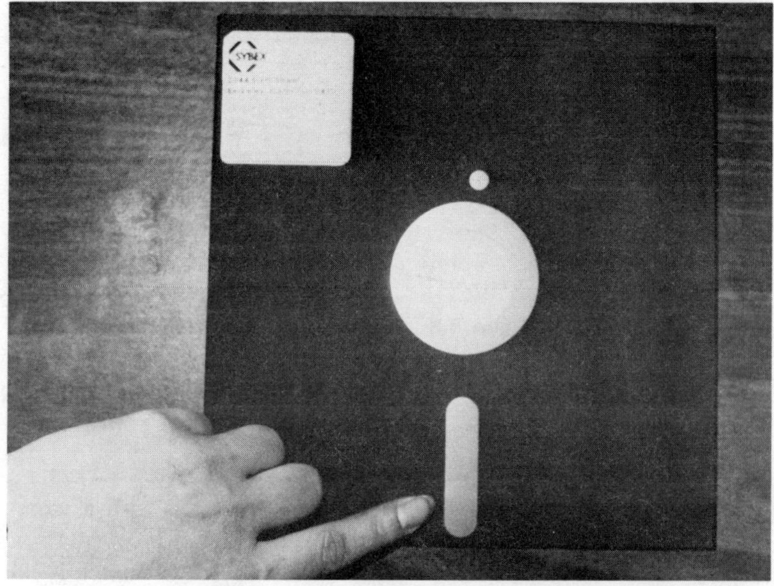

Figure 1.4: The Slot Allows the Read/Write Head to Contact the Disk.

The cardboard square (shown in Figure 1.4) contains a soft diskette of mylar coated with a magnetic oxide. When in use, the diskette rotates at high speed inside the cardboard. The central hole allows the disk drive motor to rotate the diskette. The long opening (shown in the figure) allows the read/write head to come in contact with the disk surface and to read or write information on it in the same way that a tape recorder operates. Information is recorded along concentric circles on the disk, called *tracks*. Each track is logically divided into *sectors* by CP/M (see Figure 1.5).

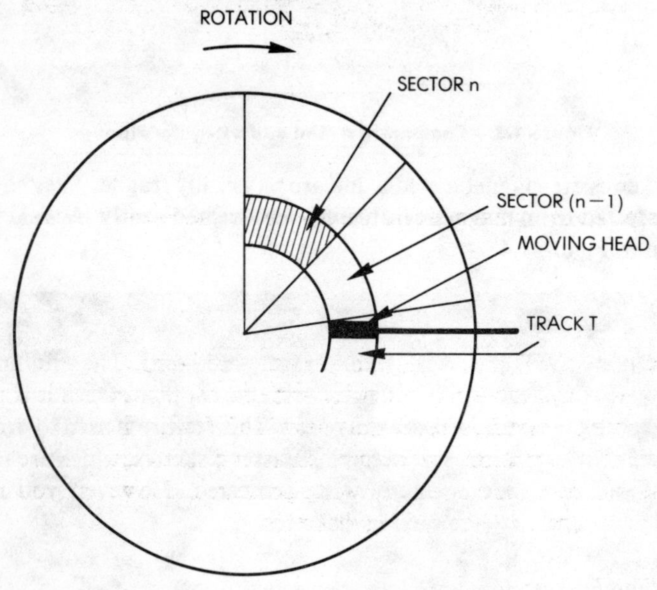

Figure 1.5: Tracks and Sectors

Diskettes are often — but not always — equipped with a *write-protect* notch. With a standard 8 inch diskette, the notch is covered by a piece of aluminized paper. If this sticker is removed, the notch is exposed and the disk drive is no longer able to write on the disk.

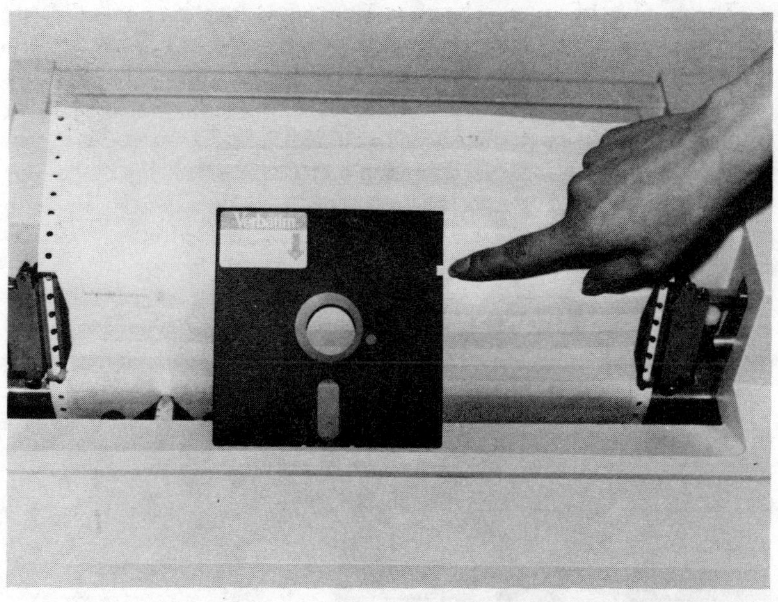

Figure 1.6: 8-inch Diskette is Equipped with Write-Protect Notch

The opposite is true with mini-diskettes (5 inch). The aluminized paper must be removed in order to write on the disk. Once it is positioned over the notch, one can only read. This feature is used to protect important information. For example, master diskettes, which are saved and stored away are normally write-protected. However, you must specify this option when buying diskettes.

Handling Diskettes

Always handle diskettes with care. Do not touch the exposed areas. Do not contaminate them with dust, or scratch them. Also, do not put any magnetic object close to a diskette (e.g., screwdrivers and telephones) as this may damage the diskette. It is important to find out how to insert diskettes into your particular diskette drive. In general, the "rule of thumb" applies: you should hold the diskette with your thumb on the square label in order to insert it correctly (see Figure 1.7). If you are practicing for the first time, use a *copy* of the System Diskette (in case you should damage it).

Figure 1.7: Inserting the Diskette Into Drive 1 (Sol)

If you turn the computer (or the drive, if it is separate from the computer) OFF while a diskette is still in a drive slot, the diskette might become unusable. Power surges may cause the computer or the drive electronics to send unwanted signals to the diskette and overwrite existing information. If you leave your computer and your drives ON when inserting or removing diskettes, you will not have this problem (unless there is a power failure). Similarly, when you want to turn the system off, always be sure to remove the diskettes first.

We will now go through the steps involved in "bringing up" the system. Again, by "system" we mean either CP/M version 1.4, CP/M version 2.2, or MP/M version 1. These versions are similar, although CP/M version 2.2 does have some advantages over version 1.4. MP/M version 1 is almost identical to CP/M version 2.2. All three systems will be described. When we mention "the system," we mean any of the three; otherwise we will specify which system we are referring to.

Turn It On, Insert System Diskette, and Boot

The Procedure

Before we begin, note that the *System Diskette* is the special diskette that holds the CP/M (or MP/M) operating system. You probably received only one System Diskette, so you should ask for, or make a copy to use in practice sessions.

If you cannot find someone to make a copy of the System Diskette for you and must do it yourself, first finish reading this section and learn how to turn your system on, then follow the procedures described in Chapter 3 and summarized below. On the screen displays, underlined characters are characters typed in by you. A "carriage return" (a special key on the keyboard) is shown as ↲. The procedure summary is:

1. Insert System Diskette in drive A
2. Insert a blank diskette in drive B
3. Type the characters shown in this display:

```
A> SYSGEN↵
SYSGEN VER 1.4
SOURCE DRIVE NAME # (OR RETURN TO SKIP) A
SOURCE ON A, THEN TYPE RETURN↵
FUNCTION COMPLETE
DESTINATION DRIVE NAME (OR RETURN TO REBOOT) B
DESTINATION B, THEN TYPE RETURN↵
FUNCTION COMPLETE
DESTINATION DRIVE NAME (OR RETURN TO REBOOT)↵
A> PIP B:=A:*.* [V]↵
(Copying Messages)
A>
```

4. Remove the copy from drive B, label it, and insert it into drive A.

Now, let us take a copy of our System Diskette and learn how to turn the microcomputer on and off. Since different computers have different methods for turning on the system, be sure to follow the instructions provided with the computer.

In order to bring up CP/M, you should:

1. Turn on the computer and the peripherals.
2. Transfer the CP/M program from the diskette, where it is stored, into the computer's memory.

The exact procedure tends to vary slightly for each computer. Computers that were not designed for CP/M, and that are equipped with their own monitor or operating system (such as the SOL) require two successive operations to bring up CP/M. Computers that are designed to run CP/M, however, accomplish this in one simple operation. The computer's own resident monitor program automatically loads CP/M from the disk.

We will now examine an example of each case by describing how to turn on two different microcomputer systems.

Turn on the Cromemco

To turn on the Cromemco computer, press the ON/OFF switch on the back of the box, and turn the key in front to ON. Turn on your terminal, your printer (if you have one), and any other terminals (if you are using MP/M). The Cromemco's disk drives are contained inside the computer box and do not need to be turned on separately. If you have other storage devices, such as a hard disk drive, turn them on also.

Figure 1.8: Inserting the Diskette

Now, insert the System Diskette into disk drive A—drive A is the closest slot to the key (as shown in Figure 1.8). Turn the key to RESET and back to ON (see Figure 1.9). Go over to the terminal's keyboard, find the Carriage Return key (usually marked RETURN or CR), and hit

Figure 1.9: Turning Cromemco On

Figure 1.10: The Keyboard of the Terminal

it two or three times (see Figure 1.10). Suddenly, the system message and a *prompt* will appear on your screen:

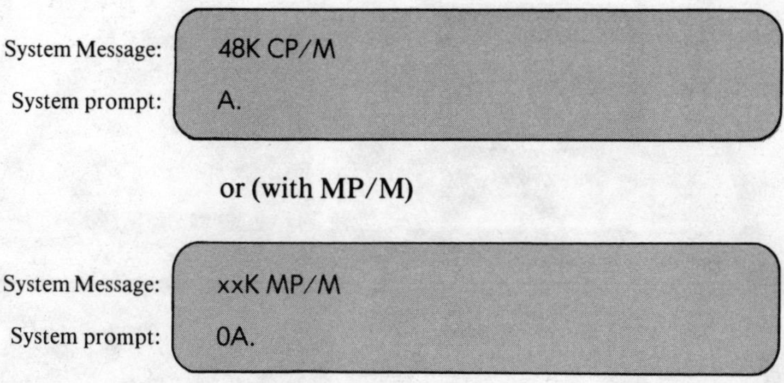
System Message:
48K CP/M
System prompt:
A.
or (with MP/M)
System Message:
xxK MP/M
System prompt:
0A.

CP/M is now up and running and waiting for your commands.

Turn on the SOL

To turn on the SOL computer (an older system) use the switch on the back of the terminal, and turn on the TV monitor (CRT screen). (See Figure 1.11.) Turn on the separate disk drives and insert the CP/M System Diskette into drive A (the lower slot). (See Figure 1.12.) This symbol will immediately appear on your screen:

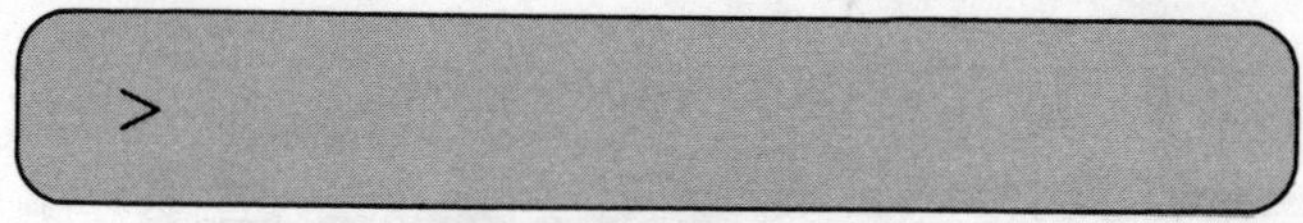
>

This is a prompt from the SOL's monitor program, not from CP/M, which is still on the diskette. Note that if the key marked LOCAL (on the SOL's keyboard) is ON, you are not actually connected to the system. Turn LOCAL off by pressing it.

To bring up the system, type the following command:

> EX E000 ↲

The symbol ↲ represents the RETURN key. The value E000 is the address of the program that loads CP/M automatically from the disk. This value varies with each disk controller. The vendor of your disk controller will tell you which address must be used with its system.

Figure 1.11: The SOL System

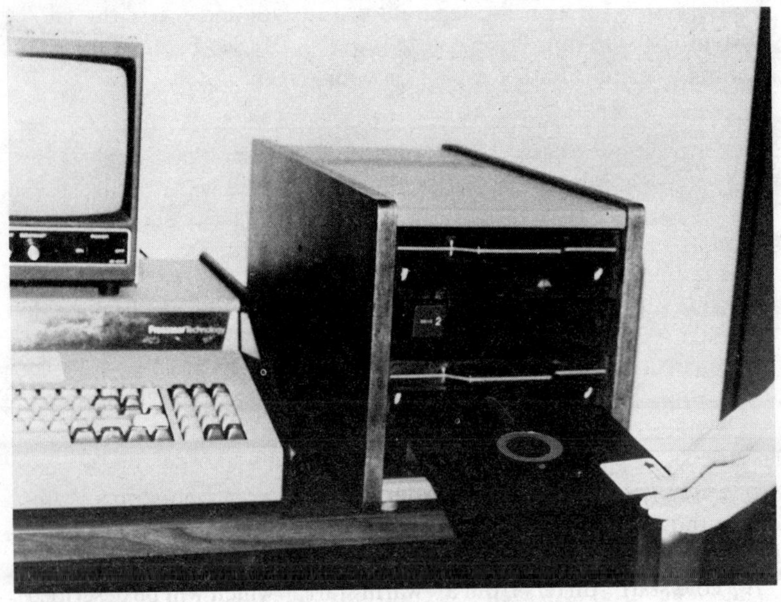

Figure 1.12: Inserting a Diskette in A

After you type the command to bring up the system, the screen will display:

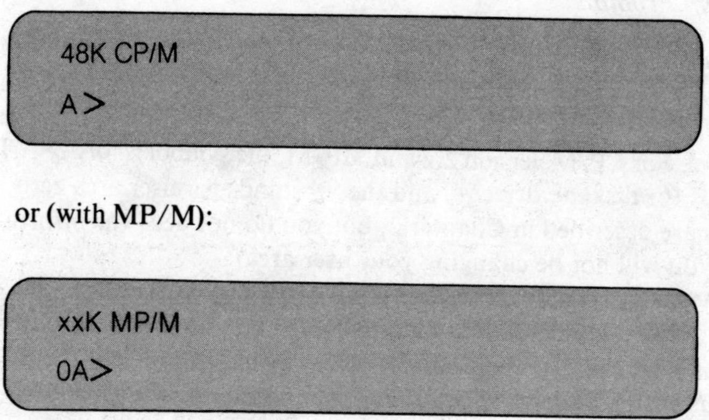

or (with MP/M):

CP/M is ready and waiting for you.

What If SOL Does Not Work or Nothing Happens

Check first to see if the LOCAL key is on (it should be OFF). If LOCAL is on, turn it off, and try typing 'EX E000' again, followed by RETURN (↲).

If LOCAL was off, and the system did not come up, check to see if the UPPER key is on. This key makes all characters UPPER CASE instead of lower case. You must type 'EX E000' in all UPPER CASE (except the zeroes). Push the UPPER key down to the on position (not the SHIFT LOCK key) and your 'EX E000' command will work.

USING CP/M

Ready to Start

You just performed a "bootstrap" operation, or "cold start," or "cold boot." Some people prefer to think machines are cold until you turn them on, or that you "bring up" an operating system by kicking it. The term "bootstrap" actually came from the idea that if you were strong enough, you could "pull yourself up by your bootstraps." Actually, the resident monitor "pulls CP/M off the diskette and starts it," i.e., the system "starts itself."

A "cold start" differs from a "warm start," which will be described later.

Now what does this 'A' (or '0A') mean, and what is a prompt?

System Prompts

A *prompt* is a message or a symbol that the system displays when it is ready for your next command. All systems have prompts, but each uses a different symbol. For CP/M version 1.4 or below, the start symbol is 'A > '. For CP/M version 2.2 and MP/M, the symbol is '0A > '. The A stands for diskette drive A, and the '0' stands for user area zero. User areas are described in Chapter 2, but you do not need the information yet (you will not be changing your user area).

The system prompt always tells you what diskette (or disk) drive you are "in" i.e., the one that you are using. You have at least one drive, and it is labeled 'A'. Subsequent drives would be labeled 'B', 'C', etc. Let us switch to drive B, assuming that you have two drives.

You type:

```
B:↵
```

The response is:

```
B>
```

The system is now running with drive B, and the prompt is now:

```
B>
```

Let us go back to A:

```
B> A:↵
A>
```

Files

Diskettes hold information in *files*. To extract that information, you must tell the computer to go into a particular diskette or disk (via the diskette or disk *drive*) and find a file by a certain name (a *filename*). You booted the system by using diskette drive A. Since you haven't "moved" to another drive, you are still "in" A; therefore, you get the 'A>' prompt. You can move to another drive *only if* you have another diskette in the drive.

We'll show you how to put in another diskette later in this chapter.

Touring the Keyboard

Hit only the RETURN key. The system prompt should appear again. Hit the RETURN key several times, and notice how easy it is to send blank lines to the computer. The RETURN key is always used to send a command to the computer. You always type a command and follow it with RETURN, symbolized by ↲ in this book. There are only a few special cases in which you wouldn't use the RETURN key — for example, when you use the CTRL (control) key and another key simultaneously. These special cases will be explained in detail later.

Let us accustom ourselves to using the system first: type random characters and hit the return key, as in the example below:

A> ANYTHING ↲

ANYTHING ?

A>

If at any time your system fails to display an error message and the system prompt, as shown above, then hit the CTRL key (hold it down) while you hit the C key. (See Figure 1.13.) This combination (CTRL

Figure 1.13: Control C Causes a Warm Boot

AND C) produces a "warm start" (or "warm boot," or "system re-boot"). A warm start essentially interrupts whatever the computer is doing and starts the operation system over again. You will then get the system prompt back.

If this does not work, refer to the section "What's Wrong . . . ?" in this chapter.

You should practice using CTRL and C, (abbreviated ↑C in this book; ↑ stands for CTRL). Remember that CTRL must be held down when you press C. You should also practice using RUBOUT (DELETE or '←' on some terminals). When you type something, you can erase the last character you typed by hitting RUBOUT (DELETE). RUBOUT (DELETE) will erase the next character to the left. You can hold the key down on some terminals and erase the entire line.

In many CP/M versions, RUBOUT (DELETE) *re-displays* the character it erases, instead of making the character disappear. If RUBOUT (DELETE) re-displays (echoes) the character it erases, it would look somewhat like this:

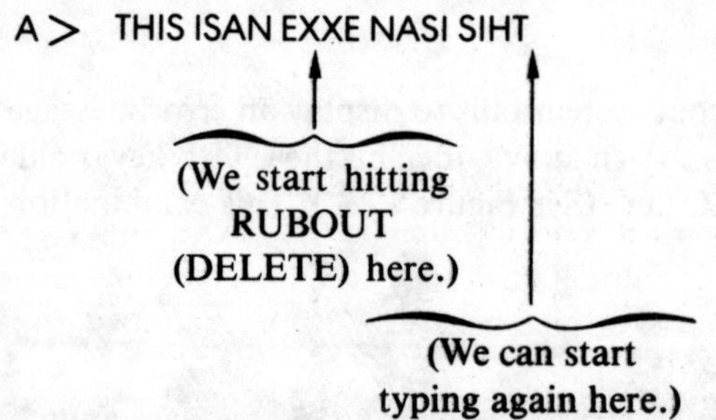
A> THIS ISAN EXXE NASI SIHT
(We start hitting RUBOUT (DELETE) here.)
(We can start typing again here.)

Another way to erase a line is to hit the CTRL and U keys "simultaneously" (i.e., holding CTRL down while pressing U). CTRL and X will do the same thing. They are abbreviated ↑U and ↑X. When you press CTRL and U (or CTRL and X), the system will display a number sign (#), meaning "everything to the left of this sign is erased":

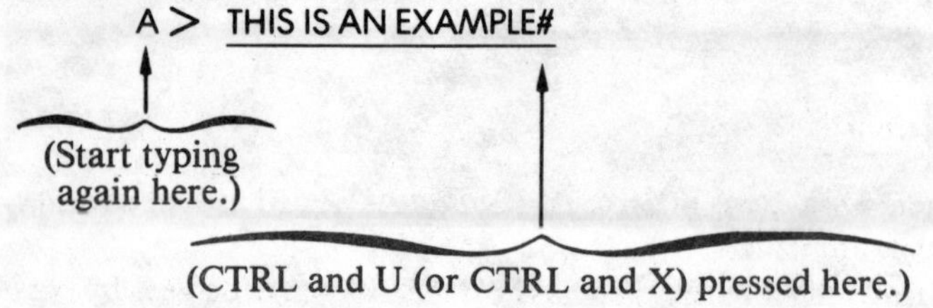
A> THIS IS AN EXAMPLE#
(Start typing again here.)
(CTRL and U (or CTRL and X) pressed here.)

You can again type as if it were a new line. You can, of course, hit RETURN to send a blank line and re-display the system prompt.

What's Wrong . . . ?

Sometimes, something unusual happens, and you may not be sure what caused it. If you hit RETURN and get no response from the computer, then the computer is busy doing something (i.e., running a program). If you inadvertently typed the name of a program you didn't know existed, and that program started running, you can abort the program (i.e., stop it) and return to the system by doing a warm start ("warm boot"): type ↑C.

If a warm start (↑C) does not bring back the system prompt (A>), check to see if any of the diskette drive lights are on. A light on means that the computer is trying to read the diskette in that drive. If the light is on, and there is no diskette, you can try to insert a diskette into the drive so that the computer has something to read. If this fails to bring back the system prompt (or resume the program), you will then have to go back to the beginning and do a cold start (refer to the beginning of this chapter for the section "Turn It On, Insert System Diskette, and Boot!").

In some systems, an interrupt facility is provided to stop the computer. In the case of the SOL, hitting UPPERCASE and REPEAT simultaneously will bring you back to the SOL's monitor.

NOTE: Be sure to remove the diskettes before turning anything off.

System Diskette

It is important to remember that your system diskette is configured for your specific system. If any of the hardware elements of your system are changed, your original System Diskette will usually not work.

In particular, if you change the printer, the CRT terminal, the disk controller, or the memory size, you will need a different System Diskette. If you change your hardware configuration from time to time, be sure to label your System Diskettes correctly so as not to mix them up.

Examining the Directory

Our System Diskette is in drive A. It contains CP/M as well as other files. Let us examine it.

You can find out what files you have on the diskette in drive A by typing the DIR ('directory') command:

```
A> DIR↵
A:PIP       COM
A:ASM       COM
A:LOAD      COM
A:PROGR     COM
A:STAT      COM
A:PROGR     INT
```

If your display goes by too quickly, press the CTRL and S keys simultaneously (i.e., ↑ S). This will stop the display. When you are ready for the list display to continue, press the CTRL and S keys simultaneously again, to re-start the display.

This is a sample display of the DIRectory command. Every diskette (or disk) has a "directory" of *filenames*, one for each file. We know that these files are on the System Diskette because we are in drive A, and the System Diskette is in drive A. Each filename is prefaced by 'A:' to show that the file is in drive A. The first name 'PIP' and the subsequent word 'COM' form a complete filename 'PIP.COM'. 'PIP' is the primary name, and 'COM' is an *extension,* indicating the type of file. They are separated by a period.

Extensions are also called *file types*. For example, all files with 'COM' as an extension are *command files* (sometimes called *transient commands*). All files with 'BAS' as extensions are BASIC source programs, and all files with 'INT' as extensions are BASIC intermediate programs. You do not need to use a specific extension for a data file or text file (a file that holds certain types of information, such as text). You can make up your own extensions to categorize your data files.

It is important to separate the different file types, as a program could appear in your directory with the same name and two or more types.

For example:

TEXT.WRK	(working file)
TEXT.BAK	(backup file)

or

PROG.BAS	(listing in BASIC)
PROG.INT	(compiled form)

Always use the complete filename (i.e., primary name *and* extension, with a period) when you refer to a file, except when you use a command file as a transient command (discussed later in this chapter). Since you now want to create a new file and not alter existing files, you should learn how to insert a new diskette and create a new file on it.

RUNNING A PROGRAM

We will now create a simple file. This file will be used in the rest of the chapter to demonstrate the correct procedures and use of CP/M facilities. The best way to create a file is to run a program that creates a file. An example of this is a word processing program, or a business program. If no one is available to show you how to use such a program, you can use ED, the *editor* that is supplied with CP/M, to create a file. We will run both a sample business program, and then show you how to use ED to create a file.

Let us first insert a blank diskette into drive B (see Figure 1.14). We will use the mailing system NAD (from Structured Systems, Oakland, California), written in CBASIC and supplied with several programs. To create a new name and address file, we type:

```
A> CRUN NADENTRY↵
```

To work, both CRUN (the CBASIC compiler) and NADENTRY must be on our System Diskette. Note that we have used an incomplete filename for NADENTRY. The CRUN program automatically assumes that NADENTRY is of type INT.

In order to describe what has just happened, we must define a new

Figure 1.14: Inserting a Diskette in B

word: *compiler.* CRUN is a compiler. In the instruction CRUN NADENTRY, NADENTRY refers to a program written in the BASIC computer language. In order to execute a program written in BASIC, the computer requires a BASIC interpreter or compiler. Here, the CRUN compiler is used. The theoretical difference between a compiler and an interpreter is that a compiler executes the program more efficiently while an interpreter allows interactive program development. Once the program executes, the effect is identical, regardless of whether an interpreter or a compiler is being used. The sequence is shown below (the dialogue has been abbreviated for clarity).

```
A > CRUN NADENTRY↓
CRUN VER 1.04
NAD   VER 2.0
```

We create a new file called NAMES on drive B (there must be a diskette in drive B):

ENTER FILE NAME: NAMES

ENTER DISK DRIVE: B

We enter a name and address (A specifies "add" a name):

```
ENTER FUNCTION (A, C, D, E, S, OR STOP): A
RECORD NUMBER IS: 7
ENTER NAME: CHARLES FRIEND
ENTER LINE ONE OF ADDRESS: ABC COMPANY
ENTER LINE TWO OF ADDRESS: 123 LUNAR DR
ENTER CITY: PALO ALTO
ENTER STATE: CA
ENTER ZIP: 90010
ENTER PHONE: 408 123 4567
```

We save it on the disk. The 'S' command is specific to NADENTRY and means "Save":

```
ENTER FUNCTION (A, C, D, E, S, OR STOP): S
1 RECORD SAVED
ENTER FUNCTION (A, C, D, E, S, OR STOP): STOP
NADENTRY COMPLETED
A >
```

We are back in CP/M. The action of saving the entry has created a file on B called NAMES. This file contains the name and address of CHARLES FRIEND.

CREATING A FILE WITH ED

A simple text file can also be created by using the CP/M editor, ED. If you have another editor that is easier to use and runs on CP/M, and if its documentation is easier to read, try using your other editor; otherwise, follow along with our simple ED session.

The ED command is a *transient command*, which means that it exists on diskette as a command file (as ED.COM). The System Diskette in drive A should have ED.COM on it. You can check this by using the DIR command:

Type:

A: ↲ (to return to drive A)

Then type:

DIR ↲ (to examine the directory; you should see ED.COM listed)

Type:

B: ↲ (to return to drive B)

Since you are presently in drive B, you must specify drive A in the filename when you refer to ED.COM.

Note that when you are using Cromemco's CDOS, you do not need to specify the drive when typing a command. You can type: 'ED ↲' on drive B. CDOS will look for it on drive B, then automatically look on A (if it is not found on B). This is a convenience feature.

When typing a transient command, you must not type the extension '.COM' with the primary name. To execute 'ED.COM', you only have to type 'ED' or 'A:ED' depending on the disk you are on. (In fact, if you type 'ED.COM', you will get an error!)

First, think of a filename for your file, like SAMPLE.TXT (always separate the primary name SAMPLE from the extension TXT with a period). The extension TXT is not required, but it helps to identify the file.

Execute the ED command by typing: 'ED', a space, and then your new filename:

```
B>  ED SAMPLE.TXT ↲
ED?
B>
```

Wait! We forgot to specify drive A with the ED command (because ED.COM is on drive A, and we are on drive B). Let us try it again:

```
B>  A:ED SAMPLE.TXT↲
NEW FILE
*
```

It worked. Do not forget to type SAMPLE.TXT after ED!

The asterisk (*) is the *editor's prompt*. It indicates that the ED program is up and running and ready for your next ED command. The ED commands are described in detail in Chapter 4, but you can learn a few of them here: The I command *inserts* new text into a file, the B command puts you at the *beginning* of the file, and the T command displays the contents of the file ('*Text*'). The E command *saves* the file and *ends* your session with ED ('End').

You can use ED to create and modify text files. A text file is just like any other file, where the information is represented in binary code called ASCII. Each character on the keys of the terminal's keyboard has an ASCII code number — they are shown in Appendix C. You will probably never need to use the code number, but it helps to know how they're "coded" — in case you should ever see strange numbers in your file, surrounded by strange symbols.

To insert new characters into your new file, use the I command, then type the lines of text. End each line with a carriage return (RETURN or CR), just like on a typewriter. Use ↑Z when you are finished inserting text.

```
*I↲
THIS IS MY NEW TEXT FILE, CALLED SAMPLE.TXT↲
↑Z
*
```

Now add a second line:

'THIS IS LINE TWO'.

If you want to re-display what you've typed, use this sequence of commands:

```
*B↲  (go to beginning of file)
*#T↲  (display contents)
THIS IS MY NEW TEXT FILE, CALLED SAMPLE.TXT.
THIS IS LINE TWO.
*
```

The B command puts you at the beginning of the text file, and the T command "types" or displays a line of text, or the entire file (if you type a '#' before the T).

You should now save the file by using the E command:

```
*E↲
B>
```

The E command saves your file and stops the ED program. You return to the system and your file is on the diskette in drive B. IF YOU DON'T EXECUTE THE E COMMAND, YOU WILL LOSE THE INFORMATION YOU JUST TYPED INTO THE FILE. Use the E command frequently! This is because the text that you type is stored in the computer's internal memory, where it can easily be accessed and modified. When you type E, it is copied onto a more permanent medium, the disk.

If you exit from ED, by turning the system off, or by rebooting (hitting ↑C), you will lose the contents of the computer's internal memory. Only what has been explicitly saved on the disk will remain accessible. This is true for any editing program. That is why we used 'S' at the end of NADENTRY in the previous section.

As a general recommendation, save frequently, especially if you have a tendency to hit ↑C by accident, or if you leave the terminal unattended. You can save as many times as you want. This will update your disk file, and will not result in multiple copies.

MANIPULATING FILES

Displaying the File

To display the file when you are back in the operating system, use the TYPE command, and specify the filename:

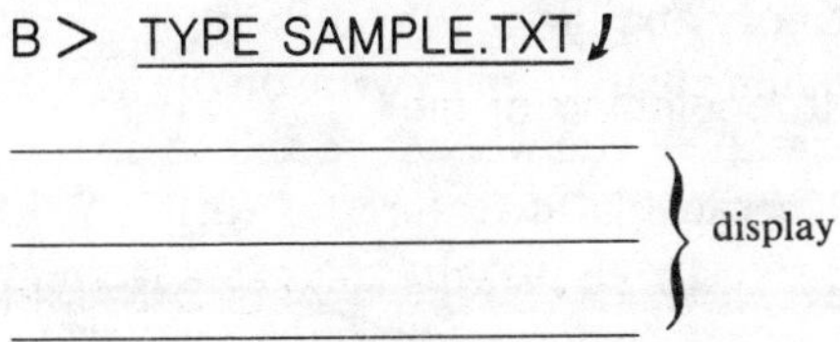

You should practice creating files using ED, and ED's commands. You will find a complete description of ED in Chapter 4. Note, however, that other editor (and word processor) programs are available to run under CP/M or MP/M, and that the other editor programs have different commands and different file structures. Use the editor that best suits your needs. Some are very simple, while some are more complicated and have more features.

If you have more than one editor program, remember which editor you used to create the file, and use that editor to modify the file.

RENAMING FILES (REN)

The REN command is used to change a filename. It is written as:

```
REN Newname = Oldname
```

Always use complete names. For example:

```
REN FILE2.TXT = OLD.TXT
```

Or:

```
REN BETTER.NAD = NAMES.NAD
```

After executing REN, 'OLD' will no longer exist. It will have been replaced by 'FILE2'. Similarly, 'BETTER' will have been substituted for 'NAMES'.

Remember, always use the complete filename, including the period and extension.

LOADING A NEW DISKETTE (PERFORMING A WARM BOOT)

Soon we will want to make copies of diskettes and change the diskette in drive B. To do this, we must first learn how to perform a "warm boot."

When a diskette is inserted, CP/M automatically reads the directory in the computer's memory and "logs" the diskette. If you change the diskette in B and then immediately try to write on the new diskette in B (to create a file, for example), you will not be able to do this. This procedure will not work because of a feature (of early CP/M versions) which is intended to protect your diskettes from inadvertent erasures.

Therefore, once you have changed a diskette, you must specifically authorize CP/M to write on it. This is done by restarting CP/M and is called a *warm boot.*

Let's see how this works. Keep your System Diskette in drive A, and insert a new diskette into drive B. (Let's assume, for example, that you had previously used drive B to make a copy.) Now, go back to your terminal and hit ↑C to "reboot" (do a "warm boot" on) the system.

A warm boot (↑C) reorients the computer to the new diskette. The computer puts information on a diskette by following a map in its memory. When you remove a previous diskette and put in a new one, the map for the previous diskette is still in the computer. Because of the feature (previously mentioned) on CP/M that will not allow you to write on a diskette if there was another one in the same drive before (to avoid accidents), you must type ↑C to authorize CP/M to write on the new diskette. A warm boot (↑C) is performed to *change the map* so that the computer can put information on the new diskette.

If you are only *reading* from a new diskette (i.e., looking up files and their contents) a warm boot is not necessary to introduce the new diskette. If you are writing (i.e., creating a file, creating a copy, or sending data to a file) to a new diskette, in a drive that housed a previous diskette, you *must* perform a warm boot to create a new map for the new diskette. A warm boot is required whenever a new diskette is inserted, with the intention to write on it, unless our instructions specify otherwise (only in special copy operations).

It should be noted that MP/M does not allow you to change diskettes, or insert a new diskette, unless you do a *disk reset* (described later). Also, under Cromemco's CDOS, the feature requiring a warm boot has been removed, and you no longer have to reboot every time you change diskettes in a drive.

After performing a warm boot (↑C), you should get the system prompt (A>). You are now free to access and write files in either drive A or drive B, or other drives if you have them.

You can switch from drive A to drive B by typing 'B:' as a command:

```
A> B:↲
B>
```

You are now in drive B. Use the DIR command to determine what files you have in the diskette in drive B:

```
B> DIR↲
NOT FOUND
B>
```

The message 'NOT FOUND' means that DIR did not find any files on the diskette. This is because we have a blank diskette in B. When referring to a file, CP/M assumes (unless told otherwise) that the file is in the current drive. At this point, to refer to a file in drive A, you can either move back to drive A, or specify 'drive A' in the filename. For example, if you wanted to refer to PIP.COM in drive A, you would say:

```
A:PIP.COM
```

The DIR command can be used to find a specific file. To do this you should type the filename after the DIR command (separated by a space):

```
B> DIR A:PIP.COM↲
A:PIP     COM
B>
```

Another way to find PIP.COM on drive A is to move to drive A, and then execute the DIR command:

```
B> A:↲
A> DIR PIP.COM↲
A:PIP       COM
A>
```

If you switch to a diskette drive that does not contain a diskette, the system will "hang" (the light on the disk drive lights up, then nothing happens, and the keyboard goes dead) until you perform a cold start (see "Turn It On, Insert the System Diskette, and Boot!" at the beginning of this chapter).

If you have only one disk drive, you have no choice — you must remove the System Diskette in order to insert a new diskette. Since this is more complicated, see Chapter 2 for instructions. With CP/M, you cannot make copies of files unless you have more than one drive. However, special programs on your computer may allow you to copy an entire diskette.

Making a Copy of a File

You will always want to make copies of files. In fact, as soon as you have created or obtained a new file or program, you should make a copy of it, and store it in a separate location (in case any mishap happens to the original diskette).

The correct procedure is the following:

- When obtaining a new program or file, make a copy of it before doing anything else. Put the master diskette in a safe location, and work on the copy only.
- When creating or updating a file, make a copy of the file before leaving the system. Label it clearly. Indicate the date. File it in a safe location.

The PIP command is used to perform the copy operations. PIP stands for the "Peripheral Interchange Program." It is a program (written in machine language) that you execute by typing 'PIP'. In order to execute it, PIP must already exist on your diskette as a file with the name PIP.COM (usually residing on the System Diskette).

If you have been following the examples, then you have a text file SAMPLE.TXT in drive B. Make a copy of this file, and put the copy on the diskette in drive A. If this is a valuable file, you should copy it on a new blank diskette. This will be explained later.

Now, let's try using PIP. You should move to drive A first, because PIP.COM is in drive A:

```
B>A:↲
A>
```

Now you can execute PIP:

A> PIP ↲
*

The asterisk (*) prompt is the PIP program's prompt, and it tells you that PIP is up and running. You can now type a PIP expression that performs a copy operation. Simple PIP expressions take this form:

d:copyname = d:originalname

The 'copyname' and 'originalname' arguments are actual filenames, and the 'd' stands for the letter of the drive. PIP always copies from an original file to a copy file. Thus, the original file must already exist; PIP creates the copy file with the name you supply. For example:

*A:COPY.TXT = B:SAMPLE.TXT ↲

This expression tells PIP to make a copy of SAMPLE.TXT, which is on drive B, and to name this new copy COPY.TXT and put it on drive A.

Since you are already in drive A, you can abbreviate the above expression:

*COPY.TXT = B:SAMPLE.TXT ↲

PIP assumes that the copy file is to be created on the *current* drive i.e., the one that you are currently "in"). Since SAMPLE.TXT is in drive B, you have to specify the drive letter. At this point, always use the drive letter when practicing using PIP, so as to familiarize yourself with copying from drive to drive.

After PIP finishes copying SAMPLE.TXT into the new COPY.TXT, it returns with the asterisk (*), PIP's prompt. Hit the Carriage Return (RETURN or CR) key to exit from the PIP program and return to the system:

* ↲
A>

No matter what drive you copy to or from, PIP should return you to the drive that you executed the command from. Since we executed PIP from drive A, we return to A.

If you want to perform only one PIP operation, you can use a shorter command and type the PIP expression and the PIP command in one line:

```
A> PIP A:COPY.TXT = B:SAMPLE.TXT ↵
A>
```

When PIP stops copying, the system prompt will again appear.

Notice how the light on drive B goes on, then off, and the light on drive A goes on, then off, as each disk is accessed. PIP copies the file in segments called *blocks*. If the file is large, it has to keep going back to the original file to get more blocks.

You now have a copy of SAMPLE.TXT called COPY.TXT in drive A. Let us make a copy of COPY.TXT and put it on drive B:

```
A> PIP B:=A:COPY.TXT ↵
A>
```

We did not have to specify a copy filename ('B:') because we want our copy of COPY.TXT to have the *same name* as the original. You will probably want to do this type of copy operation more often than any other. The above command is equivalent to:

```
A> PIP B:COPY.TXT=A:COPY.TXT ↵
A>
```

Both commands create a new COPY.TXT on drive B that is a copy of COPY.TXT that exists on drive A. You do not have to specify a filename for the copy if you want it to have the same name as the original file. You must, however, specify the drive, and the drive must be a different one than the original file's drive if the name of the new file is identical to the source.

This is because you cannot have two files on one diskette with the same name. If you tried to make a copy of a file without specifying either a new filename or a different drive, you would get the statement 'INVALID FORMAT', followed by the part of the expression that caused the error. If you get this error, hit the RUBOUT (or DELETE) key to clear the error.

Most copying involves diskette to diskette transfers (or disk to diskette, and vice-versa), because you want to make backup copies of files on disks or diskettes. Since you are about to learn the ERAse command, you should learn how to backup your entire diskette (in case you make a mistake with the ERAse command).

COPYING AN ENTIRE DISKETTE

You just learned how to copy the file COPY.TXT on drive A to COPY.TXT on drive B:

```
A> PIP B:=A:COPY.TXT ↵
A>
```

You just made a *backup* copy of COPY.TXT.

To copy an entire diskette with one command you need to use a *filename match* (an expression that tells the computer to "perform this instruction on any file that matches this name"). The filename match to use for all files in the diskette is '*.*'. For example:

```
A> PIP B:=A:*.* ↵
```

The symbol '*' will match any name in its field. This command copies all files that match '*.*' (all files on the diskette) on drive A to new files with the same names on drive B. (Note that with MP/M and newer versions of CP/M, '*.*' will only match all files in the current user area.)

When copying an entire diskette onto B, it is best at this stage to have an empty diskette in drive B. Otherwise, two problems could occur:

1. If B already has files, it must have enough space left to accommodate all of those of A. A standard diskette can store up to 270K bytes, including the directory. (If you execute DIR, it will tell you how much space on the diskette has already been used.)
2. If B already has a file with the same name as the one being copied onto B, the copy operation will stop.

Since you are in drive A (in the above example), you can abbreviate the above command:

```
A> PIP B:=*.*↵
```

Both commands search drive A (the current drive in this example) for files that match '*.*', and create copies of the files on drive B using the same filenames. If a file already exists on drive B with the same name, it is deleted.

Remember, filenames can have ten characters to the left of the period, and three characters to the right of the period. The '*' symbol matches any ten characters to the left of the period, and the '.*' symbol matches any three characters to the right of the period.

When using the above command, remember that all files (and only files) on the diskette will be copied. The CP/M program is not a file. It is stored on two reserved tracks on the disk. If CP/M is the only thing on a diskette, the DIR command will show an 'Empty Diskette.' This is because CP/M is a special program which is not stored as a file. PIP will only copy files. If CP/M must also be copied, a special command must be used, i.e., SYSGEN (described later).

A Practical Hint

Anytime that you edit a file, it is preferable to use the copy the next time around: the copy will be loaded much faster by the editor program than the original diskette. This is due to the technique used to allocate disk storage in blocks. On the original diskette, the file is spread over non-adjacent blocks. On the copy, it is nicely compacted on common tracks, therefore the data is accessed much more rapidly.

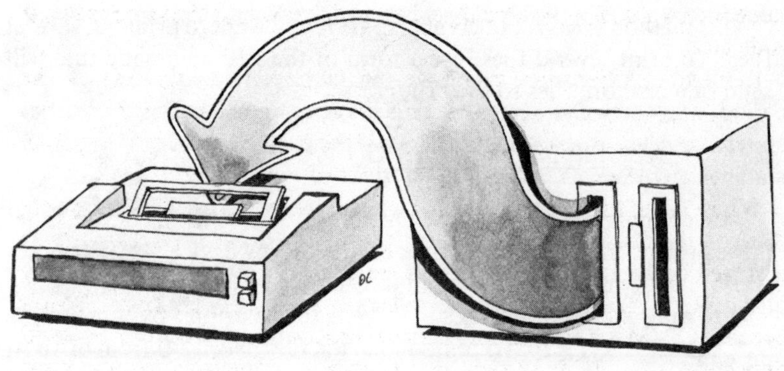

PRINTING THE FILE

You might have two copies of COPY.TXT (SAMPLE.TXT and COPY.TXT on drive B), but before you play with the ERAse command, you should also learn how to send the file to the printer. There are two easy ways.

The easiest way is to hit the CTRL and P keys simultaneously. Now type a "line feed". Notice that your printer (if it is on) will jump a line. Now, anything you type at the keyboard, and anything that appears on the screen will also be printed on paper. Try typing, and using the DIR command to verify the correct operation of the printer. Then, use the TYPE command:

```
A> TYPE SAMPLE.TXT ↵
   ____________________
   ____________________  } display
   ____________________
   ____________________
A>
```

On your screen and at the printer, the TYPE command typed your file. Now, hit CTRL and P simultaneously again. You just turned the print operation off. Use the TYPE command again, and your file appears only on the screen of the terminal (at a much faster speed).

This method is easy, but cumbersome if you want to print out several files. To print several files, use a form of the PIP command that will send one or more files to the printer:

```
A> PIP LST: =COPY.TXT ↵
```

This command sends the file COPY.TXT to the "listing device" that is the printer. 'LST:' is always used as the "listing device." If it does not work, check the STAT command in Chapter 2.

You can send all of the files in drive A to the printer by substituting '*.*' for 'COPY.TXT'. To print out all the files in drive B from drive A, use the following command:

```
A> PIP LST: =B*.*↵
```

ERASING FILES

Now that you have COPY.TXT on drive A, and COPY.TXT and SAMPLE.TXT on drive B, you can afford to erase one of them. Always check your directory first to see what you have:

```
A> DIR↵

______________________
______________________   } display
______________________

A> B:↵
B> DIR↵
SAMPLE      TXT
COPY        TXT
B>
```

Use this command to erase file COPY.TXT:

```
B> ERA COPY.TXT↵
```

If the file does not exist, you will get 'File Not Found' as an error message. If you want to erase a file or another diskette, you can specify the drive letter with the filename:

```
B> ERA A: COPY.TXT
```

This command erases the file COPY.TXT on drive A.

To erase *all* of the files on a diskette, use a filename match for all files:

```
B> ERA *.*
```

This command will erase all of the files on drive B. In MP/M and newer versions of CP/M, the filename match '*.*' will only match all files in the *current user area.* (See Chapter 2 for a discussion of user areas and filename matching.)

UNDERSTANDING CP/M

The Internal Mechanism

You just learned how to bring up a CP/M (or MP/M) system, create files, rename and erase files, copy files and diskettes, and print files; but what actually happened?

CP/M reacts to a variety of instructions: "Look in this diskette for that file by that name, display it, make a copy of it, etc." Let us look more closely at two of those operations: displaying a file, and copying it.

When you tell CP/M to 'TYPE SAMPLE.TXT', you are executing a series of instructions called 'TYPE'. The operating system program accepts what you have typed and reads it when you hit the RETURN key. It reads 'TYPE', and then goes looking for the TYPE program instructions. Then, it reads 'SAMPLE.TXT' and off it goes looking for a file by that name. It looks only in the current drive for SAMPLE.TXT because you did not tell it to look in another drive. Once SAMPLE.TXT is found, the operating system starts to send parts of it to the "console device." The file is sent block by block, until the entire file is sent. Since your "console device" is your terminal, you receive the file on your screen. If you enabled the printer to repeat (echo) everything sent to the "console device," then it would also come out of the printer.

CP/M is a complex program that executes simpler utility programs. The system reserves an area of memory inside the computer's internal memory (in the box) to temporarily store programs and execute them. For example, to copy a file, you have to execute the PIP program. When you type PIP, the system loads the PIP program into this internal memory and starts to execute it. PIP is called a transient command or transient program. It is a program (written in machine language) that executes like a command, except that it is not part of the CP/M "core" and must exist as a file in your diskette with a '.COM' extension (PIP.COM). Other commands, like STAT, SUBMIT, SYSGEN, etc. are also transient commands.

Transient Commands

Transient commands (command files) are actually programs written in machine language (assembly language). After being "assembled" and tested, a machine language program was LOADed (using the LOAD command) into the system's internal memory (called the TPA — Transient Program Area). The load command also provided the '.COM' extension, and the program became a transient command. Now you can execute the program by just typing its primary name (without the '.COM' extension).

For example, PIP.COM is a transient command. Execute it by typing:

```
A> PIP↲
```

You can add your own (purchased) commands to the diskette, such as a word processor, or a language like BASIC (CBASIC, MICROSOFT BASIC, etc.). For example, WORDSTAR, a word processor from Micropro International in San Rafael, California, has two transient commands: WSU.COM and WSMSG.COM. WORDSTAR is executed by typing:

```
A> WSU↲
```

WORDSTAR thereby becomes another facility within the CP/M (or MP/M) system. Another example would be Microsoft BASIC, which has the transient command MBASIC.COM. To execute the Microsoft BASIC system, you just have to type:

```
A> MBASIC↲
```

Always consult the manuals provided with new software for actual execution instructions.

Turning the System Off

When you are ready to turn off the system, first take out your file diskette (in drive B) and then the System Diskette (in drive A). Do not turn off the system with diskettes still in the drive slots, as you may erase them.

After you take the diskettes out, you can safely turn off your computer system by turning off the devices and then turning off the computer itself.

NOTE: do not turn the system off without first making back-up copies of any new files you have created.

A USER CHECKLIST

The following user checklist summarizes the precautions and procedures you should always observe. They are very important. Take the time to learn the instructions in this list before using your computer.

USER CHECKLIST

TURNING THE SYSTEM ON.

Make sure that:

☐ Diskettes are out of the disk drives when applying power.

☐ The proper system diskette is available

☐ One or more blank diskettes is available

☐ All cables are properly connected

☐ All settings are correct on the printer and the terminal

USING THE SYSTEM.

It is important that you:

☐ Have a copy of all diskettes you are using

☐ Frequently save your file onto the disk during editing

☐ Label diskettes promptly with the title, date, and contents, using a felt-tip pen

USING A NEW PROGRAM.

You should:

☐ Make a copy before using your program.

☐ File away the original of the new program in a safe location.

LEAVING THE SYSTEM.

It is important that you:

☐ Have a back-up copy of all new files created

☐ Remove diskettes from the drives.

SUMMARY

You have now learned how to turn the system on and off, how to get CP/M started, and how to use the basic CP/M commands and utilities, such as DIR, REN, ERA, PIP, ED, as well as special functions, such as DELete and CTRL-C.

You have also learned how to list a file on the printer or screen, and make copies of your files as well as of CP/M.

You may be surprised to learn that you now know enough about CP/M to run most application programs without problems. However, if you want to learn more about your operating system and its resources, read on.

2

CP/M AND MP/M FACILITIES

INTRODUCTION

This chapter will teach you all of the CP/M commands, including ERA, REN, STAT, DIR, and the control characters. Assembling, loading, dumping, executing, debugging and saving programs (ASM, LOAD, DUMP, DDT, SAVE), and submitting a file for execution (SUBMIT and XSUB) will also be covered. A summary of the control facilities and the commands available with CP/M will be presented. Each command and its use will be examined in detail. It is not necesary, at this point, to memorize the commands, but you should review them, as they may soon prove helpful.

Even if you are just a casual CP/M user, you should learn the following:

- The five control characters used most often (described in the next section)
- How to erase files with ERA
- How to change filenames with REN
- How to know your file space with STAT
- How to copy your CP/M "system" with SYSGEN

It is useful, although not absolutely necessary, to read this chapter in its entirety once. However, as you use CP/M, you should read this chapter again if you want to take full advantage of the resources CP/M and MP/M offer.

The material presented in this chapter will enable you to use all of CP/M's commands (and most of MP/M's commands). You will probably refer to this chapter frequently, until you are completely familiar with CP/M's actions and command conventions. You will then find Chapter 6 to be a useful reference guide.

Command descriptions are based primarily on CP/M version 1.4. CP/M version 2.2 has a few enhancements, whereas MP/M version 1.0 has many. Since most users have version 1.4, we will focus our discussions and examples of CP/M on that particular version, and describe version 2.2 and MP/M afterwards in a special section in this chapter. If you are using version 2.2 of CP/M, or MP/M, you should read this section first. CP/M version 2.2 and MP/M enhanced commands are also included in the summary, and in Chapter 6.

The conventions used by CP/M will be described first: control characters, built-in commands, transient commands, and filenames. Then, each of the built-in commands: DIR, TYPE, REN, ERA, and SAVE; and transient commands: SYSGEN, PIP, ED, STAT, ASM, LOAD, DUMP, DDT, SUBMIT, and MOVCPM, will be presented. Several important features of CP/M version 2.2 and MP/M will also be described.

COMMANDS

As a convention for describing command formats throughout this book, each command will be shown in UPPER CASE letters. The "arguments" that must be supplied with the commands will be shown in lower case letters. If the "arguments" are in *italics*, then they are optional. If two "arguments" are enclosed in brackets { }, then you must choose between them. These conventions are also used in Chapter 6.

The symbol ↲ stands for the RETURN key, sometimes called CR, which confirms the command to the system (i.e., causes execution of the command) and also moves the cursor to the next line (i.e., generates a carriage return/line feed). The symbol ↑ stands for the CTRL (control) key, and is used to symbolize holding down the CTRL key while hitting another key (e.g., ↑X means "hold down CTRL and hit the X key").

Let us begin by introducing the control characters. They are described in Figure 2.1.

Control characters may be used while typing any CP/M command line. For example, assume that you started typing:

A > <u>PIP B:NEW.NCD =</u>

However, you actually meant to type NAD, not NCD. If you hit the DEL key three times, you can erase the last three characters:

A > <u>PIP B:NEW.NCD == DC</u>

and complete the command, except for the RETURN:

A > <u>PIP B:NEW.NCD == DCAD = A:OLD.NAD</u>

Function	Key(s) to Hit	Operation
Erase the last character typed:	RUBOUT (also called DELETE) CTRL-H†	Cursor repeats character (echoes)
Erase the entire line:	CTRL-U	CURSOR moves to next line and displays '#' to signal for new command
	CTRL-X†	Cursor moves back to beginning of line, deleting the line
Re-type current command line:	CTRL-R	Types a clean line Used after corrections
Transmit (execute) the command line:	RETURN (sometimes called CR) or CTRL-M or CTRL-J (LINE FEED)	Current command is executed Cursor moves to next line for new command
Type a long command line (longer than the terminal's line length):	CTRL-E	Cursor moves to next line without transmitting or executing command
Restart (warm boot) system:	CTRL-C	Restarts CP/M Stops many processes being executed
Restart (warm boot) to allow writing on a newly-inserted diskette:	CTRL-C	Allows you to write on a new diskette replacing the previous one
Abort an MP/M process (program) running:	CTRL-C††	Aborts the process and restarts MP/M
End PIP (copy) operations:	RETURN (CR) or CTRL-M	Terminates PIP Returns control to CP/M or MP/M

† indicates CP/M version 2.2 and MP/M only
††indicates MP/M only

Figure 2.1: Control Characters

Function	Key(s) to Hit	Operation
End DDT (debugger) operations:	G0 followed by RETURN	Returns control to CP/M or MP/M
End ED (editor program) operations:	E, followed by RETURN	Saves text in source file and buffer
End ED inserting operation:	CTRL-Z	Restores control to ED
Detach a running program (process) from a terminal:	CTRL-D††	Restores control to MP/M (program runs detached)
Send everything to be typed and displayed at terminal to printer:	CTRL-P	Printer echoes what you type and what CRT displays
Stop sending everything to printer:	CTRL-P	On/Off switch for printer echo
Stop fast displays for easy reading:	CTRL-S	Halts the display until you hit another ↑S
Start display after stopping it:	CTRL-S	On/Off switch for delaying displays

† indicates CP/M version 2.2 and MP/M only
†† indicates MP/M only

Figure 2.1: Control Characters (cont.)

This looks confusing, but try it on your computer. Use CTRL-R, and you will get a clean, retyped line:

A > PIP B:NEW.NAD = A:OLD.NAD↲

The typed command line is now correct. You can type a RETURN, and the command will execute.

Similarly, if you typed an incorrect command, you can erase the entire line with a CTRL-U (see Figure 2.1). The five control characters available for input on all CP/M versions are summarized in Figure 2.2. Be sure to familiarize yourself with all of them.

Referring back to Figure 2.1, note that it lists all of the control characters available, not just for CP/M, but for all CP/M versions when using the PIP, ED and DDT commands. It is important to know the commands available under CP/M. Depending upon the version

rubout/delete	delete and echo last character
CTRL-U or CTRL-X	delete line
CTRL-R	retype line
CTRL-E	continue on next line
CTRL-C	reboot CP/M

(Note: CTRL-P and CTRL-S are also available for printer control.)

Figure 2.2: Summary of Editing Controls

(CP/M or MP/M), there are at least five built-in commands:

TYPE

DIR

REN

ERA

SAVE

and several standard "transient" commands, which must be present as files on the system diskette in order to be executed when called. These transient commands are:

SYSGEN

ED

PIP

ASM

LOAD

DUMP

DDT

SUBMIT

MOVECPM

STAT

All of these commands are listed in Figure 2.3. Each will be described in detail in this chapter.

Handling Devices	Command	Operation
Display and alter device assignments:	STAT ↵ STAT device assignments ↵	*NOTE: STAT VAL: ↵ will display possible STAT commands
Switch from one disk drive to another	d: ↵	d is the symbol of the new drive (A, B, C, D)
Copy from one disk to another:	PIP ↵ PIP destination = source ↵	Peripheral Interchange Program Destination filenames
Print, punch, copy, combine, and do other file operations with devices:	PIP parameters	See discussion of PIP
Spool files to the printer:††	SPOOL filename filename . . . ↵	
Stop and delete the spool queue:††	STOPSPLR ↵	
Display console (terminal) number: ††	CONSOLE ↵	
Enable system operator to change disks: ††	DSKRESET ↵	The command asks other users to enable a disk change
Make a copy of the CP/M system (make a new system diskette):	SYSGEN ↵	Starts up the SYSGEN program
Create a different version of the CP/M system (reconfigure for different memory size):	MOVCPM ↵	Starts up the MOVCPM program
Make a copy of the MP/M system, or reconfigure system: ††	Use the commands MPMLDR or SYSGEN *only after* reading important information in the "MP/M Alteration Guide" of Digital Research's documentation	
Display MP/M system run-time status: ††	MPMSTAT ↵	Displays process information

† indicates CP/M version 2.2 and MP/M only
†† indicates MP/M only

Figure 2.3: CP/M Commands

Handling Devices	Command	Operation
Change user area: †	USER *n* ↵	*n* is a user area number -- see the section "User Areas" in this chapter Without *n*, USER displays the current user area
Display or set the date and time: ††	TOD ↵ TOD mm/dd/yy hh:mm:ss ↵	Displays time and date Sets time and date

Handling Files	Command Format	Operation
Creating a file on a disk:	ED filename ↵	CP/M's editor program creates text files You can also use any other editor program
Renaming a file:	REN newname = oldname ↵	Changes name of file
Erasing (deleting) files:	ERA { filename / filename match } ↵	Searches for filename or match for a filename match string
Copying a file:	PIP newcopyname = oldcopyname ↵	Copies a file and gives it a name
Copying from one drive to another (single copying):	PIP d:newcopyname = d:oldcopyname (where d is the letter of the drive) (see description of PIP for abbreviations)	
Doing many copy operations:	PIP ↵ *newcopyname = oldcopyname ↵ *d:newcopyname = d:oldcopyname ↵ * ↵	Use RETURN to terminate PIP

Figure 2.3: CP/M Commands (cont.)

Handling Files	Command Format	Operation
Display contents of text file:	TYPE filename	File contents are displayed Use ↑P to print it
Modify contents of text file:	ED filename	ED program allows you to edit text files
List filenames in directory:	DIR { *filename* / *filename match* }	DIR by itself lists all filenames
Display file and disk sizes:	STAT { d:filename / d:filename match }	This displays sizes of files and space taken up
	STAT *d:*	This displays the current disk, or, optionally, the disk *d* space that is free
Display file attributes † (indicators):	STAT *d*:filename	Display attributes like R/O for read-only or SYS for system file
Create an assembly language program:	ED filename	CP/M's editor program creates text files. Any CP/M-based editor program can be used to create text files

Handling Programs	Command	Operation
Assemble an assembly language program:	ASM filename	Creates an "object file" in machine language "Hex"
Produce a relocatable program: ††	GENMOD filename. HEX filename. PRL $bytes ↵	Produces .PRL file from .HEX file, with optional extra memory expressed in hexadecimal digits for $bytes (See Chapter 3)

Figure 2.3: CP/M Commands (cont.)

Handling Programs	Command	Operation
Create a new transient command:	LOAD filename	Creates an executable command file with a .COM extension from an "object file" in "hex" machine language
Execute transient command or program:	programname ↲	Programname is the filename of a .COM extension file without the '.COM'
Print an "object file" (file in "hex" machine language):	DUMP filename ↲	Used for hex files
Save a copy of a transient command or program (after LOADing or executing):	Save p filename ↲	p is the number of pages. One page is 256 bytes
Debug a program (using the CP/M or MP/M debugger):	DDT *filename* RDT *filename* ††	RDT is the name of the MP/M relocatable debugger
Submit a batch of commands (programs):	SUBMIT filename parm1 parm2 . . .	parm stands for parameter. This command looks for a file of many commands, substitutes parameters and executes the commands. The system displays the commands executing (unless you use †XSUB). You can abort the operation at any time using RUBOUT. †XSUB', if included as the first command in the submitted file, will process the commands and accept input for programs (if programs are set up for buffered input).
Scheduling programs for execution:	SCHED mm/dd/yy hh:mm	mm/dd/yy is the date and hh:mm is the time

Figure 2.3: CP/M Commands (cont.)

To effectively use the resources of CP/M and its standard commands, two concepts need to be understood:
— Built-in vs. transient commands
— Filenaming conventions
Let us now examine them.

BUILT-IN VS. TRANSIENT COMMANDS

As you know, when you see the CP/M system prompt (a letter indicating the disk drive, followed by a right angle bracket, e.g., 'A>'), you can type any built-in command, and the computer will respond immediately. Symbolically, all commands take this form:

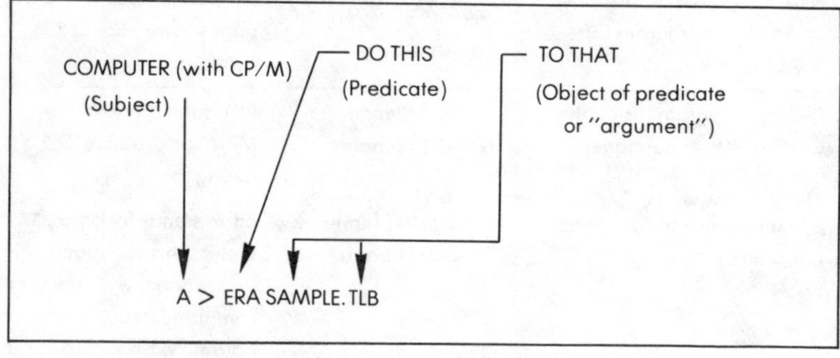

Figure 2.4: "Computer, erase the file SAMPLE.TLB."

Some commands are simple, and some are complex. All commands are actually assembly language programs (written in the language that computers "understand"). Some are "built-in" commands (not listed in the directory) and some are "transient" commands (listed in the directory). You can always execute the five "built-in" commands (DIR, ERA, REN, SAVE, and TYPE) because they are built into the CP/M operating system program. You can only execute transient commands if they exist as command files (.COM) on your disk. A transient command is actually an assembly language program that can be copied, deleted, and moved, and yet still be executed as a command. You can create your own transient command (program) if you know how to program a computer. A transient command's filename always has a '.COM' extension (e.g., PIP.COM), but you do not have to type the '.COM' when it is executed as a command. If you want to copy, delete, or move the file, you must, however, specify the entire filename with the '.COM' extension.

To find out if the transient command you want is on your disk, use the DIR command. The standard transient commands provided with CP/M are: ASM, ED, DUMP, LOAD, PIP, MOVCPM, STAT, SYSGEN, and SUBMIT. MP/M commands are *all* transient commands, or "resident programs," as described in the special section "CP/M Version 2.2 and MP/M." Although all transient commands are described, you will probably only use a few. A typical system directory is shown in Figure 2.5.

System Directory	Required	Strongly Advised	Useful	Optional
(CP/M exists but is invisible to DIR)	✓			
SYSGEN	✓			
PIP	✓			
STAT		✓		
ED			✓	
MOVCPM				✓
ASM				✓
LOAD				✓
DUMP				✓
DDT				✓
SAVE				✓
SUBMIT				✓
XSUB				✓
WORD PROCESSOR			✓	
YOUR APPLICATION PROGRAMS		✓		

NOTES:

1. As a precaution, do not store data or text files on your system diskette.
2. Also, use the write-protect feature on the system diskette.

Figure 2.5: A Typical System Diskette Directory

FILENAMES

Every system directory contains a filename for all of the files on the diskette. An example of a filename format is NAME.TTT, where NAME may have up to eight characters, and .TTT is the extension type. Filenames may contain letters, numbers and special characters. They may not, however, contain the following symbols:

<> . , : = ; * ? [ ]

For example:

PROG/22.BAK	is legal
PROG=22.BAK	is illegal

Extensions

Filenames normally have extensions (three characters to the right of a period). These extensions distinguish different types of files. Extensions are *required* for several types of files; other extensions are used for convenience (see Figure 2.6).

Whenever you use a filename as an argument to a command, you must type the *entire* filename, including the extension, if any. The only exception is when you use the file as a transient command (that file must have a .COM extension internally, even though the extension does not need to be typed to execute the command).

Filename Matches

There will be times when you want a command to act on several files or on all of the files at once. If the command allows this, its format indicates that a *filename match* (abbreviated *filematch*) can be substituted for an actual *filename* as an argument to the command. For example, the format for the ERAse command is:

$$\text{ERA}\begin{Bmatrix}\text{filename}\\ \text{filematch}\end{Bmatrix}$$

This means that you must choose between an actual filename or a filematch as an argument to ERAse.

A *filename match* is a group of characters used to refer to several files at once. The characters can be letters, digits, a period, and two special symbols '*' and '?'. These characters and symbols may be used to conveniently select the filenames of several files to be affected by the command. It is therefore important to select characters that are common to all of the filenames.

Extension	Type	Example
COM	Required Command file of a transient command (program).	PIP.COM LOAD.COM
ASM	Required for assembly language source (text) files used with ASM command.	PROG1.ASM PATCH.ASM
PRN	Required for the listing file of the assembly language program.	PROG1.PRN PATCH.PRN
PRL	Required for MP/M relocatable programs.	RDT.PRL
HEX	Required for program file in "hex" format (machine language), which is ready to be LOADed.	PROG1.HEX PATCH.HEX
RSP	Required for MP/M "resident system programs."	SPOOL.RSP
BAS	Required for BASIC program source (text) files.	PROGBAS.BAS
INT	Required for BASIC program intermediate file for execution (already compiled).	PROGBAS.INT
BAK	Created by ED (text editor) as a backup copy of file before it is altered.	LETTER.BAK
$$$	Temporary (scratch) files created and normally erased by ED and other programs.	LETTER.$$$
SUB	Text file with CP/M built-in or transient commands or programs; to be executed batch style by the SUBMIT program.	TRANSFORM.SUB

Figure 2.6: Extension Types

Try using the '?' symbol. It will match any character, but *only one for each '?'*, and *in the exact position* that the '?' symbol is placed. Here are examples:

This	Will Match These Filenames	But Not These
S?MPL?	SAMPLE SIMPLE SIMPLY	SIMPL SAMPLEY
A?B?C	AABBC ACBCC	AABBCC ABCCC

Neither '*' nor '?' can match a period. Here are some examples of multiple symbols in filename matches:

This	Will Match These Filenames	But Not These
T???Y.*	TEDDY.COM TARBY.ASM TILLY	TINY.COM TARABY.ASM TONY
????????.??? or *.*	any filename	

Recall that in Chapter 1 we used a *filenamematch* to copy an entire diskette. The command was:

A> PIP B:=A:*.* [V]↵

where '*.*' represented "all the files."
NOTE: using the '*' symbol at the beginning of the filename '*AB.*' is dangerous! Instead, use ?AB.*. Try to avoid mixing '?' and '*' in filename matches. Filename matches are commonly used with the PIP command to make copies of several or all files at once (or to send several files to a device).

BLANKS

Standard CP/M requires that a command be followed by at least one blank before any arguments are used. In the previous example:

A> PIP B:=A:*.*[V]↵

PIP must be followed by one or more blanks. (It may also be preceded by a blank.) The argument 'B:' may be followed by a blank, but this is optional.

Similarly, a blank may optionally be used after '=' or after 'A:'. In some versions of CP/M (such as North Star), *all* blanks are optional. When using a "standard" CP/M version, however, remember that blanks are mandatory after a command.

Additional blanks may be used to separate subelements of a command. Here is an example that uses additional spaces:

```
A> PIP B: = A: *.*[V] ↲
```

BUILT-IN COMMANDS

Introduction

Remember that in Chapter 1 we briefly presented all of the standard (CP/M) built-in commands (except SAVE). We will now provide specific examples of their use.

DIR (Directory)

The directory command is used to display a list of all files present on the diskette. To list all of the files on the diskette in drive A, type:

```
A >DIR ↲
```

To list the files on the diskette in drive B, type:

```
A >DIR B: ↲
```

(This method is quicker, and you remain in drive A.) Or, you can type the sequence:

```
A >B: ↲
B >DIR ↲
```

(This method takes longer, but you remain in drive B after executing the last command.) To search for a specific file on the diskette in drive B, type:

```
A > DIR B:SPECIFIC.NAD
```

To list all NAD files on the diskette in drive A, type:

```
A > DIR *.NAD
```

Use the DIR command often to check which files are on the diskette. The DIRectory should also be checked after a file is created or erased.

With CP/M 2.2, the directory is listed in a four-column format. Here is an example:

```
A> DIR
A : MOVCPM   COM : ASM       COM : DDT      COM : DUMP    COM
A : ED       COM : LOAD      COM : PIP      COM : STAT    COM
A : SUBMIT   COM : SYSGEN    COM : XSUB     COM : DISKDEF LIB
A : DUMP     ASM : SINGLE    ASM : COPY     COM : LIST    COM
A : FORMAT   COM : SAVEUSER  COM : USER     ASM : MEMR    COM
A : FILECOPY COM : SETDRIVE  COM : READ-ME  DOC : CONFIG  COM
```

TYPE

The TYPE command can be used to display any ASCII file on the screen. This is a quick and convenient way to examine any textfile. The format is:

```
TYPE d:name.type
```

where the drive name d is optional. If you want the file to be printed, push a CTRL-P before giving the command. Using the printer, however, will slow down the display.

The TYPE command can be used to check on any text you have created. While it may not provide the convenient format of a word processing or mailing list program, TYPE does print the file as it is actually stored in the computer's memory. TYPE is usually a fast way to examine a text file that has been accidentally damaged. It is a valuable tool for quick examination on the screen of a newly-created file.

REN (Rename)

This command allows you to change the name of a file. The format is:

REN new = old

For example, assume that FILE11.TXT is on the diskette in drive A. If you type:

A > REN FILE23.TXT = FILE11.TXT ↵

FILE11 will be renamed FILE23, and only FILE23 will be on the diskette in drive A. The name FILE11 will have been discarded. The file itself, however, will remain intact.

The drive specification is optional. For example, the instruction:

A > REN B:FILE.TXT = FILE.BAK ↵

is equivalent to:

A > REN B:FILE.TXT = B:FILE.BAK ↵

Note that both files must reside on the same drive. The drive specification may appear either to the left or to the right of the equal sign, and the new filename may not already exist.

A good practice when working on a file is to include the date in the name. For example, the PUB file may be labeled PUBMAY21. The next time that it is updated, the file can be RENamed PUBMAY23.

At the end of a computer session, always REName the file that you have been working on in order to:

1. Give it an identifying name
2. Avoid possible confusion
3. Include the date.

ERA (Erase)

ERA is used to erase a file. Its format is:

```
ERA d:name
```

where d is an optional drive name. An example of an ERA command is:

```
A > ERA PROG.TXT ↲
```

where PROG.TXT is erased.

NOTE: the ERA command can be dangerous! Use it carefully!

ERA can also be used to erase more than one file at a time. For example, if you want to erase all files with the '.ASM' extension in their filenames, you should substitute a match symbol for the file names:

```
A > ERA *.ASM ↲
```

In this case, the filename match is '*.ASM', and it matches up with all filenames that end with '.ASM'. The '*' symbol matches up with any number of characters, including no characters. Note that there can only be one period in a filename. The last three characters in the name (ASM) only match up with the letters 'ASM' that appear in those exact positions (first three positions to the right of the only period). Therefore, in this example, '*.ASM' will match up with 'SAMPLE.ASM,' 'ANOTHER.ASM,' '1.ASM,' and '.ASM'. It will *not* match up with 'SAMPLE,' 'ANOTHER.PRG,' 'ASM.COM,' or 'ASM' (note that the last 'ASM' is not an extension, because it is not in three positions to the right of a period).

Do not use the ERA command to practice filename matches — use the DIR command instead. DIR will only list files that match your filename match.

In practice, you will often want to create multiple copies of a file, such as VERSION1, VERSION2, VERSION3, or COPY1, COPY2. To avoid confusion, remember to ERASE all unnecessary copies before leaving the terminal.

SAVE

The SAVE command is used to store information from the TPA (main memory). This command is more complex, and will be described in detail later in this chapter.

THE TRANSIENT COMMANDS

Introduction

CP/M's ten standard transient commands are: SYSGEN, PIP, ED, STAT, ASM, LOAD, DUMP, DDT, SUBMIT, and MOVCPM. All are supplied with CP/M as .COM files. They will be described separately.

SYSGEN

Recall from Chapter 1 that SYSGEN is used to copy CP/M from one disk to another. In particular, it is used to copy a System Diskette. When you first receive a System Diskette, and use it to bring up your CP/M system, you should immediately make a copy of the system, and then store the System Diskette in a safe place. You can use the PIP transient command to transfer all of the '.COM' (and '.SYS') files to a new diskette (see Chapter 3), but you also have to copy "the system" that resides on reserved tracks of the diskette, in order to turn the new diskette into a "System Diskette." The SYSGEN transient command (program) can be used to do so.

The SYSGEN program turns an ordinary diskette into a System Diskette (with "the system" residing on its reserved tracks). To do this, SYSGEN brings "the system" *into memory* from the original diskette (*into memory* means that it is brought into the program execution area of the computer, called the TPA for Transient Program Area), and then it writes on the diskette. SYSGEN brings "the system" into memory and moves it to a new diskette; or, SYSGEN transfers whatever is already in memory to another diskette.

The sequence for using SYSGEN is:

```
A>SYSGEN↲
  SYSGEN VERSION n.n
  SOURCE DRIVE NAME (OR RETURN TO SKIP) A
  (if CP/M has been copied into memory, using
  MOVCPM, for example, you can type RETURN in-
  stead)
  SOURCE ON A THEN TYPE RETURN↲
  (this is intended to leave you time to insert a diskette
  with CP/M on it into the appropriate drive)
  FUNCTION COMPLETE
  (CP/M is now in memory, ready to be written on a
  disk)
  DESTINATION DRIVE NAME (OR RETURN TO
  REBOOT) B
  (place the new disk in B)
  DESTINATION ON B THEN TYPE RETURN↲
  (CP/M is written on B)
  FUNCTION COMPLETE
  DESTINATION DRIVE NAME (OR RETURN TO
  REBOOT)↲
  (you could now type B and make one more copy. In
  this case we finish by hitting RETURN.↲
A>
```

Remember that the diskette in drive B now contains only CP/M. It has no files (assuming that it was a fresh diskette). CP/M can be copied onto a diskette that already has files on it; this will not damage the files. If the diskette in drive B is empty, you should now copy the files separately. If you want to copy all of the files from the diskette in drive A to B, type:

```
A > PIP B:=A:*.* [V]↲
```

Otherwise, you can copy the desired files one at a time, as needed. The format for this operation is explained in Chapter 3.

At this point, you should test your new System Diskette.
MP/M users: it is important to mention here that the above example, which uses the PIP command to copy several files at once, will only copy the files in the current user area. The System Diskette supplied can be

copied using this form of PIP, because all of the necessary files are in user area zero, which is the "current user area" if you *never use* the USER command. (We recommend that you do not use the user area or the USER command unless you have a multi-user system.) (See "Enhancements in CP/M Version 2.2" in Chapter 3.)

SYSGEN can be used to make a copy of the system that can be left in the TPA (Transient Program Area) and *not* transferred to a new diskette. To do this, just hit 'RETURN' (to reboot) when the message 'DESTINATION DRIVE NAME (OR RETURN TO REBOOT)' appears.

You can also use SYSGEN in conjunction with MOVCPM to configure a new version of your system with a different memory size. In this case, when the first message 'SOURCE DRIVE NAME (OR RETURN TO SKIP)' appears, just hit RETURN (↲) and SYSGEN assumes that the system is already loaded into the memory (the TPA). When you use MOVCPM, you can load the system into memory in preparation for this type of SYSGEN. This is described in Chapter 5.

PIP

PIP is the file transfer program, explained in detail in Chapter 3.

ED

ED is the editor, presented in detail in Chapter 4.

STAT

Using STAT for Display

STAT is used to display status or change device assignments. The STAT command is a simple way to display available disk space. It can also be used to display and modify device assignments.

The simple 'STAT' command displays the sizes of remaining disk space and space allocated to files. The simplest form of the STAT command is:

```
A > STAT↲
A:R/W, SPACE: 144K
A >
```

This display shows that there are 144K bytes remaining on the diskette in drive A, i.e., 144K bytes that are not used. Most 8-inch diskettes hold only 224K bytes of file space. 'R/W' tells you that the diskette can be *written on* (i.e., you can create new files, overwrite, or delete old files). 'R/W' stands for "read-write," as opposed to 'R/O', which means "read-only." You cannot write on an R/O file, since it is "write-protected."

Bytes and Records

A *byte* is an 8-bit location in memory (a bit is either "1" or "0"). 128 bytes form a *record* (not necessarily a "data record," but a CP/M file record). This is also the size of a sector on the disk. Eight records equal 1024 bytes (or 1K). These particular values are used because they can be expressed as powers of 2 (binary numbers), i.e., they can be represented by a corresponding number of bits (n bits represent up to 2^n).

A 128-byte record is a useful convention for reading and writing sections of a file. Files exist on diskette as 16K "chunks" called "extents." These "extents" are not contiguous (next to each other) on the diskette. Each one always contains the starting address of the next one, in other words, they are "chained." You never have to find them yourself; the Basic Disk Operating System (BDOS), a part of the entire system, handles file space allocation using file control blocks (this is described in Chapter 5). Space allocation is dynamic—the system allocates new space for the file as you (or your program) write records to the file. You never have to specify a maximum length.

Assigning Devices With STAT

The STAT command provides useful information about the disks (diskettes), the transient or "scratch-pad" memory (called the Transient Program Area, or TPA), and the system's device assignments. It also enables you to *change* your device assignments and write-protect your diskette drives. In version 2.2 of CP/M, and in MP/M systems, you can also set indicators (like read-only) on *files*, receive additional status information about file size and disk size, and receive information about user areas.

Thc following form of STAT can be used to display a list of possible device assignments for the generic (logical) names CON:, RDR:,

PUN: and LST:

```
A > STAT VAL: ↲
```

The system responds by displaying:

```
CON:    =TTY:   CRT:   BAT:   UC1:
RDR:    =TTY:   PTR:   UR1:   UR2:
PUN:    =TTY:   PTP:   UP1:   UP2:
LST:    =TTY:   CRT:   LPT:   UL1:
```

Next to each logical device name (CON, RDR, PUN, LST), STAT gives a list of possible physical names for that device. These names correspond to names on the Intel MDS-800 system.

The physical device name can be used for a device that performs the same basic functions; e.g., the PTP: device (paper tape punch) could actually be the "record" (write) operation of a cassette recorder.

The actual device assignments can be displayed at any given time by typing this command:

```
A >STAT DEV: ↲
CON: =CRT:
RDR: = UR1:
PUN: = PTP:
LST : =TTY:
A>
```

This sample display shows that the CON: device is a CRT (Cathode Ray Tube), the RDR: device is a user-defined reader (number 1), the PUN: device is a paper tape punch device, and the LST: is a teletype device.

You may occasionally want to modify the four physical device names. These assignments can be changed by using the following STAT command:

```
STAT log: = dev:, log: = dev:, . . .
```

where *log:* is a logical device name (CON:, RDR:, PUN: or LST:) and *dev:* is a physical device name (PTP:, CRT:, UR1:, etc.). For example, the command

A > STAT LST: = LPT: ↲

changes the LST: device to a lineprinter (LPT:), so that all copy operations to LST: will now go to the lineprinter (unless the system is reset).

Note that the CON: device must be an input/output device that can send as well as receive data (e.g., a terminal with display and keyboard). The RDR: must be a device that can at least send data (input), and the PUN: and LST: devices must be able to receive data (output).

CP/M Version 1.4 and Later Versions

In CP/M version 1.4 and subsequent versions, a simple STAT command displays the number of bytes remaining in the current drive. You can also obtain this information for other drives by using this format:

A > STAT B: ↲

BYTES REMAINING ON B: 192K

B: R/O

A >

The display shows that the diskette in drive B is 'R/O', which stands for "read-only." You can only read this diskette; any attempt to write will result in the error message:

BDOS ERR ON B: READ ONLY

When you get this message in version 1.4, you need only hit a key on the terminal keyboard (such as RETURN), and the diskette will be reset to 'R/W', which stands for "read/write." You can now read from and write to this diskette.

You can reset the diskette to R/O (read-only) by executing the following form of the STAT command:

STAT d: = R/O

where d: is any disk drive.

To display the size of files, you use this form of STAT:

```
          ( filename       )
STAT d: <                   >
          ( filename match )
```

where d: is an optional drive letter for files not on the current disk drive. If you specify one filename, STAT will display the information for that file. If you specify a filename match, STAT will match files and display them alphabetically with the size information. The display below is a sample:

```
A> STAT B:*.TXT
RECS BYTS EXT D:FILENAME.TYP
8     1K    1   B:SAMPLE:TXT
4     1K    1   B:QUOTE:TXT
16    2K    1   B:CHAP1.TXT
A>
```

The RECS field shows how many 128-byte records were allocated to the file (thus far), the BYTS field shows how many kilobytes were allocated to the file (1K is 1024 bytes, and 128 times RECS equals the number of bytes allocated, so BYTS is equal to the result of 128 times RECS divided by 1024). The BYTS field is the most accurate allocation figure.

The EX field shows the number of 16K "extents" remaining in the file (the number in BYTS divided by 16.) In version 1.4, this may correspond to the number of directory entries on a disk for the same file, because one directory entry (one file control block) can only address up to 16K. CP/M automatically creates more entries and file control blocks as the file is extended.

CP/M Blocks and Records

CP/M always works with a minimum of 8 records when allocating space. On IBM standard diskettes, a record has 128 bytes. This is why the smallest amount of space allocated by CP/M is 1K, as shown in the STAT example above.

Double-density diskettes, however, may have 256 records. In this case, the smallest amount of space allocated by CP/M is 2K, even though the file may use only a small portion of that space. If a hard disk is used, the smallest amount of space may be 4K.

STAT in CP/M Version 2.2 and Subsequent Versions

The STAT program for version 2.0 or 2.2 of CP/M has a number of enhancements, including more complex displays. If you merely type 'STAT↲ ', the display will correspond to that of earlier versions of CP/M. Here is an example:

```
A>STAT *.* ↲

Recs  Bytes  Ext  Acc
  64     8K    1  R/W  A:ASM.COM
   8     1K    1  R/W  A:BOOTHD.COM
  20     3K    1  R/W  A:CONFIG.COM
  22     3K    1  R/W  A:COPY.COM
   6     1K    1  R/W  A:SAVEUSER.COM
```

The form 'STAT VAL: ↲ ', however, produces the following display:

```
Temp R/O Disk  : d: = R/O
Set Indicator  : d:filename.typ $R/O $R/W $SYS $DIR
Disk Status    : DSK:   d:DSK:
User Status    : USR:
Iobyte Assign  :
CON:       = TTY:     CRT:     BAT:     UC1:
RDR:       = TTY:     PTR:     UR1:     UR2:
PUN:       = TTY:     PTP:     UP1:     UP2:
LST:       = TTY:     CRT:     LPT:     UL1:
```

Note that the last four lines are identical to the ones displayed in CP/M version 1.4. The lines above them show possible STAT commands and the things that they will do. To set the R/O attribute on an entire *disk*, you use the version of the STAT command 'd: = R/O' (as in CP/M version 1.4), where 'd:' is a drive specifier (A:, B:, . . ., Y:). To set the $R/O, $R/W, $SYS or $DIR attributes of a *file,* you use the format of STAT described in the section on CP/M version 2.2 and MP/M in this chapter. To display the status of the current disk (diskette), or one or another drive, you use the format 'STAT DSK:' or 'STAT d:DSK:'. To display the current user area (and other user areas present in the system), use the format 'STAT USR:' (an example will be shown later in this section).

In version 2.2, you can add the $S argument to the STAT command to display the sizes of files by using the following format:

```
         (filename )
STAT d: {           }$S
         (filematch)
```

$S is an optional field that causes the size to be displayed. You can specify either a filename (including extension), or a filematch (filename match for several filenames). You can optionally specify a drive *d*: to display files on another disk drive. Here are some examples:

```
A > STAT PIP.COM $S

   Size      Recs      Bytes      Ext          Acc
    55        55        12K        1    R/O A:PIP.COM
```

The 'Size' field tells you how many records (128 byte units) are allocated to the file,but this is a "virtual" size, because the file might not be using all of the space yet. The 'Recs' field sums up the number of records in each extent (an extent is a 16K block). If the file was constructed sequentially, these two fields would be identical (and they would correspond to the 'RECS' field in version 1.4 of CP/M).

The 'Bytes' field tells you the only accurate allocation figure for randomly accessed files — the actual number of bytes allocated to the file. This figure corresponds accurately to the 'Size' and 'Recs' fields of sequential files. Randomly accessed files grow as data is written to them, so the 'Bytes' field gives the size in bytes allocated at a given moment, and the 'Recs' field sums up the number of records in each extent — although an extent might have unallocated "holes" that have not yet been filled with data. The 'Size' field is more accurate for the "logical number of records" in a file.

The 'Ext' field tells you how many extents (16K blocks) are allocated to the file. Unlike version 1.4, a directory entry (file control block) on a disk can address up to 128K bytes (8 logical extents) instead of only 16K (1 logical extent). The figure displayed, however, corresponds to version 1.4's display to keep the two versions compatible.

The 'Acc' field tells you what type of access is allowed — R/O (read-only) or R/W (read-write). These types of access correspond to the $R/O and $R/W file attributes described in the section on CP/M version 2.2 and MP/M (in this chapter). You can change the file attributes by supplying one attribute as an argument (to replace '$S' in the definition above) to the STAT format. For example:

```
A > STAT PROG.ASM $R/O↵
A > STAT FILE.TXT $R/W↵
```

The first STAT command puts the $R/O attribute (read-only) on file PROG.ASM. The second STAT command assigns the $R/W attribute (read-write) to file FILE.TXT.

The general format of this command is:

```
          ⎧filename ⎫   ⎧$R/O⎫
STAT d:   ⎨         ⎬   ⎪$R/W⎪
          ⎩filematch⎭   ⎨$SYS⎬
                        ⎩$DIR⎭
```

The following is another example, where ED.COM is read-only, PIP.COM is read-only *and* a system ($SYS) file, and DATA is a randomly accessed data file that has the read-write attribute:

Size	Recs	Bytes	Ext	Acc	
48	48	6K	1	R/O	A:ED.COM
55	55	12K	1	R/O	(A:PIP.COM)
65536	128	2K	2	R/W	A:TEXT.NAD

Note that PIP.COM is in parentheses to denote that it has the $SYS (system) attribute. Files not in parentheses have the default $DIR (directory) attribute. Attributes are described later in this chapter in the section on CP/M version 2.2 and MP/M.

To display information about the current (or alternate) disk (diskette), use the form 'STAT d:DSK', where d is an optional drive specifier (A, B, C, . . . , P) for an alternate drive. Here is a sample display:

```
A>STAT DSK:↲
    A:  Drive Characteristics
 3888:  128 Byte Record Capacity
  486:  Kilobyte Drive Capacity
  128:  32 Byte Directory Entries
  128:  Checked Directory Entries
  128:  Records/Extent
   16:  Records/Block
   52:  Sectors/Track
    2:  Reserved Tracks
```

This sample display is for a double-density diskette in the current drive (drive A, in this case). The total record capacity (128 bytes per record) is 3888 records (approximately 486K bytes). The kilobyte drive capacity is listed as 486 (this does not count the reserved areas of the diskette). The number of 32-byte directory entries corresponds to the actual number of file control blocks (FCBs) stored on the diskette. The number of "checked" entries is usually identical to the number of directory entries for removable media (like diskettes), because the system must check entries to detect a change in diskettes (this number is usually zero for non-removable disks). The system checks entries, unless there is an intervening warm start (↑C) or cold start (system reset, or "cold boot"). The number of records per extent ('Records/Extent') shown on the display gives the addressing capacity of each directory entry; i.e., how many records (128 byte segments) can be addressed by one directory entry (file control block on disk). The display states that 128 records can be addressed by a single directory entry (128 records equals 128 times 128 bytes, or approximately 16K bytes). The number of records per block ('Records/Block') shown on the display tells the number of records allocated to each sector (16 records equals 2048 bytes, or 2K bytes per block). This information is followed by the number of physical sectors ("blocks") per track ('Sectors/Track'), and the number of reserved tracks on the disk (diskette). Our example shows 52 sectors (blocks per track), and two reserved tracks for the system. Note that if you have a large disk that is accessed by several logical disk drives, the number of reserved tracks will be large, since the system uses these tracks to determine which areas of the disk should be accessed by which logical disk drive.

To display information about user areas, use the form 'STAT USR:↵ '. The following is a sample display:

```
A > STAT USR:↵

Active User : 0

Active Files : 0 1 3 1 0
```

The 'Active User' in this sample display is actually the number of the user area you are currently "in." In MP/M, the current user area is displayed along with the system prompt (e.g., '0A>' means current drive A, user area 0); in CP/M version 2.2, you have to determine your user area by using this form of STAT. In our example, the current user area is zero (the default user area after a cold start or system restart). The term 'Active Files' indicates the number of user areas that currently have files in them (on the current disk or diskette drive). If you move to one of these user areas (using the USER command), you will find at least one file in the user area. User areas without any files are not shown in the 'Active Files' display. User areas (and the USER command) are described more fully in the section on CP/M version 2.2 and MP/M in this chapter.

SUBMITTING A FILE OF COMMANDS FOR EXECUTION (SUBMIT AND XSUB)

Introduction

It is sometimes useful or necessary to execute a sequence of CP/M commands as if they were instructions in a program. For example, if a sequence is frequently used by an operator, it would be convenient to give a name to the sequence, and execute it with a single command, just like a program.

CP/M provides the SUBMIT transient command for conveniently executing a sequence of several commands. The SUBMIT command expects to find a file with the extension '.SUB' that contains actual command lines that include *arguments* to be replaced by *values* at execution time. The '.SUB' file is created just like a text file, by using ED or any other editor program, and lists command lines as they would be typed at the terminal. For example, SAMPLE.SUB could contain these lines:

```
DIR $1:$2 ↲
PIP A:=1$:2$ ↲
```

The '$1' and '$2' are arguments. They are like variables in a program — they will be replaced by actual values when you supply them at execution time (i.e., when you use the SUBMIT command). Here, the '$1' argument is replaced by a drive letter for a disk drive, and the '$2' argument is replaced by a complete filename (with the extension included, if any).

In this example, the file SAMPLE.SUB is executed by using the following SUBMIT command:

```
A > SUBMIT SAMPLE B FILE1.TXT ↲
```

The SUBMIT program first looks for SAMPLE.SUB, and then starts executing the commands. To execute DIR, it plugs the value 'B' into $1 and 'FILE1.TXT' into $2, and displays the filename in the directory for drive B. Then it executes PIP to copy B:FILE1.TXT onto drive A, using the same name.

The SUBMIT command takes the following form:

SUBMIT filename *v1 v2 v3* . . .

where *v1* is the value to substitute for '$1' everywhere in the '.SUB' file, and *v2* substitutes for '$2' everywhere in the '.SUB' file, etc. SUBMIT applies a '.SUB' extension on the filename supplied, so you do not have to specify the '.SUB' extension.

When you use arguments ($1, $2, . . .), you must use a dollar sign followed by an integer number. The number must start at one for the first argument, two for the next argument, three for the next, and so on. Since you use a dollar sign to denote arguments, you need to supply two dollar signs ($$) to have a normal dollar sign in a '.SUB' file (two dollar signs become one in a '.SUB' file, while a dollar sign with a number becomes an *argument*). You can also include a ↑ character to denote a CTRL-key combination (e.g., ↑C or ↑Z) in a '.SUB' file — use the up arrow character instead of the CTRL (Control). This is necessary because in most cases you cannot hit any CTRL-key sequences in an editor program while creating the '.SUB' file.

NOTE: no matter what drive you select to perform the SUBMIT operation, the '.SUB' file will not be processed until you insert the diskette into drive A (or use logical drive A) and reboot (warm start) the system (a ↑C is sufficient). You can specify an alternate drive for the '.SUB' file in a SUBMIT command by preceding the filename with a drive specifier, but the operation will not take place until the diskette with the '.SUB' file is in drive A.

You can abort a SUBMIT operation in progress by hitting the RUBOUT (DELETE) key. SUBMIT automatically creates a temporary file '$$$.SUB' to hold the commands from the '.SUB' file; this file is deleted when SUBMIT is finished, or if the system detects an error while the SUBMIT operation is happening, or if you abort the SUBMIT operation by hitting RUBOUT (DELETE). If, for some reason, this file $$$.SUB still exists after an error has occurred, any system reboot (warm start) will cause the system to execute the commands in $$$.SUB (instead of waiting for your typed commands). If this happens, abort the SUBMIT operation (by hitting RUBOUT) and erase the file $$$.SUB.

NOTE: for programmers who write programs making use of the SUBMIT facility: if your program takes over the CCP (Console Command Processor) function of reading and interpreting console input and system errors, you have to make your program erase the $$$.SUB file SUBMIT creates. Also, if you execute your program through a SUBMIT operation, you must make sure that the $$$.SUB file is either erased (if you do not want to keep doing the SUBMIT operation) or preserved for future use (by renaming it to something else). Any new SUBMIT command will replace the existing $$$.SUB file. You can, of course, imbed a SUBMIT command within the '.SUB' file as "just another CP/M command." This allows you to "chain" to another set of submitted commands.

SUBMIT With XSUB

In CP/M version 1.4, SUBMIT creates the temporary file $$$.SUB from the '.SUB' file you supply, and then the CCP (Console Command Processor) executes each line of $$$.SUB as if it was a typed command. (The CCP is the part of the system that reads and executes what you type as a command.)

In CP/M version 2.2, there is an added capability: the XSUB program (transient command). The XSUB program allows you to include input (i.e., commands) to programs (other than the CCP) that make use of CP/M's "buffered input" operation. You do not have to know how to use buffered input; you only need to know whether the program you want to execute and supply input to uses buffered input. The ED, DDT and PIP programs all do. Therefore, for example, you can use ED commands in a '.SUB' file as input to the ED program, and automatically perform a complicated ED operation repeatedly with one SUBMIT command.

Here is an example of such an operation. The file DOTHIS.SUB contains the following lines, including the 'XSUB':

XSUB	Execute XSUB
DIR $1.*	Display files
ED $1.$2	Use ED on file specified
#A	Do an ED append to fill buffer
B	Go to beginning of buffer
Copyright 1980, Sybex	Insert copyright notice
E	Terminate ED
PIP 1$.OLD = 1$.BAK	Make copy of old backup file, when CP/M system returns after ED terminates
DIR $1.*	Display all files again

A > SUBMIT DOTHIS SAMPLE TXT ↵

In this example, SUBMIT first tells the CCP to execute XSUB. The XSUB program relocates to the area directly below the CCP, and stays active until the next cold start (system reset or cold "boot"). While XSUB is active, it displays the message 'XSUB ACTIVE' above the system prompt; and as long as there are commands in the file DOTHIS.SUB, XSUB executes them (unless you intervene with a ↑C).

Next, XSUB executes the DIR command to display the files associated with SAMPLE. 'SAMPLE' is a substitute for '1$' and 'TXT' is a substitute for '2$' in DOTHIS.SUB. XSUB executes the ED program on the file SAMPLE.TXT. XSUB continues to provide input to the ED program (using buffered console input): first the #A command to tell ED to append the entire file (65535 lines) into the edit buffer, next, the B command to move ED's character pointer to the beginning of the buffer, then the I command to insert the text "Copyright 1980, Sybex" at the beginning of the buffer, and finally, the E command to save the edits and terminate the ED program. (ED commands are described in Chapter 4.)

The XSUB program remains active after ED terminates, executing the PIP command to copy SAMPLE.BAK into the new file SAMPLE.OLD (making a backup copy of SAMPLE.BAK). XSUB then executes the DIR command to display all of the files associated with the name SAMPLE.

When the submit file is exhausted for commands, the CCP takes over and waits for more commands to be typed at the terminal. However, the XSUB program remains active (the message 'XSUB ACTIVE' still occurs after each command execution) unless a program is executed that intentionally overwrites the area occupied by XSUB (i.e., directly below the CCP, or until you do a cold start or system reset). While XSUB is active, the SUBMIT command can be used to execute other '.SUB' files. The other '.SUB' files do *not* have to have 'XSUB' as a command line if XSUB is already active. Therefore, you can create '.SUB' files *without* XSUB to keep them compatible with earlier versions of CP/M, and execute XSUB as a command whenever you want it to be active while submitting '.SUB' files.

ASSEMBLING (ASM), LOADING (LOAD), AND DUMPING (DUMP) PROGRAMS

Introduction

In the world of assembly language, ASM, LOAD, and DUMP are standard terms for operations that allow assembly language programs to work like commands. You can use the commands ASM and LOAD to turn an assembly language source program (written into a text file) into a do-it-yourself transient command, and you can use DUMP to display the contents of the transient command. The term "dump" is often used to describe large-scale copy operations (e.g., the "daily dump" operation on minicomputers and mainframes) and the act of sending the contents of a program to the printer. CP/M's DUMP command only "dumps" the memory area of a program (in hexadecimal) onto the terminal display. To send a file to the printer, or to do large-scale copy operations, you must use the PIP transient command.

To write assembly language programs for a CP/M (or MP/M) system, you need to know the host computer's assembly language. Standard CP/M runs on microcomputers using the Intel 8080, 8085 or 8086, or Zilog Z80 or Z8000 microprocessors. Other software vendors offer CP/M on 6502-based computers like the Apple and Pet.

Assembling

The ASM command executes Digital Research's 8080 Assembler, residing in the file ASM.COM. This assembler program translates an assembly language source file (written in the assembly language of the 8080) into a *machine language* file. (See Figure 2.7.) A machine language file contains instructions in *binary* — the language of the microprocessor; however, most displays or printouts of the file will be in *hexadecimal* notation.

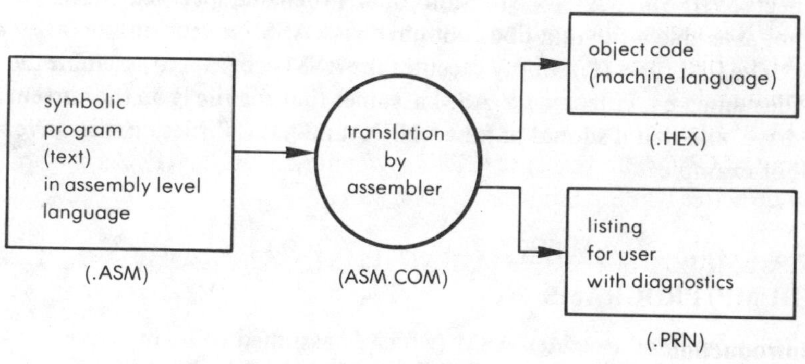

Figure 2.7: The Assembly Process

There are other assembler programs that can perform assembly languages for other microprocessors, and there are more powerful assemblers for the 8080 as well. These assemblers would all exist as '.COM' files in your system, and you can execute any one in the same manner as you would execute ASM.COM.

The assembler program assembles a source file that has an '.ASM' extension (e.g., PROG.ASM). The assembler then uses the '.HEX' extension to denote the assembled machine language file it creates (e.g., PROG.HEX). The assembler also uses a 'PRN' extension (e.g., PROG.PRN) to create a printable file. You can send this '.PRN' file to the printer to obtain a printout of the program. The '.PRN' file contains the lines from the original '.ASM' source file, along with error messages and the resulting machine code (in the standard Intel hexadecimal notation).

The '.HEX' machine-code file produced by ASM is now ready to be loaded into the system (using the LOAD command) and become a transient program that is executed as a command.

To execute ASM, you can use one of these forms:

1. ASM filename
2. ASM filename.*shp*

In both forms, you only have to specify the primary name of the source file. The file must have an '.ASM' extension — the ASM program expects to find an '.ASM' extension for any filename specified. ASM will not assemble a file that does not have an '.ASM' extension.

The first form (1.) simply executes the ASM program to assemble the file named by "filename." ASM assumes that the file is on the current drive, and that it should put the '.HEX' and '.PRN' files on that drive. For example:

A > <u>ASM PROG</u> ↲

This command executes ASM (which is assumed to be on drive A as ASM.COM) to assemble file PROG.ASM (which is also assumed to be on drive A). ASM will produce files PROG.HEX and PROG.PRN and also put them on drive A.

The second form (2.) allows you to specify disk drives other than the current drive if the source file is on another drive, you want to put the '.HEX' or '.PRN' files on another drive, or you want to tell ASM to skip the operation of creating the '.HEX' or '.PRN' file.

In the format, *.shp* consists of three letters preceded by a period following the filename argument. The *s* may be any of the letters A through P. The *h* may be any of the letters A through P, or Z; the *p* may be any of the letters A through P, or X or Z. The *s* is a letter that indicates which drive (A, B, . . . , Y) contains the disk with the source file. The *h* is a letter that indicates which drive (A, B, . . . , Y) should receive the '.HEX' file, or, if the letter 'Z' is used, that tells ASM to skip creating the '.HEX' file, and only generate the '.PRN' file. The *p* is a letter that indicates which drive (A, B, . . . W, Y) should receive the '.PRN' file. If an 'X' is used, that sends the '.PRN' file only to the display of your terminal, or, if a 'Z' is used, that tells ASM to skip the function of creating the '.PRN' file and only create the '.HEX' file.

Here are some examples of the second form:

```
A > ASM PROG1.ABZ ↲
```

This command assembles file PROG1.ASM, which is the source file on drive A. It also creates PROG1.HEX on drive B (and thus skips the process of creating PROG1.PRN).

```
A > ASM PROG2.BZX ↲
```

This command assembles file PROG2.ASM, which is the source file on drive B, and sends the PROG2.PRN file to the display of the terminal (without creating PROG2.HEX).

NOTE: ASM's error messages may take the form of an assembly language source line, in which a letter indicates an error code. (These codes are explained in the assembler's documentation.) Errors are corrected by modifying the program under the debugger DDT (or another debugger), or by correcting the source file and reassembling. These ASM errors are also flagged in the '.PRN' file. Other errors that can occur are shown in Figure 2.8.

NO SOURCE FILE PRESENT	— ASM cannot find the source file, or you specified a file that doesn't have an '.ASM' extension.
NO DIRECTORY SPACE	— The disk (diskette) directory is full; erase non-essential files (or make copies) and try again.
SOURCE FILE NAME ERROR	— Improperly typed filename to the ASM command. You cannot use filename matches in ASM commands.
SOURCE FILE READ ERROR	— Source file cannot be read by ASM for some reason. Use the TYPE command to find the incorrect line in the source file.
OUTPUT FILE WRITE ERROR	— Output file ('.HEX' or '.PRN' file) cannot be written out to disk (diskette); most likely because the disk (diskette) is full.
CANNOT CLOSE FILE	— Output file ('.HEX' or '.PRN' file) cannot be closed (updated); check to see if the disk (diskette) is write-protected (i.e., read-only).

Figure 2.8: Assembly Errors

Loading

When you have a '.HEX' file produced by ASM (or another assembler), you can turn it into a '.COM' file (executable transient command) by "loading" it into the system using LOAD. (See Figure 2.9.)

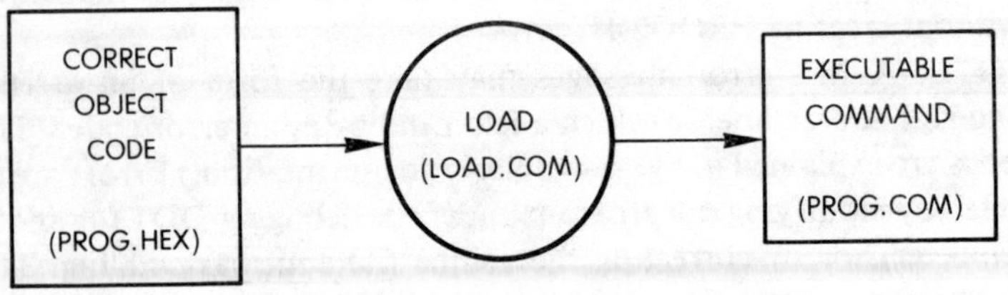

Figure 2.9: Loading the Object Code

The LOAD command is itself a transient command, existing as LOAD.COM. You execute it by typing 'LOAD', followed by a filename of a '.HEX' type file, as in the following example:

A > LOAD PROG ↵

This command looks for PROG.HEX on the current drive, creates a memory-image of this file (in hexadecimal format), and calls the new file PROG.COM. This new program can be executed by typing 'PROG↵ '.

Since LOAD creates a '.COM' file, you only have to LOAD a '.HEX' file once. The '.HEX' file must contain valid Intel "hexadecimal format" that is created by ASM or any similar assembler.

You can also load files from another disk drive by specifying the drive as part of the filename. For example:

A > LOAD B:GAMES ↵

This command loads the file GAMES.HEX in drive B and creates GAMES.COM on drive A (the current drive).

Since you can use PIP to transfer files in "hexadecimal format" from readable devices, you can also LOAD a file that was assembled at some earlier time and was recently transferred to your system via PIP.

NOTE: for assembly language buffs: the '.HEX' file must have valid hexadecimal records that begin at 100H ('H' for hexadecimal, i.e., address 100_{16}). 100H is the beginning of the TPA (Transient Program Area). Addresses of the '.HEX' file must be in ascending order (gaps in unfilled memory regions are filled with zeros by LOAD as it reads the hexadecimal records). Thus, LOAD is only used to create '.COM' files that execute in the TPA. Programs that will *not* occupy the TPA (special programs) can be loaded by using DDT (or another debugger).

Dumping

The DUMP command displays the contents of a file at the terminal in hexadecimal form. Any file can be DUMPed, since all data is a binary value that can also be represented in hexadecimal (base 16) form. All hexadecimal numbers end with 'H' in this book, just like they do in Intel mnemonics. The 'H' stands for the 16 subscript (e.g., 10H is 10_{16}).

In a DUMP command you must give the entire filename (including extension):

A > DUMP B:PROG.HEX ↲

The example above displays the contents of PROG.HEX (which is on drive B).

EXECUTING, DEBUGGING (DDT), AND SAVING (SAVE) PROGRAMS

Executing

Once a '.HEX' program is LOADed, and a '.COM' file is created for it, you can execute the program by typing the filename as a command (without its '.COM' extension). For example:

A > PROG ↲

PROG.COM is assumed to be on drive A.

You could also execute the program from another drive:

A > B: ↲

B > A:PROG ↲

When you execute a program or a transient command, it is brought into the computer's main memory ("scratch-pad" memory, or TPA).

Debugging

"Bugs" are errors in a program. The errors flagged by ASM (or another assembler), PIP or LOAD, or the "run-time" errors (errors while executing) can usually be corrected by using a "debugger" program such as DDT. DDT.COM is supplied with the standard version of CP/M (or MP/M). DDT will bring any file into main memory and perform the operations available as DDT commands. DDT can be used to correct errors, or to bring a file into the main memory in order to save a memory image of it (by using SAVE). To execute DDT on any file, use the following form:

DDT { filename.HEX | filename.COM }

You can specify a drive letter as part of the filename (if the file exists on another drive).

In both cases, DDT replaces the CCP (Console Command Processor) as the "operating system" that reads the command line-by-line. The CCP is described in Chapter 5. When the DDT program replaces the operating system's CCP program, the DDT program takes on the job of reading the command line. (Like the ED program, DDT has its own set of commands.)

If you specify a filename (of type '.HEX' or '.COM') with DDT, then the debugger brings the program into the TPA (wiping out whatever was there before). If you do not specify a filename, DDT will occupy the TPA, and wait for a DDT 'I' command to input a file to the TPA.

When executed, DDT displays a sign-on message (which can be different for each installation), and then its prompt: '-'. You can now type DDT commands (use the documentation supplied with DDT). In later versions of CP/M, DDT also displays the 'NEXT' and 'PC' values that are discussed with DDT's 'R' command below.

Several DDT commands will be discussed here: the I (input) command, the R (read) command, and the G0 command (stop debugger and return to the operating system).

The I command inputs a '.HEX' or 'COM' file into the TPA. Essentially, it is the same operation that is performed when you supply a filename of '.HEX' or '.COM' type with the DDT command. You can also add another file to the file existing in the TPA by using this command.

The R command reads the file in the TPA and displays a "load message" that consists of:

```
NEXT   PC
nnnH   pc
```

This display occurs automatically in later versions of DDT. The number under the NEXT column is the next address following the loaded program. You use this value to calculate the number of "pages" (256-byte blocks) to use in a SAVE command. The number is in hexadecimal notation.

The G0 command terminates DDT, but leaves the program in TPA so that you can use the SAVE command to save a memory image of the file. Just type:

<u>G0</u>↲

Saving

The SAVE command takes one or more "pages" of the TPA (main memory) and places it on a disk as a file with the name that you specify. (Note that one "page" is 256 bytes.) (In MP/M, this operation is implemented *within* the debugger program — DDT or SID.)

You use the SAVE command to create a memory image file of whatever is currently in the TPA (the most recently executed program). If you use DDT on a program, and it starts working correctly) or even if *part* of it works correctly), you will want to SAVE it as a file that can be copied, debugged, or executed.

NOTE: in version 1.4, you cannot perform two consecutive SAVEs on the same contents of the TPA, because the first SAVE causes a directory operation that changes several areas of the TPA. In version 2.2, however, this problem has been corrected — you can perform two consecutive SAVEs on the same TPA contents.

The SAVE command takes this form:

```
SAVE p filename
```

You supply the number of memory pages as p (a decimal number). p is calculated by using DDT and DDT's R command to display the address under the NEXT column — the next (higher) address that follows the program in the TPA. This address is actually the last address of the TPA *plus* 1. Therefore, if you subtract 1 from this displayed value (subtracting in hexadecimal arithmetic), you will have the last TPA address (end of the program), which you can convert to "pages" in decimal.

An easy method for converting the NEXT address into the value for p is: if the NEXT address ends in two zeros (e.g., 1200H), subtract 1H ('H' is for hexadecimal) to get 11FFH, then ignore the last two digits ('FF') and convert 11H to decimal ($1 \times 16^0 = 1$, and $1 \times 16 = 16$, so 11H $= 17_{10}$). If the NEXT address does *not* end in two zeros, *do not* subtract 1H from it; simply convert the first two digits (e.g., 1205H becomes 12H, which equals 18 pages).

Here is an easy example:

(Value under NEXT in DDT's R command display):

```
3FFH
```

NOTE: 'F' is the decimal value "15" in hexadecimal notation. 'H' stands for hexadecimal, and is *not* a digit.

To convert to *pages* (256-byte blocks), ignore the first two digits 'FF' and use the digit '3'. This is the "high order byte," and can be expressed as 3H. 3H converted to decimal is 3_{10}. Therefore, you use 3 as the decimal value for pages in the SAVE command.

Here is a more difficult example:

(Value under NEXT in DDT's R command display):

```
 1D00H
   -1H
 -----
 1CFFH
```

NOTE: D is the decimal value '13'. Subtract 1H because '1D00H' ends in two zeros. D (13) becomes C (12).

To convert to pages, use the high order byte '1C' and convert it to decimal:

$$
\begin{array}{llcr}
 & CH = 12 \text{ times } 16^0 & = & 12 \\
+ & 10H = 1 \text{ times } 16^1 & = & \underline{16} \\
= & \dots\dots\dots\dots\dots\dots & & 28
\end{array}
$$

NOTE: the decimal value 28 equals the number of pages of memory between addresses 100H (start of the TPA) and 1CFFH.

Here are examples of SAVE commands:

A	<u>SAVE 4 PROG.COM</u>↵	Saves memory from 100H through 4FFH and puts it in PROG.COM on drive A. Next higher address after 4FFH is 500H.
B	<u>SAVE 10 KLUDGE.COM</u>↵	Saves memory from 100H through 0AFFH to file KLUDGE.COM on drive B. Next higher address after 0AFFH is 0B00H. AH is 10 decimal.

A	SAVE 40 B:WORKS.COM↵	Saves memory from 100H through 28FFH to the file WORKS.COM on drive B. Next higher address after 28FFH is 2900H. 28H is (2 times 16) + 8 = 40 decimal.

CP/M VERSION 2.2 AND MP/M

An Introduction to MP/M

MP/M is an operating system designed for time-sharing. A time-sharing system can execute several *processes* or programs simultaneously. However, the simultaneity is only apparent. In fact, the computer executes one user program, and then another in rapid succession, so that each user has the impression that he/she is the only one using the computer.

Therefore, when MP/M is used at a single terminal, the system essentially behaves like a single-user CP/M system. MP/M offers additional facilities, however, by allowing a single user to execute several programs simultaneously. For example, programs may be attached to and detached from the console, allowing a single user to interact with the console while other programs are executing.
NOTE: if you plan to use MP/M as a single-user, single-program facility, you do not need to know about MP/M. Reading the text on CP/M version 2.2 should fulfill your needs.

One of the problems to be solved by a time-sharing system is *program scheduling*. Each program should be scheduled to run in turn on the processor. The *round-robin* scheduling technique is the simplest one used to do this. With this technique, each program gets an equal slot of computer time, in turn. This technique is illustrated by a rotating pointer in Figure 2.10.

In order to make efficient use of the processor, however, some programs (or processes) should be run before others. In any good scheduling system, each process must be equipped with a *priority level* that will determine when it will run. For example, when data becomes available from the disk, it should be read promptly by a transfer program, or a long delay will be incurred as the head moves past the proper point on the disk. This transfer process should have a high priority.

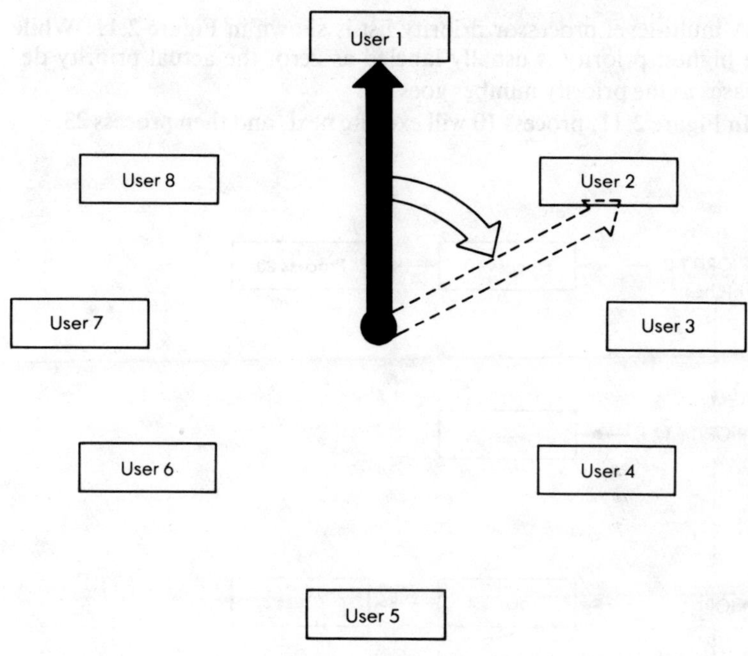

Figure 2.10: Round Robin Scheduling

Conversely, a process that prints on a slow printer can be delayed by a few milliseconds, or even seconds, at no great loss. Therefore, the printing process should generally have a low priority.

In order to set priorities, two classes of processes are usually distinguished: those that perform input/output functions (I/O operations), and those that perform computations, (CPU operations).

Whenever a process executes on the CPU (the processor), it may request an input or an output operation. This type of operation is very slow by CPU standards, as it typically requires several milliseconds, and a CPU instruction operates in microseconds. When an I/O operation is requested, the process in execution is generally *blocked*, and becomes *dormant*. An I/O operation is then started. I/O will proceed concurrently with the CPU. When the I/O operation is completed, it will awaken the original dormant process. The CPU process then resumes its position in the scheduling list. It has become *active* again.

A multi-level processor priority list is shown in Figure 2.11. While the highest priority is usually labeled as zero, the actual priority decreases as the priority number goes up.

In Figure 2.11, process 10 will execute next, and then process 23.

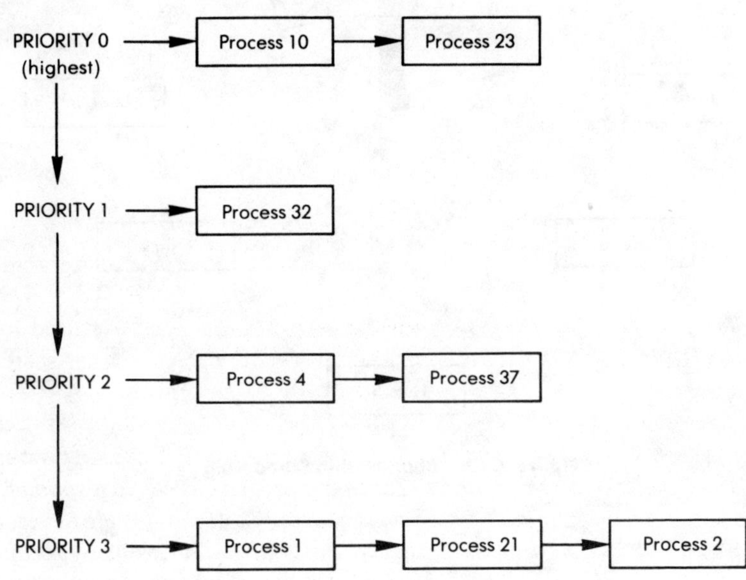

Figure 2.11: A Four-Level Priority List

While process 23 is executing, a new process could be entered at priority 0 (see Figure 2.12). In this case, process 40 will execute next. When all processes at level 0 have completed execution, those at level 1 will execute, and so on.

A process has not been formally defined here because each operating system uses a somewhat different definition. A process may be a program, or a subprogram, or other program entities. Thus, a user may activate a variety of processes.

In the example in Figure 2.11, only *active processes* are shown. A similar list is maintained for *dormant processes* that have been blocked. When awakened, a dormant process will become active, and enter the active list.

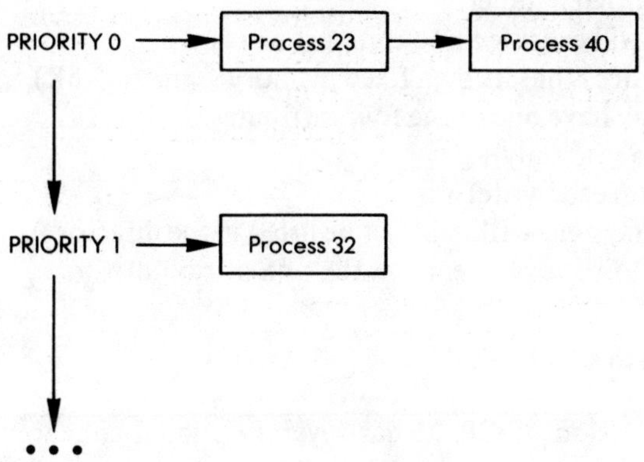

Figure 2.12: A New Process is Entered at Priority 0

The scheduling system that has been described is generally used for the processor. However, competition may take place for other scarce resources within the system, such as the disk or the printer.

Generally, processes will queue up for the printer and will be serviced on a first-come first-served basis. This is called a FIFO list (First-in First-Out). The corresponding scheduling program is called a *spooler*.

Similarly, requests for the disk are generally queued up. However, a program will attempt to optimize disk access by reading as many sectors as possible while moving the head as little as possible. As a result, processes in the disk-waiting queue may be serviced in any order, if the block they need comes up under the disk head.

Simultaneous processes sharing common resources require additional mechanisms:

— The processes must be synchronized. This is done by flags and interrupts.

— The processes must operate in a reasonable order when competing for a common device. This is the function of a scheduler program for that device.

— Protection mechanisms must be provided so that a single process malfunction does not damage other processes.

— The memory space must be allocated efficiently so that processes occupy memory space only when needed.

MP/M is a simple time-sharing system that provides a good set of facilities. However, in order for a time-sharing system to reside in a limited amount of memory, many of the resources have been provided for in a simplified manner:

- MP/M will execute up to eight processes
- Each process has its own fixed memory segment (48K)
- Files may have one of the four attributes:
    - R/O (read only)
    - R/W (read/write)
    - SYS (system—file will not be listed in the directory)
    - DIR (directory—removes the SYS attribute)

Introduction to CP/M 2.2

The new version of CP/M has several optional enhancements designed for an easy transition to MP/M, a multi-user system. In a multi-user environment, where several people are using the same machine at the same time, more protection is needed for your files, because you have to *share* your system's resources — the printer, the disk (or diskette) drives, and the computer (CPU) itself. If you have CP/M version 2.2, you can use several features actually designed for MP/M, and still maintain compatibility, that is, your files and programs will be usable on both systems.

The new features are:

- User areas and the USER command to segregate your files from other user's files
- File attributes (assigned by using STAT) to protect your files from accidental deletions or overwrites, including an attribute to store a file secretly.

NOTE: if you *do not* use these features, your files and programs will be compatible with previous versions of CP/M as well as CP/M version 2.2 and MP/M.

In addition to these features, MP/M has features that are not found in CP/M version 2.2, and *only* used in multi-user environments:

- CONSOLE command to display the current console (terminal) number in a system with more than one terminal
- DSKRESET command to regulate changing of disks in a multi-user system
- GENMOD command to produce a relocatable program (essential in multiprogramming systems)
- SPOOL command to regulate traffic to the lineprinter (STOPSPLR is used to cancel a SPOOL)
- SCHED command to schedule programs to execute at a later time
- TOD command to display or set the time and the date

— Ability to detach a running program from your terminal and attach to it later; use along with MPMSTAT to display system information.

MP/M 1.0 Characteristics

MP/M requires at least 32K bytes of memory. MP/M can handle up to sixteen consoles and sixteen disks, each disk drive containing up to eight megabytes of information. MP/M allows up to eight memory segments of 48K.

User Areas and the USER Command

In CP/M version 2.2 and MP/M, you can segregate files on a single disk (diskette) into "user areas" numbered zero to fifteen. The files are not actually segregated — they just need to be referred to by using a "user area number" that is internally prefixed to their names. The assumption is that you would choose a user area, and put your files in that same area on all of the disks (diskettes). Figure 2.13 demonstrates this placement.

	Disk A	Disk B	Disk C
user 0	system files	system files	system files
user 1			
user 2 (you)	your files	your files	your files
user 4			

Figure 2.13: File Placement in User Areas

When initially accessing MP/M, the following message appears on each console:

```
MP/M
nA >
```

where n is the user number for that console. n is 0 for console 0, 1 for console 1, etc. For example, the display on console 3 (assuming that 4 consoles or more are connected) is:

```
MP/M
3A>
```

Any user number in the range 0 to 15 may be assigned to any console using the USER command described below.

The 'A' refers to disk drive A, and may be changed at will, just like in CP/M.

How to Put a File Into a User Area

When you are "in" a "current user area," the files that you create are put into that user area, and you must be "in" that user area to access the files. If you need to "get" a copy of a file that is in another user area, use the PIP parameter G provided in CP/M version 2.2 and MP/M (described in Chapter 3).

When you first bring up CP/M version 2.2 or MP/M, your current user area is user area zero. In MP/M, this is emphasized by the system prompt, '0A>' (for drive A, user 0). In CP/M version 2.2, you must use the form of STAT, 'STAT USR: ↵ ', to determine the current user area number.

How to Move to Another User Area

If you stay in user area zero (i.e., if you do not use the USER command), your files and programs will be compatible with earlier versions of CP/M and MP/M's user area zero. If you wish to go to another user area, you must use the USER command; the files you create in that user area must be copied to user area zero (using PIP's G parameter) to be compatible with earlier versions of CP/M.

The USER command's format is:

```
USER n
```

where n is an optional argument in MP/M, but necessary in CP/M version 2.2. In both systems, if you supply an n in the range of zero to fifteen, the USER command will move you to that user area. For example,

```
0A> USER 2↵
2A>
```

NOTE: this is an MP/M example. In CP/M you must use 'STAT USR: ↲' to display the current user area. In both cases, the user is moved to user area 2 of the same disk drive.

When you move to another user area, you stay in that user area until another USER command is performed or until the system is reset (cold start). After a cold start, you are always put in user area zero.

Points to Remember About User Areas

A user area does not become active until you move to it. Note, however, that the disk drive remains active wherever you go within it — and user areas are within the logical disk drive. User areas are really designed with large disks in mind (hard disks may be used). The user area ceases to exist when you erase *all* of the files, including files with the $R/O and $SYS attributes (discussed later in this chapter). You erase all of the files by using the ERA command with the filename match '*.*', which erases all files in the current user area except files with the $R/O (read-only) attribute.

Since the ERA command only erases files in the current user area, you can only erase files in one user area at a time, unless you write a program that erases everything on the disk (diskette). The form 'ERA *.* ↲' only erases files in the current user area (the one that you are currently "in"). It will not erase files with the $R/O attribute (read-only) until you change their attribute to $R/W (read-write).

If you use the DIR command to see if any files still exist in the current user area, you might be missing the files with the $SYS attribute (called "system files"). These files will not appear in a DIR display, but will only appear in parentheses in a display produced by 'STAT *.* $S ↲'. Use the STAT command to change file attributes (discussed next) in order to erase all of the files and close out a user area.

File Attributes

Ordinarily, your files are already "directory" files that can be *read* or *written to.* Optionally, you can prevent a file from being listed in a DIR display by replacing the "directory" attribute with a "system" attribute. You can also prevent a write or delete operation to a file if you change its "read-write" attribute to "read-only."

In CP/M version 2.2 and MP/M, each file is created with the $DIR attribute to signify that it is a "directory file" which the DIR command can find and display. Each file is also created with the $R/W (read-write) attribute to signify that you can *read* and *write to* (and *erase*) the file.

When a file has the $SYS attribute (the opposite of $DIR), the DIR command and the PIP command cannot find it. (PIP cannot find it unless you use PIP's R parameter, described in Chapter 3.) The $SYS attribute is used to "hide" files from DIR and PIP, and thus prevent other users of the system from knowing about or copying the file. Note, however, that the STAT command can be used by other users to display even "system" files, so this protection (from PIP and DIR) is not enough. You must *also* affix the $R/O (read-only) attribute to the file (the opposite of $R/W), and then hide the documentation for the STAT command. Essentially, these files are only protected against *your accidental* misuse of the system. If you misuse your disk media, then you have another problem.

NOTE: the ERA command *will* find "system" files, but will not delete read-only files. You have to use STAT to change the $R/O attribute to $R/W in order to delete any $R/O file.

Here are examples using STAT to change and display file attributes:

```
A > STAT SAMPLE.TXT $R/O ↲
```

This command changes SAMPLE.TXT to be read-only.

```
A > STAT B:TEMP $R/W ↲
```

This command changes TEMP on drive B to be read-write (from read-only).

```
A > STAT SAMPLE.BAK $R/O ↲
A > STAT SAMPLE.BAK $SYS ↲
```

This command changes SAMPLE.BAK into a read-only and "system" file, one not found by DIR:

```
A > DIR SAMPLE.BAK ↲
NOT FOUND
A > STAT SAMPLE.* $S ↲
 Size   Recs   Bytes   Ext    Acc
  48     48     6K      1     R/O   A:SAMPLE.TXT
  48     48     6K      1     R/W   A:SAMPLE.JNC
  48     48     6K      1     R/O  (A:SAMPLE.BAK)
```

The file SAMPLE.BAK is in parentheses because it has the $SYS attribute, as well as the $R/O attribute (shown in the 'Acc' column, and representing a file access method). The other files have the $DIR attribute, and SAMPLE.TXT has the $R/O attribute (read-only), while SAMPLE.JNC has the $R/W attribute (read-write).

If you copy a read-only or "system" file, PIP creates the new copy with the default read-write ($R/W) and directory ($DIR) attributes. You must use STAT to actually assign new attributes.

MP/M Operations

In a multi-user MP/M system, each user has a terminal, and can operate the system. An MP/M system with only one user can be identical to a CP/M version 2.2 system. With more than one user, however, MP/M can appear as a separate CP/M system for each user. In some environments, it may be necessary to have a "system operator" handle all resources and manage the system for users. A system operator might perform the following operations:

- Change diskettes (use the DSKRESET command)
- Spool files to the lineprinter or other device (SPOOL and STOPSPRL commands)
- Schedule programs to be executed at a later date (SCHED command)
- Set the time and date (TOD command)
- Display information about the system (MPMSTAT command).

DSKRESET (MP/M)

Although you can walk up to any diskette drive and take out a diskette, this would not be wise in an MP/M system, where other users might be accessing files on the diskette. MP/M has the DSKRESET command to inform other users that someone wishes to change a diskette. DSKRESET, like other MP/M commands, exists on the system diskette as a '.COM' or '.PRL' ("page relocatable") file, and can be executed by simply typing its primary name:

```
0A >DSKRESET↵

Confirm reset disk system (Y/N) ?Y
```

The message "Confirm reset disk system" appears on every terminal hooked up to the system. Each user must respond with a 'Y' (for yes) to allow a disk reset.

Spooling (MP/M)

When more than one user wants to send files to the printer, or when one user wants to send several files, the user can *spool* (line up, one after another, in a *queue*) the files to the device. However, only text (ASCII) files or data files filled with ASCII text can be sent. (Note that source files, listings, '.PRN' files and any files created by a text editor like ED, or a word processor, are all text files.

To send files to the spool queue, use the SPOOL command, which takes the following form:

SPOOL filename *filename filename . . .*

The first filename is required; the subsequent ones are optional. The filename must include the extension, if any. Here is an example:

0A > SPOOL PROG.PRN SAMPLE.TXT TEMP.LST↵

This command sends the files PROG.PRN, SAMPLE.TXT, AND TEMP.LST to the LST: device (usually a printer).

To stop a spool operation and empty the spool queue, use the command STOPSPLR. Here is an example:

0A > STOPSPLR↵

MP/M has the ability to keep time, and provide the correct date, if you set these values properly. Using the time and date, you can schedule programs to run at a specified time on a specified date. The system constantly monitors the time and date to manage scheduled programs.

Scheduling Execution (MP/M)

The SCHED program can be used to schedule execution of another program. The SCHED program has either a '.PRL' or '.COM' extension. When you execute it as a command, you must supply the arguments shown in the following format:

SCHED mm/dd/yy hh:mm program

Supply your date as mm/dd/yy, your time in hours (hh) (expressed as zero to twenty-four), and minutes (mm) (expressed as zero to sixty). Your program is assumed to be a filename with a '.COM' or '.PRL' (page relocatable) extension (which it is not necessary to supply). Here is an example:

```
0A > SCHED 12/31/80 23:59 EIGHTY↲
```

The program EIGHTY.COM (or EIGHTY.PRL) will execute on December 31, 1980, at 12:59 P.M., if the system is running and if it encounters that date. Note that since the time indicator can be set and reset at any time, anyone could interfere and reset the time and date. All users must, therefore, cooperate in order to rely on this operation.

Time of Day (MP/M)

To display the time of day, use the simple form of the TOD command:

```
0A > TOD↲
Sat 12/29/80 02:20:14
```

To reset the time and the date, use this form of the TOD command:

```
0A > TOD 12/29/80 02.22.00↲
Strike any key to set time
Sat 12/29/80 02:22:00
0A >
```

NOTE: the TOD program displays the 'Strike any key' message; you may then hit any key when you are ready.

Aborting a Program (MP/M)

To abort the program currently attached to the console, type ↑C. (This has no effect on a detached program.)

The ABORT command will abort any program, even if it belongs to another console.

For example:

```
2B > ABORT LISTING 2 ↲
```

aborts the program LISTING belonging to the console at which the command is typed (console 2).

It is also possible to type at console 4:

4A> ABORT LISTING 2↲

to abort the program LISTING. Note that the console number may be optionally specified after the program name.

Attaching and Detaching a Program (MP/M)

A program may be detached from the console by typing ↑D. It will continue to execute "invisibly" until it is reattached to the console. This frees the console for the execution of another program or the entry of text or data.

Typing a ↑D will detach the program from the console, provided that the program checks the console status, i.e., reads the command. A program may also detach itself automatically by making an XDOS detach call.

Conversely, a program is attached to its console with the ATTACH command. It must always be reattached to the same console from which it was detached.

For example:

0A> ATTACH PROG↲

NOTE: typing ↑D when the TMP (Terminal Message Process) is executing at a console results in the activation of the next process, which qualifies it as being ready to run, and at the highest priority level of those waiting for the console. Note also that TMP is in execution whenever a command can be, or is being typed.

Console (MP/M)

Since a user number does not necessarily correspond to the console number, the CONSOLE command is provided to examine the number of the console being used.

For example:

2A> CONSOLE↲

CONSOLE = 1

The above example shows that user number 2 is using console number 1.

Directory (MP/M)

The DIR command works in the usual way and has one extension, the "S option". For example:

```
0A> DIR *.* S ↲
```

will include all files that have the system attribute set.

Erase (MP/M)

The usual form of the ERAse command is provided, as well as a new form. The ERAQ command may be used to erase a set of files that match a specific pattern. For example:

```
1B> ERAQ PROG. *↲
B: PROG COM? 4
B: PROG INT? 4
```

Typing a File (MP/M)

To execute the typing of a file, the usual TYPE command is provided. In addition, a pause mode may be used. When this option is utilized, the command:

```
0A> TYPE PROG.TXT P15 ↲
```

will display fifteen lines of PROG.TXT, and then pause until a ↲ is typed.

MP/M Control Characters

MP/M provides the usual line-editing functions of CP/M for the user typing in commands, plus some additional functions. The control characters are listed in Chapter 6.

MPMSTAT (MP/M)

A special STAT command is provided by MP/M to display the complete run-time status of MP/M proper. The command is:

```
0A> MPMSTAT ↲
```

A typical output is shown below.

```
****** MP/M Status Display *****

Top of memory = FFFFH
Number of consoles = 02
Debugger breakpoint restart # = 06
Stack is swapped on BDOS calls
Z80 complementary registers managed by dispatcher
Ready Process(es):
  MPMSTAT  Idle
Process(es)    DQing:
  [Sched    ]  Sched
  [ATTACH   ]  ATTACH
  [CLiQ     ]  cli
Process(es)    NQing:
Delayed Process(es):
Polling Process(es):
  PIP
Process(es) Flag Waiting:
  01 - Tick
  02 - Clock
Flag(s) Set:
  03
Queue(s):
  MPMSTAT    Sched    CliQ      ATTACH    MXParse
  MXList    [Tmp0   ] MXDisk
Process(es Attached to Consoles:
  [0] - MPMSTAT
  [1] - PIP
Process(es) Waiting for Consoles:
  [0] - TMP0      DIR
  [1] - TMP1
Memory Allocation:
  Base = 0000H   Size = 4000H   Allocated to PIP   [1]
  Base = 4000H   Size = 2000H   *  Free  *
  Base = 6000H   Size = 1100H   Allocated to DIR   [0]
```

NOTE: a detailed interpretation of this status display goes beyond the scope of this chapter. The display is included primarily to make the text more complete, and can be skipped during a first reading.

The simplified meaning of the display is as follows:

Ready Process(es): This list shows all of the ready processes in order of priority. The process with the highest priority is the one that is running.

Process(es) DQing: Each queue is shown, along with the processes that have executed a read operation on the queue. The processes are listed in order of priority and are waiting for a message to be written to the queue.

Process(es) NQing: Same as above, except that processes wait for a buffer to write a message to the queue.

Delayed Process(es): Lists the processes delayed for a specified length of time (clock ticks).

Polling Process(es): Lists the processes that poll an I/O device waiting for a ready status.

Process(es) Flag Waiting: Lists the processes opposite the corresponding flag number.

Flag(s) Set: List of the flags that are set.

Queue(s): Lists the queues in the system. Upper case characters are used for those queues that may be accessed via a console command. 'MX' at the beginning of a queue name denotes mutual exclusion.

Process(es) Attached to Console: Lists the processes and corresponding console numbers.

Process(es) Waiting for Consoles: Lists the processes by console and priority. The processes have been detached and are now waiting for their console in order to resume execution.

Memory Allocation: Displays a memory map showing the base, size, bank (if applicable), and the resident process, along with the console number.

Additional MP/M Commands

MP/M is equipped with three additional commands that are complex in appearance, and are used only by assembly-language programmers: GENMOD, GENHEX, and PRLCOM.

They are listed here to complete the text, but may be skipped during a first reading.

GENMOD (MP/M)

This special command transforms FILE 1 that contains two concatenated hexadecimal files (of type HEX), offset from each other by 0100H bytes, into a FILE 2 which is page relocatable (of type PRL).

The command format is:

```
0A> GENMOD d: FILE1.HEX d:FILE2-PRL $DDDD ↵
```

where $DDDD is an optional parameter that specifies, in hexadecimal, the additional amount of memory required by the program.

GENHEX (MP/M)

This command transforms a COM file into a HEX file. This command is often used before a GENMOD. An offset may also be specified. For example:

```
0A> GENHEX B:FILE.COM 200 ↵
```

PRLCOM (MP/M)

This command transforms a PRL file into a COM file:

```
0A> PRLCOM B: FILE1.PRL A: FILE2.COM ↵
```

GENSYS (MP/M)

This command is used to generate an MP/M system. It prompts the user for all the required information and parameters, and creates the MPM.SYS file. The MPMLDR command (described next) may be used afterwards to load and execute the MPM.SYS file.

The dialogue is shown below. A dash denotes a user response.

```
A> GENSYS ↵

          MP/M SYSTEM GENERATION

______________________________________

______________________________________

Top page of memory = __
Number of consoles = _
```

Breakpoint RST# = __

Add system call user stacks (Y/N)? __

Z80CPU (Y/N)? __

Bank switched memory (Y/N)? __

Memory segment bases, (ff terminates list)

: __ __

: __ __

: __ __

: __ __

Select Resident System Processes: (Y/N)

ABORT ? __

SPOOL ? __

MPMSTAT ? __

SCHED ? __

NOTE: the above dialogue varies slightly if Bank Switched Memory is specified.

SUMMARY

All of the facilities offered by CP/M, from control characters to built-in and transient commands, were presented in this chapter. Recall that you should know all the control characters, four of the five built-in commands (DIR, TYPE, REN, and ERA), and four of the nine transient commands (PIP, ED, SYSGEN, and STAT). The other commands will be useful to you only if you plan to write and execute assembly level languages (ASM, LOAD, DUMP, DDT, SAVE), or if you want the convenience of a SUBMIT file.

A complete summary of all of these commands will be presented in reference form in Chapter 6.

PIP

3

HANDLING FILES WITH PIP

INTRODUCTION

The PIP command was briefly introduced in Chapter 1, where it was used to copy a file. PIP's primary use is to copy, or more precisely, transfer files. It can, however, do much more.

In this chapter, you will learn about all of the facilities offered by PIP. While you will probably only use a few of these facilities, it is important to know all of the options available. You are therefore encouraged to read through this chapter completely, and then go back and study in detail the sections of specific interest to you.

You may be surprised at the range of facilities PIP offers. To mention just a few, you will learn:

- How to join files (concatenation)
- How to print formatted text (using tabs)
- How to cut off lines that are too long for the screen (D option)
- How to print a group of files with just one command (using a PRN specification)
- How to automatically print text in formatted pages (P option)
- How to read a file up to a specified word, without using the assembler (Q option)

UNDERSTANDING PIP

PIP is a file transfer program. The letters PIP stand for "Peripheral Interchange Command." As its name indicates, PIP allows the transfer of files between any two devices. Thus far, we have performed file transfers from disk to disk only. We will now learn to use additional options available with PIP. In particular, PIP can also process files as it transfers them.

We will first present a complete description of PIP's most important function: copying files. Then, we will study PIP's facilities for transferring files between the various devices connected to the computer system.

COPYING FILES

Copying A Single File

PIP may be executed in two ways:

1. As a single line command
2. As a "program"

Here is an example that uses PIP as a single line command:

```
A> PIP B : COPY1.BAK = FILE1.TXT ↵
A>
```

It is assumed that FILE1.TXT is on the current drive, A. This command directs PIP to make a copy of FILE1.TXT, name the new copy COPY1.BAK and put COPY1.BAK on drive B. Then, CP/M returns with the system prompt (A>). This is a quick way to copy a single file.

PIP can also be executed as a "program," and used to perform a sequence of copy operations:

```
A> PIP ↵
*B:COPY2.BAK = FILE2.TXT ↵
*A: = B:SAMPLE.BAS ↵
*A: = B:PROG.FOR ↵
* ↵
A>
```

Once the PIP program executes, it displays the PIP prompt '*'. PIP commands may then be executed. The first line in the example makes a copy of FILE2.TXT, which is on drive A, calls the copy COPY2.BAK, and then puts COPY2.BAK on drive B. The next line makes a copy of SAMPLE.BAS, which is on drive B, uses the original name (SAMPLE.BAS) for the copy, and puts the copy on drive A. The next expression also copies a file from drive B to drive A. A simple RETURN (carriage return) terminates PIP, causing a return to CP/M: the usual CP/M prompt 'A>' appears on the screen again.

We will now present the rules for performing such transfers. To make a copy of a file from one diskette to another, use this form of a PIP expression:

d:copy = d:original

where 'd' is a drive letter, 'copy' is the new name for the copy file, and 'original' is the name of the original file. The two d's above may refer to the same drive, or to two different ones. The 'd' on the right may be omitted, since PIP will assume that the file is in the current drive. The 'd' on the left may also be omitted, as long as the 'copy' name is supplied. If you want the copy file to have the same name as the original file, use this abbreviated form:

d' = d:original

where d' is a different drive letter than d:. The copy name may be omitted — PIP will just assume that the name of the file in the new drive is the same as the original. However, this will only work if the copy file's drive is a different drive from the original file's drive, because you cannot have two files with the same name on the same diskette. For example:

```
*B: = A:TEST.INT
```

will copy TEST.INT from A to B.

Let us study some examples. Assume that we are in drive A. Assume that FILE1.NAD is in drive A and PROGRAM.TXT is in drive B. Are the following PIP commands legal?

```
    A> PIP
(1) *A: = B:PROGRAM.TXT
(2) *B: = FILE1.NAD
(3) *A:FILEREV.NAD = A:FILE1.NAD
(4) *A:FILE1.TXT = FILE1.NAD
(5) *B:FILE1.NAD = FILE1.NAD
```

All of the above are legal. In (2), notice that the command is equivalent to:

```
B: = A:FILE1.NAD
```

Remember that the current drive may be omitted. It is then assumed by PIP to be the current drive, i.e., A. The A could have been omitted in

(3). FILE1.TXT in (4) is *not* the same as FILE1.NAD. This is legal. (5) could have been abbreviated to look like (2).

Copying Multiple Files

Multiple PIP commands are used to copy several different files. For example, let us copy the three files:

```
FILE1.NAD
LETTER.TXT
PROGRAM.INT
```

from B to A:

```
A> PIP ↵
*A:=B:FILE1.NAD ↵
*A:=B:LETTER.TXT ↵
*A:=B:PROGRAM.INT ↵
* ↵
A>
```

In special cases, however, this procedure can be simplified with the use of PIP's *matching symbols*. To facilitate copying multiple files, PIP permits the use of two special symbols: '?' and '*'. The '?' may be used in a file name, and will match any character that might appear in its place.

For example:

FILE?.NAD

will match:

FILE1.NAD

FILE2.NAD

FILE3.NAD

but not: FILE44.NAD (one character too many)

We will now copy the three files:

FILE1.NAD

FILE2.NAD

FILE3.NAD

from drive B to drive A. Here is the command:

A > PIP A: = B:FILE?.NAD ↵

which will accomplish the three transfers in just one command by using the special matching character. B's directory will be examined by PIP until all possibilities of making a match are exhausted. Note that if there were another file on B called

FILES.NAD

it would also be transferred.

The second matching character, '*', is even more powerful. It will match anything in its field, *regardless of length.* For example, assume B contains:

FILE1.NAD

FILE12.NAD

LETTER.TXT

CBASIC.INT

FILE1.BAK

Then, the characters *.NAD will match:

FILE1.NAD

FILE12.NAD

And FILE1.* will match:

FILE1.NAD

FILE1.BAK

It is also possible to write '*.*', which will simply match all of the files on the diskette in drive B. This will be used in the next section to copy all files.

For example, if we want to copy all COM type programs from drive A to drive B, we can simply type:

```
A > PIP B: = *.COM ↵
```

and all commands will be successively copied to drive B.

We have now learned how to copy a single file and a group of files. Next, we will learn how to copy an entire diskette.

Copying All Files

Note that this section is titled "Copying All Files," and not "Copying An Entire Diskette." This is because CP/M is not stored as a file. In order to copy CP/M, a special command, SYSGEN, must be used (described in Chapter 2). If a diskette contains only files, then we will be copying all files. If the diskette also contains CP/M, however, we will only be copying the files, not CP/M.

You cannot know whether CP/M is on a diskette by simply examining the directory with the DIR command; CP/M is not a file, and is not listed as a file. If you want to check whether or not CP/M is on a diskette, you will have to try executing CP/M from it by doing a CNTRL-C, for example.

Let us now use PIP's matching facility to copy all files. A *filename match* may be used as a filename in the *original* filename arguments only. For example, if you want to copy all of the files from diskette drive A to diskette drive B, you would type this command:

```
A > PIP B: = A:*.* ↵
```

Use this form of PIP to make copies of diskettes:

```
PIP d': = d:*.*
```

where *d'* is the letter of the drive holding the new diskette,and *d* is the letter of the drive holding the old diskette. The filename match '*.*' will match *all filenames. d'* must be different from *d*.

In practice, when copying all files, it is recommended that you type:

```
A > PIP B:=A:*.* [V]
```

'V' is a PIP option that specifies "verify"; it checks to see if the copy is identical to the original. This is the best command to use for safety. However, the copy process takes much longer with the [V] option, so that many users do not use it unless a file is very valuable.

NOTE: remember that the PIP command:

```
B:=A:*.*
```

will copy all files on A, but only the files. If A contains a "system," i.e., CP/M, CP/M will not be copied, as it is not a file. Recall that CP/M itself must be copied with the SYSGEN command.

Copying A Diskette

On many computers, a special utility program is available to copy *entire diskettes* at high speed. If this option is used, then the second disk will be a complete copy of the first, including CP/M, if CP/M was on the first one. This is usually the quickest way of copying a complete diskette.

On the other hand, when PIP copies a file, it copies it on adjacent "blocks" or "sectors" on the diskette. As a result, the copied file will be accessed much more quickly by programs such as an editor (or word processor) or an interpreter (BASIC).

In summary, using PIP to copy a diskette will result in a "cleaner" file. Using a disk-copying program, however, will save time on the copy operation.

CP/M Version 2.2 and MP/M

The expression '*.*' for a filename match might not be sufficient for your installation if you have separate *user areas* (user areas are discussed in Chapter 2). If you make use of these areas, then your system should have a special program that will duplicate diskettes. If you get an "invalid format" error, hit any key *except* the RETURN key to bring back the PIP prompt. If the PIP operation does not occur, try it again.

If you hit RETURN, PIP terminates, and the operating system returns with the system prompt.

Copying Onto A Fresh Diskette

The Two Methods

If you have three disk drives or more, simply insert a new diskette in drive C, and "PIP" your file from B to C, i.e., from the second to the third drive. If you have only two drives, however, the copying process is more complicated. We will assume that the system disk is in drive A, and that the file to be copied is in drive B. We want to copy it onto a new diskette. Two methods may be used: transferring through A, and diskette swapping.

Transferring Through A

This method is safe, but slow, and works only if the diskette in drive A has enough space left on it. (We will later see how to check the space available with the STAT or DIR commands.) The method used is quite simple:

1. The file is transferred from B to A
2. A new diskette is placed in B
3. The file is transferred from A to B, onto the new diskette.

Remember that ↑C must be executed before step 3, so that CP/M is able to write on a new diskette. For example:

```
A> A:=B:FILE.INT↲
(place a new diskette in B)
↑C
A> B:=A:FILE.INT↲
```

Then, verify that your file is on the diskette in drive B by checking B's directory (using 'DIR'), and erase the extra copy from A ('ERA').

Disk Swapping

This method directly transfers the file onto a fresh diskette. In order for the transfer to occur, three conditions must be met simultaneously:

1. PIP must be executing
2. The source file must be in a drive
3. The destination diskette must be in a drive.

PIP is loaded from the diskette into the computer's memory. Then, the system diskette is removed, and PIP is executed in memory. In other words, once the PIP command has been invoked, the PIP program is loaded into the computer's memory, and the System Diskette may be replaced by another diskette for the transfer.

Assuming that the System Diskette with PIP is in drive A, the process is as follows:

1. Insert a fresh diskette in B
2. Hit CTRL-C to perform a "warm boot." This allows CP/M to recognize a new diskette in B, and to write on it
3. Invoke PIP by typing: 'PIP(CR)':

```
A> PIP↲

*↲
```

PIP is now in the memory, and ready to execute.

At this point you can remove the System Diskette for a *moment*, and insert the original diskette (the one that you are copying) into drive A. It may sound surprising to suggest removing the System Diskette on which PIP resides. Remember, however, that whenever a COM type program is executed, it is loaded from the disk into the computer's memory.

PIP has been invoked by typing:

```
A> PIP↲
```

A copy of PIP is now in the computer's memory. We no longer need the diskette, and we can remove it until we want to exit from PIP.
NOTE: do not terminate PIP until you put the System Diskette back in.

Do not type a return after a prompt, once PIP has been activated:

```
*↲      (DON'T!)
```

as this will terminate PIP. Also, don't use CTRL-C until you have put the System Diskette back in. Refer to "Practical Hints" in Chapter 7 to learn an effective safeguard against accidental exit from PIP.

Now, insert the diskette to be copied into drive A. At the PIP prompt

'*', you can type a PIP expression. Bear in mind that the original diskette is in drive A, and that the fresh diskette is in drive B. If you are copying the entire original diskette, you should type this expression:

```
*B:=A:*.*
```

Or, if you prefer:

```
*B:=A:*.*[V]
```

with the verification option.

The '*.*' is a filename match for all files (under CP/M version 2.2 and MP/M, the '*.* [V]' matches all files in *your user area* only). This PIP expression copies all files from drive A (the original diskette) to drive B using the same names for the copies of the files. After executing, you will have a copy of every file on the fresh diskette, and the files will have the same names as before.

Now you are ready to bring back the system. Before terminating PIP, remove the original diskette from drive A, and put the System Diskette back into drive A. You can now terminate PIP by simply hitting the RETURN key:

```
*
A>
```

If the system does not return, check drive A. If the drive A light is on, you can insert the System Diskette, and the system will return. If the light is off, you must insert the System Diskette and restart the system, as described in Chapter 1.

Installations that have only two drives must use the method just described:

1. Put a fresh diskette into drive B
2. Execute PIP
3. Take out the System Diskette
4. Put the original diskette into drive A
5. Execute PIP expressions for copy operations
6. When finished, take out the original diskette
7. Put the System Diskette back in
8. Then, terminate PIP.

Remember to put the fresh diskette in drive B, and the original in drive A. If there was another diskette in B before, execute a CTRL-C before doing anything, or CP/M will refuse to write on a diskette that it does not "know." CTRL-C will force CP/M to log in the fresh diskette. Note that this does not work the other way around. If, instead of the System Diskette, we had placed the new diskette in A, CP/M would refuse to write on it, as we did not log it in.

Once the system diskette has been removed, you can no longer execute a CTRL-C, so there is no way to log in the new diskette in A. However, here is a practical hint: make a copy of CP/M and PIP on your new diskette; then you can place it in either drive and make convenient copies from it.

Cromemco CDOS

CDOS does not require a CTRL-C to write on a new diskette; therefore, the process of copying may be simplified. With the system in drive A, and the diskette to be copied in drive B, execute 'PIP ↲' as before, then:

1. Remove the system diskette
2. Insert the new diskette in A
3. Perform the transfer
4. Remove the new diskette
5. Put the System Diskette back in A
6. Hit "return" to terminate PIP.

The Recommended Procedure

As long as you are inexperienced with CP/M, you should transfer your file by using the first method (copying through A), as it is safer. Better still, copy CP/M and PIP on all of your diskettes so that swapping is no longer required. While you may want to try the second method of transferring a file, remember that you may damage your original diskette if you exit from PIP too soon by hitting return without having removed the original diskette housing the files.

Aborting A Copy Operation

Pressing any character on the keyboard during a PIP transfer will normally abort it. PIP confirms this by displaying the message 'ABORTED.'

COPYING TO DEVICES

Introduction

Printing a file is one example of a transfer operation: the file is copied from the disk onto the printer. PIP provides general-purpose transfer capabilities and allows a file to be transferred not just from disk to disk, but between various devices.

These general capabilities will be described next. We will learn how to transfer between any two (reasonable) devices that may be attached to the computer. We will introduce new features of PIP such as concatenation, which may be used on all file transfers, including disk to disk. Even though you may not plan to use a card-reader, it is important to read this section completely, as it also applies to printing and file copying.

We will first consider the most frequently used operation, printing.

Printing A File

A file may be printed by PIP, or by other programs. If you are using a word processor or other special program that has a "printing facility" (the ability to send a file to the printer) included, you should use that program to print files created and accessed by the program. For example, if you created and added data to a "name and address" file by using a "name and address" software package, chances are you also have a way of printing the file by using a special program provided as part of the same "name and address" software package.

The major advantage of a specialized printing program is that it prints your file in a specific format. A printing program, for example, may provide automatic formatting, tabulations, line spacing, pagination, and other printing options.

The CP/M command TYPE may also be used to type an alphanumeric file (refer to Chapter 1). For example:

```
A> ↑P
A> TYPE FILE.TXT ↵
```

The CTRL-A turns the printer "on," if it was "off" before. This command is easy to use, and provides "raw" typing, in other words, the file appears on the printer exactly as it is on the disk without any reformatting.

Only one formatting facility is provided by TYPE; it will expand any tab characters (CTRL-I) contained in the file, and assumes a tab position at every eighth column. The TYPE command is used for fast typing, looking at the beginning of a file, or, most often, displaying a file quickly on the screen rather than on the printer. The CRT terminal can display text at a speed of 9600 baud vs. 300 to 600 baud for a printer (approximately). TYPEing on the screen will therefore display text much faster than if it was listed on the printer.

Files may also be printed with PIP as part of its general file transfer capabilities. This process will now be described.

Transferring Files

A file can be sent to any device capable of receiving it. For example, a file can be sent to a disk unit, a printer, a video monitor, a paper tape punch, and a cassette recorder. It may not be sent to a card reader or a keyboard.

A printer without a keyboard can only receive files. A printer with a keyboard becomes a terminal, and the keyboard may generate a file.

Figure 3.1 shows how a user can "input" (read) from a device and "output" (write) to a device. The computer executes all programs and transfers all information.

To list a file on the printer, the computer first reads the file from the disk (input), and then transfers it to the printer (output). Most programs read files from the disk in blocks (one sector at a time), so that they can transfer a large file while using only a small amount of internal memory. This is shown in Figure 3.2.

Characters or files can also be input from the keyboard, or output to the display. They can be output to the disk as a disk-to-disk transfer as well. Specific file transfer programs must be available to provide these facilities. Often, specialized programs accomplish one of these functions within applications packages. However, the PIP program (a command) may be used as a general facility to send a copy of a file to a device, or receive information from a device to put in a file. Several PIP expressions, combined with special keywords used to represent devices, can perform powerful and complex copy operations. They will be described here.

In order to learn the valid PIP expressions, devices must be properly designated. The PIP conventions for specifying devices will be examined first.

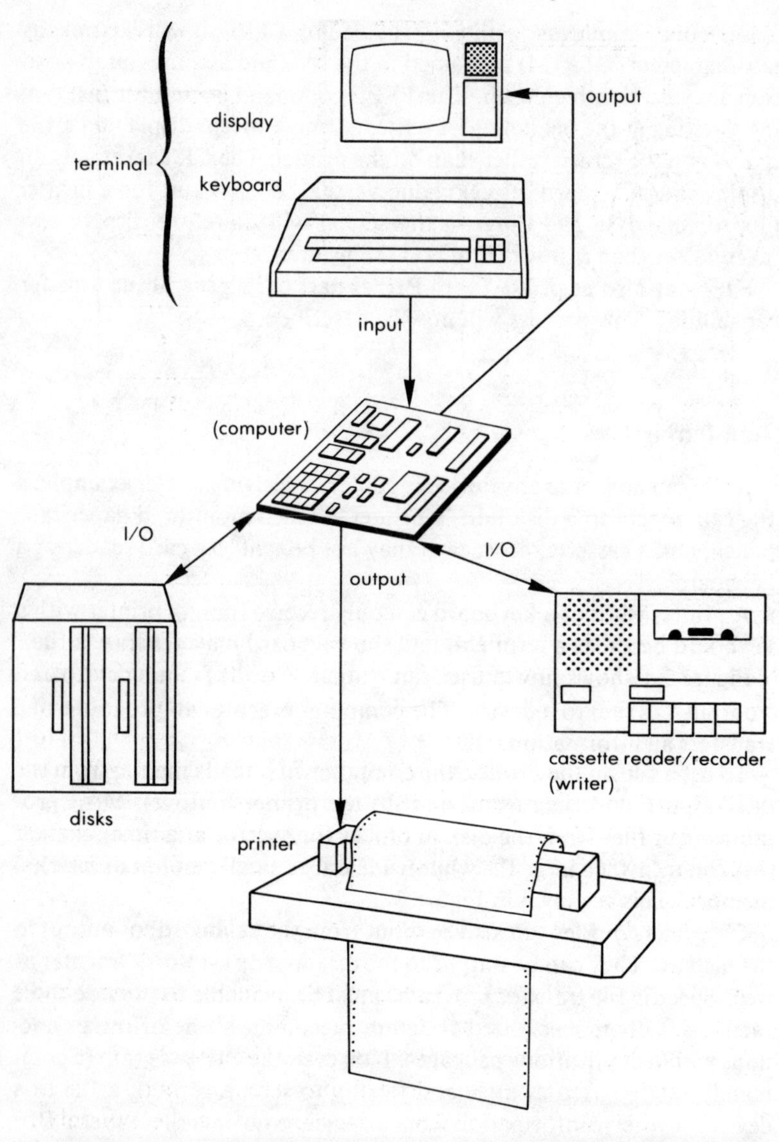

Figure 3.1: The Elements of a System

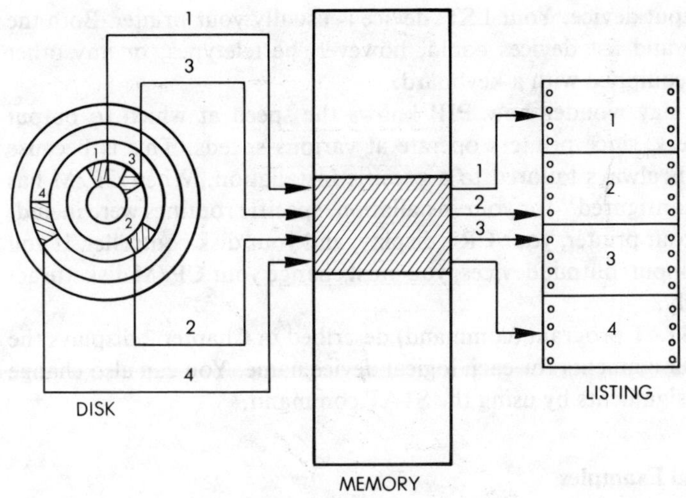

Figure 3.2: Transfers Through Memory

Specifying the Device

The keywords used in PIP expressions are "logical" as well as physical device names. A *physical* device name is the actual name of a device attached to your system. A *logical* device name is like a "generic" name that can actually be one of several devices assigned to the system. For example, LST: is the name of the "list" device, which is usually the printer, but which could be another device like a teletype, or a modem used to communicate over a telephone line. You do not have to know the brand name of the device (such as Teletype or Hazeltine), just the logical name.

The logical device names allowed in PIP expressions are:

- CON: for "console" or terminal, including keyboard and display (Input/Output)
- RDR: for paper tape or card reader (input only)
- PUN: for paper tape or card punch (output only)
- LST: for "listing" device like a line printer (output only).

Note that your assignments for RDR: and PUN: will probably not be paper tape or punched card devices, since those devices are quickly becoming antiques. They are used mostly for "batch" input and output (discussed in Chapters 2 and 4). Also, your CON: device is usually your CRT terminal (Cathode Ray Tube) with a keyboard, hence it is an input/output device. Your LST: device is usually your printer. Both the console and list devices could, however, be teletypes, or any other printer equipped with a keyboard.

You may wonder how PIP knows the speed at which to output characters, since printers operate at various speeds. This is because CP/M is always tailored to a specific installation. When CP/M has been "configured" for your installation, specific routines were included for your printer, your CRT display, and your disk controller. If you change input/output devices, you must change your CP/M diskette accordingly.

The STAT program (command) described in Chapter 2 displays the device assignments for each logical device name. You can also change these assignments by using the STAT command.

Practical Examples

You can use the logical names (described previously) in PIP expressions. For example:

```
A> PIP ↵
*CON: = SAMPLE.TXT ↵
*LST: = B:SIMPLE.BAK ↵
*PROG.BAS = RDR: ↵
*PUN: = PROG.BAS ↵
* ↵
A>
```

The first PIP expression sends a copy of the file SAMPLE.TXT (which is in the current drive [A]) to the console device (probably your display terminal). This is illustrated in Figure 3.3.

The second expression transfers a copy of the file SIMPLE.BAK in drive B to the current list LST: device (usually the line printer or teletype device). This is illustrated in Figure 3.4.

The third PIP expression reads the information coming from the reader device RDR:, and creates the file PROG.BAS. This is usually a program on paper tape, punched card, or cassette that can be read into the system and stored in a disk file by using this PIP expression (see Figure 3.5).

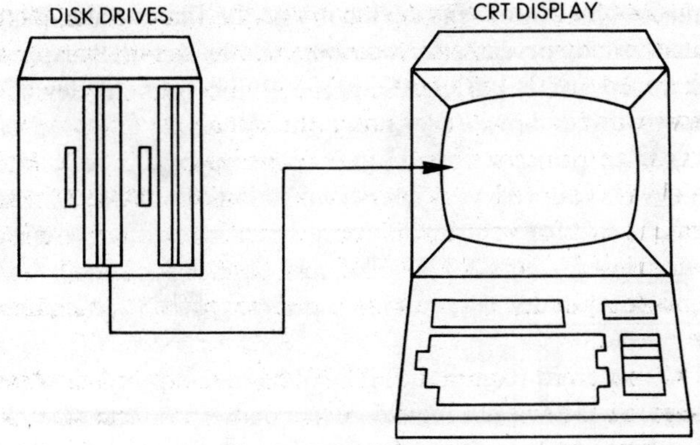

Figure 3.3: A File is Transferred to the Console: CON: = SAMPLE.TXT

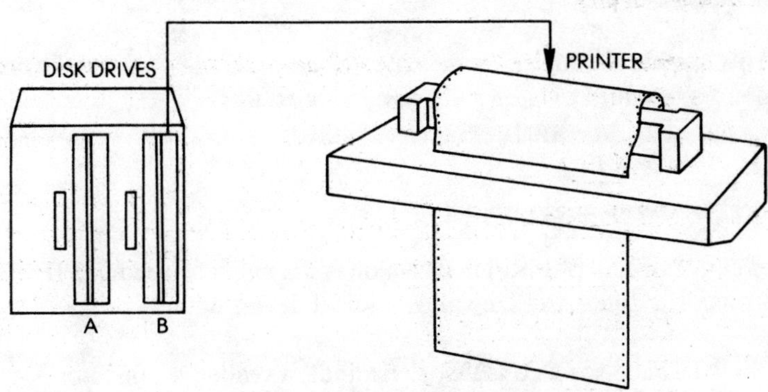

Figure 3.4: LST: = B: SIMPLE.BAK

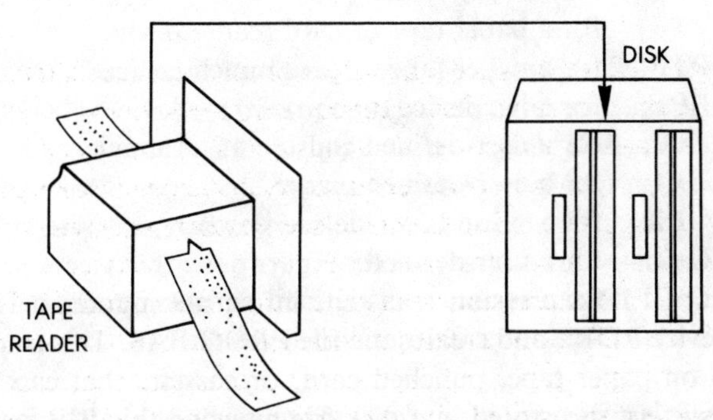

Figure 3.5: PROG.BAS = RDR:

The opposite operation, sending a copy of the file to the paper tape punch, card punch, or cassette recorder, is the last PIP expression that sends a copy of PROG.BAS to the PUN: (punch) device (see Figure 3.6).

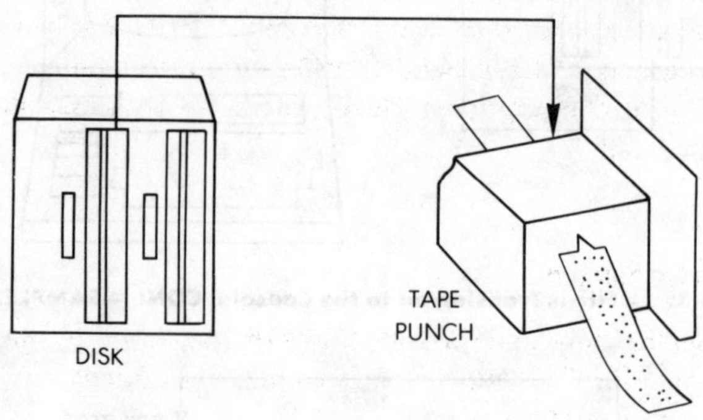

Figure 3.6: PUN : = PROG.BAS

Physical Device Names

For convenience, physical device names may also be used in PIP expressions. The following are valid physical device names:

- TTY: for a console or terminal, a reader, a punch or a list device (teletype)
- CRT: for a console or terminal, or list device (Cathode Ray Tube)
- PTR: for a paper tape or card reader device
- PTP: for a paper tape or card punch device
- LPT: for a list device (line printer)
- UC1: for a user-defined console or terminal
- UR1: for a user-defined reader
- UR2: for a second user-defined reader
- UP1: for a user-defined output (punch) device
- UP2: for a second user-defined output (punch) device
- UL1: for a user-defined listing device

NOTE: BAT: is not included, since it only reassigns the values for RDT: and LST:

SPECIAL COPY OPERATIONS

Introduction

We have now learned how to perform all of the simple copy operations. In this next section, we will learn how to perform more complex transfer operations on text files and "hex files." PIP is not just a simple "copy" program, but a general transfer program equipped with a number of processing options. These processing options will now be described in detail.

Special Device Names

Special device names are provided by PIP that result in the special processing of a file. The following additional device names may be used when performing PIP transfers:

NUL: send 40 "nulls" (ASCII code 0) to the device, usually a punch device for output. Example (where PROG.HEX is sent to the punch):

```
*PUN: = PROG.HEX,NULL: ↲
```

EOF: send an end-of-file (ASCII ↑Z) to the device (sent automatically by PIP during ASCII text file transfers, and only needed for special cases). Example:

```
*PUN: = NUL:,X.ASM,EOF:,NULL: ↲
```

This example sends 40 nulls to the punch device, followed by a copy of the file X.ASM, followed by the end-of-file character (↑Z) and 40 more nulls.

PRN: same as LST: (send to the printer), except that tabs are expanded every eighth character, lines are numbered (as in the ED program), and page ejects (form feeds) are inserted every 60 lines (to advance the printer paper to the next page), with an initial page eject. Example:

```
*PRN: = SAMPLE.TXT ↲
```

INP: special input device code which can be "patched" into the PIP program itself (you must write the patch in assembly language and add it to PIP). PIP receives the input character by calling a location in memory (103H) and storing the data starting at location 109H (parity bit must be zero — use the Z parameter).

OUT special output device code that can be "patched" into the PIP program itself, like INP: described above. PIP calls location 106H and sends the data in register C (each character).
NOTE to assembly language programmers: locations 109H through 1FFH of PIP memory image are not used and can be replaced with code for special purpose device drivers (use DDT— the CP/M Debugger supplied by Digital Research with CP/M or MP/M). Examples:

```
*MODEL.CLK = INP: ↵
```

(input from special device is stored in file MODEL.CLK)

```
*OUT: = MODEL.CLK ↵
```

(copy of MODEL.CLK is sent to the special device)

Text (ASCII) Files Sent to Devices

Most data files and *all* of the text files created by editor programs or word processing programs are text files in ASCII format. Other files, like command (.COM) files, BASIC intermediate (.INT) program files, and machine language (.HEX) files are actually programs written in a high level language (like BASIC) or in an assembly language where binary codes represent actual numbers or instructions, *not* text.

It is important that you know the differences between files if you perform special copy operations, like translating upper case characters to lower case, or deleting characters while copying, or copying portions of a file. You can only do these things with ASCII text files, because PIP expects a certain character (the character produced by hitting CTRL and Z simultaneously, i.e., ↑Z) to be at the end of the file, so that it can easily search for characters. You can also concatenate (join) several ASCII text files by using PIP (described later in this chapter).

Certain devices can only receive or send ASCII text files. You can only send text files to printers and console displays, for example, but other devices (RDR: and PUN:) can send or receive any kind of file. The information in a file may be coded in a number of ways. For example, a text file is normally coded in ASCII format, where an 8-bit code (a "byte") is used to represent each character, including the special control characters. This code is shown in Figure 3.7.

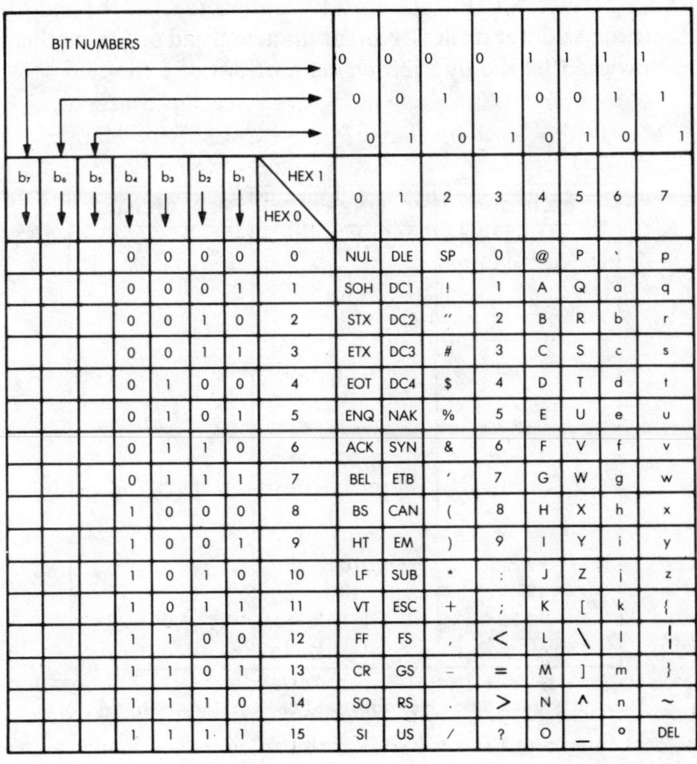

BIT NUMBERS															
b_7								0	0	0	0	1	1	1	1
b_6								0	0	1	1	0	0	1	1
b_5								0	1	0	1	0	1	0	1
b_7	b_6	b_5	b_4	b_3	b_2	b_1	HEX 1 / HEX 0	0	1	2	3	4	5	6	7
			0	0	0	0	0	NUL	DLE	SP	0	@	P	`	p
			0	0	0	1	1	SOH	DC1	!	1	A	Q	a	q
			0	0	1	0	2	STX	DC2	"	2	B	R	b	r
			0	0	1	1	3	ETX	DC3	#	3	C	S	c	s
			0	1	0	0	4	EOT	DC4	$	4	D	T	d	t
			0	1	0	1	5	ENQ	NAK	%	5	E	U	e	u
			0	1	1	0	6	ACK	SYN	&	6	F	V	f	v
			0	1	1	1	7	BEL	ETB	'	7	G	W	g	w
			1	0	0	0	8	BS	CAN	(	8	H	X	h	x
			1	0	0	1	9	HT	EM	)	9	I	Y	i	y
			1	0	1	0	10	LF	SUB	*	:	J	Z	j	z
			1	0	1	1	11	VT	ESC	+	;	K	[	k	{
			1	1	0	0	12	FF	FS	,	<	L	\	l	¦
			1	1	0	1	13	CR	GS	–	=	M	]	m	}
			1	1	1	0	14	SO	RS	.	>	N	^	n	~
			1	1	1	1	15	SI	US	/	?	O	_	o	DEL

NUL — Null
SOH — Start of Heading
STX — Start of Text
ETX — End of Text
EOT — End of Transmission
ENQ — Enquiry
ACK — Acknowledge
BEL — Bell
BS — Backspace
HT — Horizontal Tabulation
LF — Line Feed
VT — Vertical Tabulation
FF — Form Feed
CR — Carriage Return
SO — Shift Out
SI — Shift In
DLE — Data Link Escape
DC — Device Control
NAK — Negative Acknowledge
SYN — Synchronous Idle
ETB — End of Transmission Block
CAN — Cancel
EM — End of Medium
SUB — Substitute
ESC — Escape
FS — File Separator
GS — Group Separator
RS — Record Separator
US — Unit Separator
SP — Space (Blank)
DEL — Delete

Figure 3.7: ASCII Conversion Table

However, programs that have been processed by a compiler are usually represented in a more compact code, called hexadecimal, which uses only 4 bits to represent 16 symbols. See Figure 3.8.

When transferring a file to a printer or a display, it is essential to specify whether it is hexadecimal (two digits per byte) or ASCII (one character per byte). PIP transfers a file until it reaches the end-of-file character in ASCII text files (↑Z), or the actual end of file in other files (except where PIP is only transferring portions of a file).

DECIMAL	BINARY	HEXADECIMAL
0	0000	0
1	0001	1
2	0010	2
3	0011	3
4	0100	4
5	0101	5
6	0110	6
7	0111	7
8	1000	8
9	1001	9
10	1010	A
11	1011	B
12	1100	C
13	1101	D
14	1110	E
15	1111	F

Figure 3.8: Hexadecimal Conversion Table

Concatenating Text Files

Concatenation is an important command used to group several text files into one. Note, however, that the space available on the disk must be sufficient to accommodate the final file.

The simplest example is to concatenate two files:

```
A> PIP ↵
* BIG.TXT=PART1.TXT, PART2.TXT ↵
```

You can also join several text files at once:

```
A> PIP↲
*FINAL.ASM=SUB1.ASM,SUB2.ASM,TEMP.ASM↲
*B:NEW.ZOT=A:OLD.ZAP,B:OLD.ZOT,A:NEW.ZAP↲
*↲
A>
```

In this example, copies of the files SUB1.ASM,SUB2.ASM and TEMP.ASM (all on the current drive, drive A) are joined in that order (i.e., SUB1.ASM is first, SUB2.ASM is second, etc.) into one copy called FINAL.ASM. The second PIP expression joins a copy of OLD.ZAP on drive A with OLD.ZOT on drive B and with NEW.ZAP on drive A, and the resulting copy is put on drive B and called NEW.ZOT.

PIP always assumes that these are *text* files, each ending with the end-of-file character (ASCII ↑Z). If they are text files, PIP will have no trouble joining them (removing the ↑Z characters and putting one on the end of the new copy to denote end-of-file). If they are *not* text files, however, you should read the next section, "Concatenating Non-Text Files."

Another way to concatenate is to specify the "leading" file as the *copy*. For example:

```
A> PIP FIRST.TXT=FIRST.TXT,SECOND.TXT,THIRD.TXT↲
A>
```

This command will *not* change the initial contents of FIRST.TXT or the other files, but will *append* (add to the end) to FIRST.TXT the files SECOND.TXT and THIRD.TXT. The final file FIRST.TXT will contain at its beginning the old contents of the initial FIRST.TXT.

Concatenation may be used to list or examine several files at once, with a single command. For example:

```
A> PIP LPT:=FIRST.TXT,SECOND.TXT
```

will print the two files in sequence on the printer.

When using Cromemco's XFER instead of PIP, the control characters are different from PIP and should be learned specifically. In

particular, XFER requires a control character to concatenate files (or the CRTL-Z will be left in at the end of each file).
A practical hint: when concatenating files, make sure that there is enough room on your diskette for the resulting file.

Concatenating Non-Text Files

When you are concatenating (joining) non-text files, each file does *not* have an end-of-file character, therefore PIP will not copy after it reaches an actual end of file (i.e., if there is no end-of-file character, just an end of the file). To force PIP to copy the next file, and join it to the previous file, you must use a "transfer parameter" shown here as "X" (discussed in "Parameters in Copy Operations" in this chapter). Parameters are enclosed in brackets ([ ]), and they must appear in the PIP expression after the file or device they apply to. For example:

```
A> PIP FINAL.HEX=TEMP1 [X], TEMP2 [X], TEMP3 ↲
```

This PIP command concatenates copies of the files TEMP1, TEMP2, and TEMP3, and calls the resulting copy FINAL.HEX. The X parameters force PIP to overlook the actual ends of files TEMP1 and TEMP2, and perform the concatenation (used with non-text files only).

Copying Hex Files

Files that are hexadecimal are generally created by an *assembler.* An assembler translates an assembly language program into *machine code* (sequences of binary numbers corresponding to instructions), which is stored in a hexadecimal file.

The CP/M assembler creates a HEX file, i.e., a file with a HEX extension. The HEX extension has a special meaning to PIP: PIP assumes that the file is in the Intel "hex format," and PIP automatically checks for proper format, legal hexadecimal values, and checksums. The HEX extension should, therefore, be used with care.

If you want to make a copy of a HEX-type file, you can use a PIP expression with the H or I parameter (for *hexadecimal* data transfer). When you use the H parameter, PIP checks all of the data to ensure proper Intel hexadecimal format. If there is an error in the data (i.e., it does not have the proper hex format) PIP prompts your terminal to seek corrective action. The H parameter also removes non-essential characters between hexadecimal records during the copy operation.

The I parameter automatically sets the H parameter (it does what H does, and more). If you use the I parameter, PIP ignores the ':00' records in the original hexadecimal-formatted file (Intel hex), and checks for improper hexadecimal format.

If you are copying *from a device* to a file with an explicit 'HEX' extension, PIP checks the data for improper Intel hexadecimal format *and* checksum records. In other words, if you are copying from a paper tape reader to a new file SAMPLE.HEX, you don't need to use the H parameter to check for proper hexadecimal format (you do, however, need the I parameter to ignore ':00' records).

If PIP senses an invalid format or a checksum error, it reports the error to your terminal and waits for corrective action. If you are copying from paper tape, you can usually pull the tape back about 20 inches and rerun the tape. When the tape is ready, type a single RETURN and PIP will attempt to copy from the tape.

NOTE: if the device is the RDR:, you can enter the end-of-file (↑Z) character from your terminal keyboard while the PIP operation is copying. PIP reads from the device while monitoring your keyboard, and waits for you to type a ↑Z to terminate the copy operation.

Here are examples of PIP expressions using this extension:

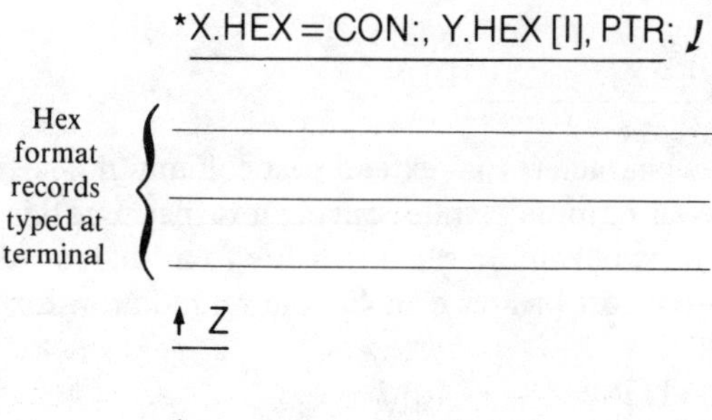

In this expression, PIP copies into X.HEX first from the CON: device (your terminal) until you type a Z. Then, PIP copies from Y.HEX and ignores '.00' records. Finally, PIP copies from the paper tape reader PTR: until it encounters an end-of-file (↑Z).

```
*PROG.X = KLUDGE.HEX [H]
*
```

This expression copies the hexadecimal format file KLUDGE.HEX into PROG.X and checks for invalid hexadecimal format during the transfer.

PARAMETERS IN COPY OPERATIONS

The Parameters

We will now describe some of the processing options available during transfers. Even though you will generally only use a few, it is important to know that they exist. Parameters are special letters enclosed in brackets that follow a filename in a PIP expression and affect the copy of that file. You can specify more than one parameter in a PIP expression. Some parameters require another letter or letters or digits. These are all advanced copy operations, and knowledge of them is not required for the casual PIP user.

B Block mode transfer. PIP puts data in a buffer until it reads an ASCII 'X-off' character (↑S) from the device. PIP then clears the disk buffer and returns for more data. The size of the buffer depends on the size of your system (see the documentation provided with your system). Use this parameter to transfer data from a continuously reading device like a cassette player or reader. Example:

```
*SERVE.TXT = RDR: [B] ↲
```

Dn PIP deletes characters that extend past column 'n' (vertical columns on your terminal) while copying text files. Use this to truncate long lines if you are sending a file to a "narrow device," such as a low-cost printer or a 40-column monitor. Example:

```
*PRN: = LONG.TXT [D40] ↲
```

This command may also be used to "cut off" comments from a program, if they appear in a specific position.

E Echo (redisplay) all copy operations on the terminal screen as they are being performed. Example:

```
*COPY.TXT = SOURCE.TXT,S2.TXT,S3.TXT,S4.TXT [E] ↲
```

This is useful in the case of a sequence of transfers.

F PIP filters form feeds from the file (i.e., removes them). You can also use the P parameter to insert new form feeds. This allows you to "clean up" a file after modifying it for neat printing.

H Hexadecimal data transfer: PIP checks all data for proper Intel hexadecimal format. This requires a .HEX file.

I Ignore ':00' records in the transfer of Intel hex format files (automatically sets the H parameter). This requires a .HEX file.

L Translate all UPPER CASE characters to lower case.

N Add line numbers to each line copied into the new file (starting at line 1). Each line number is followed by a colon. Leading zeros (e.g., 003) are deleted, unless you specify the 'N2' parameter. 'N2' leaves the leading zeros and inserts a tab space after the numbers. You can expand tab spaces by using the T parameter. This is useful for referencing a listing.

O Object file transfer (for non-ASCII files): PIP ignores the physical end of the file during concatenation (see "Concatenating Files").

Pn PIP includes page ejects at every 'nth' line (with an initial page eject). If n is 1 (or if you don't specify 'n'), page ejects occur every 60 lines. (This is called a *default* specification.) If you also use the F parameter, PIP removes the form feeds before inserting page ejects. This is a convenient method for printing onto a set page format.

Q string ↑Z PIP quits copying from the device or file when it finds the 'string' of characters you specify (a 'string' is a group of characters; e.g., STRING105%). You end your 'string' with a ↑Z (CTRL and Z simultaneously). See "Copying Portions of Files" in this chapter. This is a convenient way to list a portion of a file.

S string ↑Z PIP starts copying from the device or file when it finds the 'string' of characters you specify. End your string with a ↑Z. See "Copying Portions of Files" in this chapter. This is a convenient way to list a portion of a file, starting at a given location.

Tn Expand the tab space to every 'nth' column during the transfer of text files. You create a tab space in a text file using ↑I; this parameter expands the tab space from its usual fixed column amount (vertical columns on your terminal screen).

U Translate all lower-case characters to UPPER-CASE during the copying of text files.

V PIP verifies that data has been copied correctly by re-reading the new copy file afterwards (copy file cannot be a device), and displaying a message if the copy was successful. This parameter should be used whenever an important backup copy is made.

Z Turn the parity bit to zero on inputs of ASCII characters. Use this parameter especially if you are inputting from the INP: patch device.

Here are examples of PIP expressions with parameters:

```
*LST: = SAMPLE.TXT [NT8P60] ↲
```

This expression sends the file SAMPLE.TXT to the list device (LST:), with line numbers ('N') tabs expanded to every eighth character column ('T8') and page ejects at every 60 lines ('P60'). The PRN: device assumes these parameters; if the listing device was assigned to PRN:, the above example could be rewritten:

```
*PRN: = SAMPLE.TXT ↲
```

You can override the PRN: "assumptions" (default parameters) by providing your own parameters:

```
*PRN: = SAMPLE.TXT [P59] ↲
```

This expression sends SAMPLE.TXT to the PRN: device with the usual default parameters (i.e., NT8), *except* that the usual P parameter is changed to 59 lines.

Here is another example:

```
*LPT: = PROG.ASM [NT8U] ↲
```

This expression sends PROG.ASM to the listing device with line numbers ('N'), expanded tabs to every eighth column ('T8'), and with lower case characters translated to upper case ('U').

Copying Portions of Files

Inevitably, you will some day interrupt a long listing on your printer either by accident (hitting a character on the keyboard), or because of a printer problem (no more paper, or other mechanical problems). You will want to restart your listing where it was interrupted, rather than list the entire file again. This is the simplest example of a partial transfer. PIP provides the convenient option of listing and transferring portions of files.

You can instruct PIP to only copy *portions* of text files by specifying *starting* and *stopping* strings of characters. (Recall that a "string" is a sequence of characters.) Use the S parameter to specify a starting string (i.e., where PIP should start copying), and the Q parameter to specify a stopping string (i.e., where PIP should stop copying). PIP will automatically search for each string of characters.

You must end both strings with the ↑Z character (hitting CTRL and Z simultaneously). Here is an example that copies the file SAMPLE.TXT from its beginning to the string 'Extra':

```
A> PIP ↲
*NEWSAMPLE.TXT = SAMPLE.TXT [QExtra↑Z] ↲
* ↲
A>
```

This PIP operation stops when it encounters the string 'Extra.' Note that 'Extra' is in upper and lower case, and that we executed PIP as a program, not as a one line command. If we had typed:

```
A> PIP NEWSAMPLE.TXT = SAMPLE.TXT [QExtra↑Z] ↲
```

PIP would translate the string 'Extra' to 'EXTRA' automatically. IF YOU EXECUTE PIP AS A ONE LINE COMMAND, IT WILL ALWAYS TRANSLATE YOUR STRING TO UPPER CASE. If you execute PIP as a program and type a PIP expression, it will leave your string the way you typed it.

Here is another example of the use of the S and Q parameters:

```
A>PIP↲
*EXTRA.TXT=SAMPLE.TXT [SExtra↑Z QAnother extra↑Z]↲
*↲
A>
```

This PIP operation starts copying SAMPLE.TXT when it finds the string 'Extra', and *stops* copying when it finds the string 'Another extra'. The file EXTRA.TXT contains the portion of the file between the strings 'Extra' and 'Another extra', including 'extra' but not 'Another extra'.

Note that we executed PIP as a program in order to preserve the upper-lower case strings. IF THE STRINGS WERE ACTUALLY ALL UPPER CASE IN THE FILE, then the upper-lower case strings would not be found by PIP.

ENHANCEMENTS IN CP/M VERSION 2.2

Enhancements

If you have CP/M version 2.2, there are certain restrictions preventing you from performing copy operations that are "normal" in CP/M version 1.4. For example, if you are making use of version 2.2 *user areas,* you might have noticed already that you cannot create a copy in another user area, nor can you make a copy of a file that is in another user area.

The enhancements to PIP allow you to "get around" the *other* enhancements to the rest of CP/M version 2.2 and MP/M. The section on CP/M version 2.2 and MP/M explains user areas and file attributes, but here is a quick summary:

User areas: Any disk (diskette) can contain files separated into distinct user areas (i.e., user 0, user 1, user 2, etc.) Of course, your disk (diskette) could have only one user area (user 0) to be compatible with earlier versions of CP/M, but version 2.2 allows you to separate files into user areas, and to jump from one user area to another using the USER command, in order to *prepare* you for MP/M (so that your disks and diskettes will be compatible with future releases of MP/M). MP/M is a multi-*user* system, and there is a need to separate user's files. You do not have to use this feature, and it is not recommended unless your system will have many simultaneous users.

File attributes: In CP/M version 2.2 and MP/M, you can choose to put a special indicator on a file, called a *file attribute*. File attributes regulate the use of the file, and include: read-only, read-write, system, and directory. These attributes are set with the STAT command (described in the section for CP/M version 2.2 and MP/M).

If a file is read-only (abbreviated 'R/O'), it cannot be *changed* (updated) or *deleted*; i.e., the system cannot write to the file (or over-write the file). You must first change the R/O file attribute to R/W (read-write) by using STAT.

If a file is a "system" file (abbreviated '$SYS'), it is *not* displayed by the DIR command, and you cannot read from the file (which also means that you cannot copy it). If you also set the R/O attribute (i.e., $SYS and R/O), it is well-protected. You must change the $SYS file attribute by using STAT to the attribute '$DIR' (for "directory"), so that the file can be accessed as a regular file. If you also set the R/O attribute, it stays in effect until you change it to R/W. File attributes are discussed in the section dealing with CP/M version 2.2 and MP/M (in Chapter 2.).

PIP has several new features to "get around" these file attributes, and to move files from one user area to another. These features are in the form of parameters:

Gn Get file from user area 'n', where 'n' can be from zero to fifteen

W Overwrite (delete) read-only files (ignore the R/O attribute)

R Read (copy) system files (files with $SYS attribute)
This parameter also allows a W (ignore R/O attributes)

Copying From User Areas

Use the G parameter to copy a file that is in another user area. (Remember, you cannot create a copy in another user area, only in your own). You do not need this parameter to copy a file from one disk (diskette) to another if the file to be copied (and the copy to be created) have the same user area number. For example, if ORIG exists in user area 2 on drive A, you can copy it into a new file COPY in user area 2 on drive B. From user area 2, you can copy any file in any other user area by using the G parameter, but your new copy can only be created in the *current user area* (i.e., the user area that you are currently "in").

You change your current user area with the USER command, described in detail in the section on CP/M version 2.2 and MP/M.

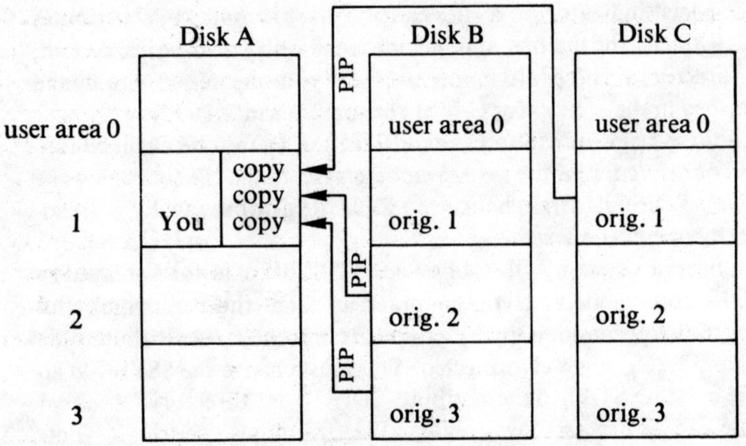

Here is an example of a PIP expression using the G parameter:

```
*A:=B:JIM.TXT [G3]
*
2A>
```

This PIP expression copied the file JIM.TXT, on drive B in user area 3, to drive A in the current user area. The current user area is 2, as shown by the system prompt (after the PIP program has been terminated by a RETURN).

NOTE: to remain compatible with earlier versions of CP/M *and still* be compatible with new and future releases of CP/M and MP/M, use only user area 0. This is the "default" user area that will go unnoticed in new and future releases, yet will not cause problems with earlier releases.

If you do use other user areas, you have to first copy PIP.COM to each user area that receives copies of files. Once you have a copy of PIP.COM in each user area of one disk drive, you can easily invoke the PIP program from another drive by specifying the drive letter. If PIP.COM does not exist in your current user area of at least one active disk drive, then you cannot execute the PIP command. To initially copy PIP into user areas, use the following sequence of commands involving DDT (dynamic debugger) and SAVE (both commands are described in Chapter 2):

A> USER 0 ↵	(Specify user area 0—change from user area 2.)
A> DDT PIP.COM ↵	(Execute DDT on PIP.COM—debugger.)
DDT VERS. xx.xx	(DDT sign-on message.)
NEXT PC 1C80 xxxxxx -G0 ↵	(DDT displays next address after end of PIP.COM. You use this address to calculate the number of pages to use with SAVE.
A> USER 3 ↵	(Change to user area 3, where you want to put a new copy of PIP.COM.)
A> SAVE 28 PIP.COM	(SAVE creates a new file, PIP.COM, in user area 3 of disk drive A, with 28 pages of memory—equal to the original PIP.COM. You derive '28' from the hexadecimal value '1C' where 'C' equals 12, and '1C' equals 28. 1C is the "high order byte" of the hexadecimal value under the NEXT display of DDT, 1C80.)

Read-Only and System Files

PIP will not overwrite (delete and recreate) a file that has the read-only 'R/O' attribute set. If you try, the PIP program replies with a question:

```
A> PIP B: COPY = ORIG ↵
DESTINATION FILE IS R/O, DELETE (Y/N)? Y
A>
```

In this example, we tried to make a copy of ORIG called COPY—but COPY (the old COPY) already exists on drive B with the R/O attribute (if it did not have the R/O attribute, it would have been deleted by PIP and replaced with the new COPY). PIP displays the message that COPY (the destination file) is read-only, and asks if we want to delete the old COPY ('Y/N' stands for "yes" or "no"). We reply 'Y' to delete the old COPY and replace it with the new COPY. (When you answer 'Y' or 'N', you do not have to hit RETURN (↵).)
NOTE: The new COPY will *not* have the R/O attribute automatically set.

If we had answered 'N' for no, the old COPY would *not* have been deleted, and PIP would have displayed the message:

```
**      NOT DELETED       **
```

If you want to *override* this PIP action of displaying a message if the file is R/O and asking you for verification, you can use the W parameter. The W parameter tells PIP to ignore the R/O attribute. You can use the W parameter at the end of a PIP expression if you want it to apply to all of the files in a file concatenation:

```
A> PIP WHOLE.TXT=PART1.TXT,PART2.TXT,PART3.TXT[W] ↵
A>
```

If either the original file or the copy file has the $SYS (system) attribute, then PIP cannot find the files in the disk directory. You can use the R parameter to ignore the $SYS (and R/O) attributes so that PIP can find the original file or create the copy file. Use the R attribute in the same manner as the W attribute was used above.

SUMMARY

PIP is a powerful general-purpose file transfer facility. Although most CP/M users use it only for simple disk-to-disk transfers, it can do a lot more:

- Transfers between devices and disks
- Multiple file transfers
- File processing, verification, and formatting.

PIP can be used to advantage to obtain portions of a file, or to join several files. It can also be used to obtain clean, paginated, tabulated printouts. A working knowledge of the relevant parameters is a definite advantage. Every CP/M user should therefore read this chapter completely through once, then read again the details on the options he/she may use most often.

4

USING THE EDITOR

INTRODUCTION

Chapters 1 and 2 were designed to teach you everything you need to know to begin using CP/M. Chapter 3 described the most important utility program, PIP. This chapter will teach you how to use another important application program that comes with the CP/M operating system: the editor, ED. You will be shown how to use an actual editor program, and you will follow the data transfers between the disk, the computer's memory, and the terminal.

It is not important to remember the specific commands provided by ED. These commands are summarized in the Appendix section. What is important, however, is for you to understand how an editor operates, and what it can do. If you achieve this goal, you will find most other application programs simple to understand (if they are well-designed and documented). Also, you will probably be able to easily use a word processing program, a very useful application program on any computer.

This chapter is useful, but not indispensable. If you feel you are not interested in learning about the editor, you can go on to the next chapter.

WHAT IS AN EDITOR PROGRAM?

A good editor program allows you to create and edit text files — letters, novels, poems, business forms, or anything comprised of characters. The program should also let you move from line to line easily, and change characters by retyping over them, or by deleting and inserting characters in one motion. It should also be able to find any group of characters you specify in a file, and do substitutions. A good editor program should allow you to merge two files as well as interweave lines of text from two files.

When you type text using a good editor program, you will type a line and end it with a Carriage Return (RETURN or CR on some keyboards), just as you would on an electric typewriter. In the future, an editor program might even make it easier than that; we have certainly not yet seen the best editor program nor the easiest one to use.

ED, the editor program provided with CP/M, is only a minimal editor and is not as easy to use as most other editor programs. If you plan to do a significant amount of editing or word processing, you should obtain a more powerful editor. There are many editor and "word processing" programs on the market today that will run on CP/M or MP/M.

A *word processor* is a program that includes both an editor program (for typing text) and a program that runs the printer (for printing text), making it backspace, underline, justify margins, expand tabs, and type in boldface type. Take note, however, of exactly what you are buying. There are some so-called "word processors" that are only printing programs designed to be used with CP/M's ED program. These are only formatters, and are not convenient or powerful enough for general use as word processors.

Shop around as if you were buying a typewriter. You might want bells and whistles; or, you might want a portable, inexpensive model that requires more effort but will do the job. However, ease of use should be your primary consideration (especially if you use one for writing). After reading this chapter, you will know what the minimum set of facilities provided by an editor should be. ED is sufficient for most simple applications.

ED, THE EDITOR

The editor program ED.COM usually resides on the System Diskette, and is executed by typing 'ED', followed by the name of the text file that you are creating or modifying. For example, if you want to create or modify the file SAMPLE.TXT, type:

A > ED SAMPLE.TXT ↵

Do not type just 'ED'. This is a common error, and will not work. You must supply a file name.

NOTE: if you get the message 'FILE IS READ/ONLY', or 'SYSTEM FILE NOT ACCESSIBLE', then you have to use the STAT command on the file first (CP/M version 2.2 and MP/M). See the section on CP/M version 2.2 and MP/M in Chapter 2.

If ED cannot find the file that you specify, it assumes that you are creating a new file. This file, specified in your command, becomes the "source" file. Subsequent ED commands will then bring the source file's text into the *edit buffer,* as shown in Figure 4.1.

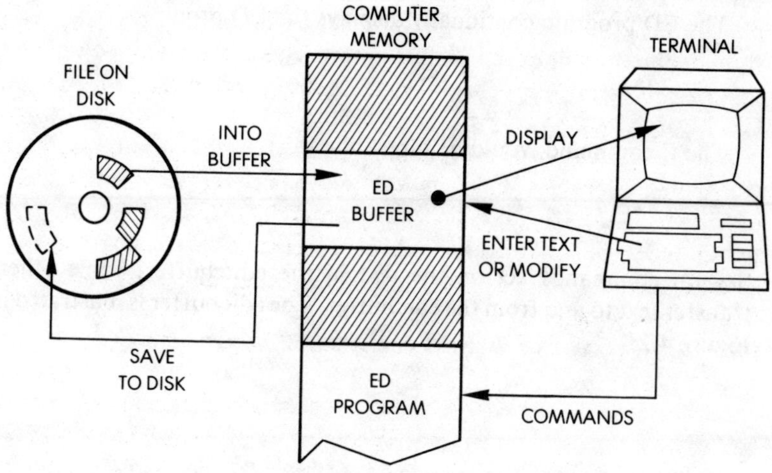

Figure 4.1: ED's Buffer

The *buffer* is a block of memory inside the computer reserved for ED's text processing. If your text file is large, you can load only one block of it at a time into the buffer. (Note that this is an inconvenience inherent to ED that does not exist in more powerful editors.)

You can only type new text in the edit buffer, or change text that is already in it. However, the buffer is not copied back to the disk automatically. If you terminate ED (or if you turn off the system) without *saving* the text that is in the buffer on a disk file, you will lose the text in the buffer. Since ED *copies* the text file into the edit buffer, your original file (i.e., before it was used with ED) is untouched but your new text and modifications are lost. Therefore, you should periodically save the text in the edit buffer, and always remember to save the buffer before leaving the ED program. You save the buffer by using ED's 'E' command (E ↲). The E command also copies the rest of the source file into the new "source" file that it creates. (This is explained in more detail later in this chapter.)

Most of ED's commands consist of a special letter preceded by a number or symbol determining an amount. These commands are executed by typing them as you would type CP/M commands: the command, followed by a RETURN (↲), which transmits the command. Other "commands" are special key combinations (like CTRL and Z (↑Z), CTRL and C (↑C), etc.) that are transmitted automatically and do not require a RETURN.

The ED program continually displays the ED prompt:

*

The E command would be typed like this:

*E ↲

Several commands act on the text in the edit buffer, while others transfer text to and from the edit buffer. The edit buffer is illustrated in Figure 4.2:

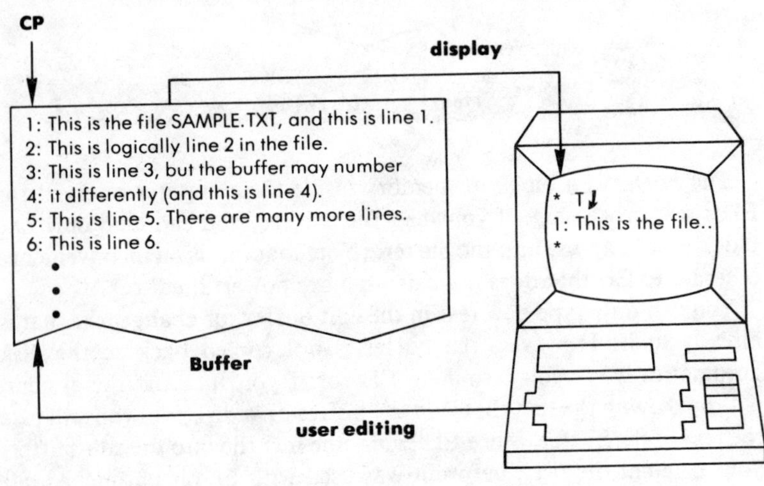

Figure 4.2: Text Being Processed

THE 'CP' (CHARACTER POINTER) AND LINE NUMBERS

The 'CP' in the illustration is the "character pointer." It is not actually displayed on the screen, but is used by the ED program, and is moved by ED commands. The pointer always points at one character, and the ED commands usually refer to the characters following (and including) the character pointed to by the CP, or the characters trailing the CP. In other words, you move the CP to the *right* to go forward in the text, and you move the CP to the *left* to go backwards. You will see examples illustrated in subsequent sections of this chapter.

In addition to the imaginary CP, each line has an imaginary *line number* that is not actually part of the text. If you have the newer version of ED, it automatically displays the line numbers with the text (and you can move to any line of text by specifying the line number as a command, as shown later). If you have the older versions of ED, you have to *turn on* the display of line numbers by executing the V command (the command -V (negative V) turns it off). If you have even *older* versions, you might not have line numbers at all (which is unfortunate, since they do make it easier to move around in the edit buffer). The line numbers, like the CP, only exist in the edit buffer and are used only to move around in the buffer. They would not appear in a print-out of the file.

WHAT ED DOES TO YOUR TEXT FILE

For example, assume that the file SAMPLE.TXT already exists, and contains the text shown in Figure 4.3:

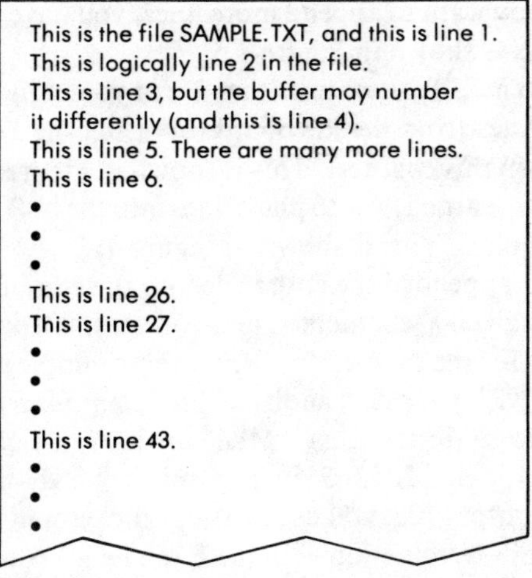

```
This is the file SAMPLE.TXT, and this is line 1.
This is logically line 2 in the file.
This is line 3, but the buffer may number
it differently (and this is line 4).
This is line 5. There are many more lines.
This is line 6.
•
•
•
This is line 26.
This is line 27.
•
•
•
This is line 43.
•
•
•
```

Figure 4.3: A Sample File is in the Buffer

When you execute the CP/M command:

A> <u>ED SAMPLE.TXT</u> ↲

ED sets aside a space in the *transient program area* (scratch-pad memory—this will be explained in Chapter 5) for the edit buffer, creates a temporary output file called SAMPLE.$$$ (to store the edited file without damaging the original one), and prepares SAMPLE.TXT to be copied into the edit buffer. The copying is actually done by using the A (append) command—this will "append" a certain number of lines into the edit buffer, as shown in Figure 4.4:

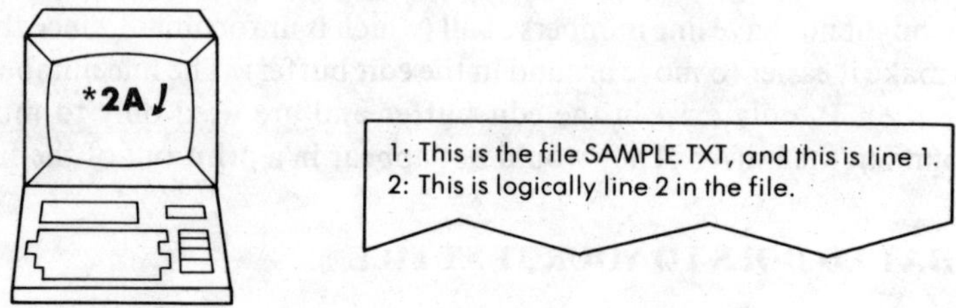

Figure 4.4: The Append Command is in A

The ED command '2A' appended the first two lines of the text file into the buffer. If you want to append more lines, you have to do another A command. This is shown in Figure 4.5.

Now you can modify these lines that are in your edit buffer. You can also add new lines from the keyboard (by using the I command, described later on in this chapter). This is shown in Figure 4.6.

You have now learned how to place lines into the buffer from the disk file or the keyboard. This is shown in Figure 4.7.

You could have appended the entire file into the edit buffer (unless the file has more than 6000 characters, and you are not using a 16K version of CP/M), but for the sake of simplicity, this example sends the newly-modified text (with your new additions) to a *temporary output* file, so that you can append more text to the edit buffer. ED calls this temporary output file SAMPLE.$$$. To send the newly-modified text to the temporary output file, you use the W (write) command, or you perform a "normal" termination with the E (end edit) command or the H (end and reopen) command. Figure 4.8 shows the use of the W command.

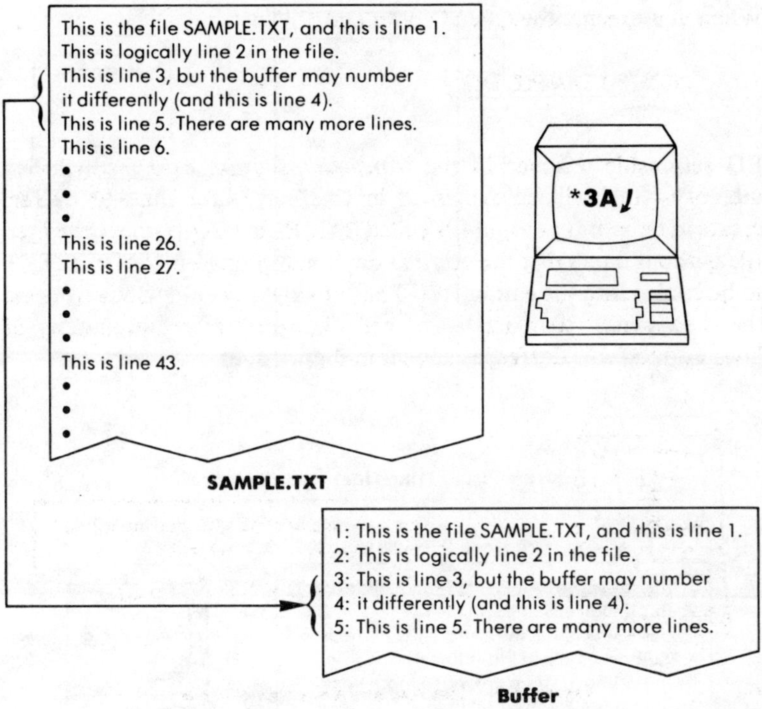

This is the file SAMPLE.TXT, and this is line 1.
This is logically line 2 in the file.
This is line 3, but the buffer may number
it differently (and this is line 4).
This is line 5. There are many more lines.
This is line 6.
•
•
•
This is line 26.
This is line 27.
•
•
•
This is line 43.
•
•
•
SAMPLE.TXT
*3A↵
1: This is the file SAMPLE.TXT, and this is line 1.
2: This is logically line 2 in the file.
3: This is line 3, but the buffer may number
4: it differently (and this is line 4).
5: This is line 5. There are many more lines.
Buffer

Figure 4.5: Appending Three More Lines

1: This is the file SAMPLE.TXT, and this is line 1.
2: This is logically line 2 in the file.
3: This is line 3, but the buffer may number
4: it differently (and this is line 4).
5: This is line 5. There are many more lines.
: *I↵
6: This is a newly-inserted line.
7: This is another added line.
8: ↑Z
: *

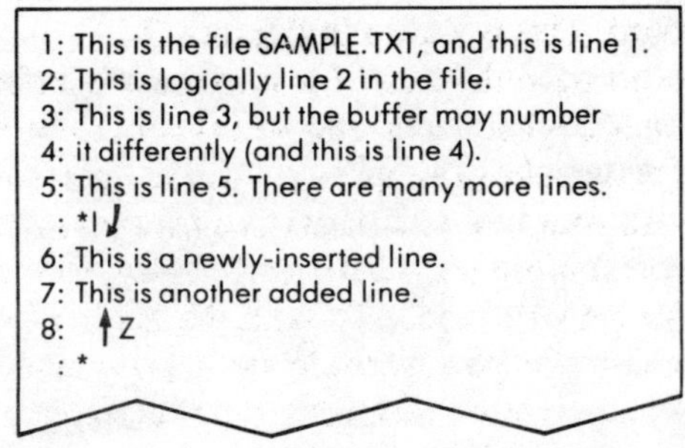

Figure 4.6: Adding Two New Lines From the Keyboard

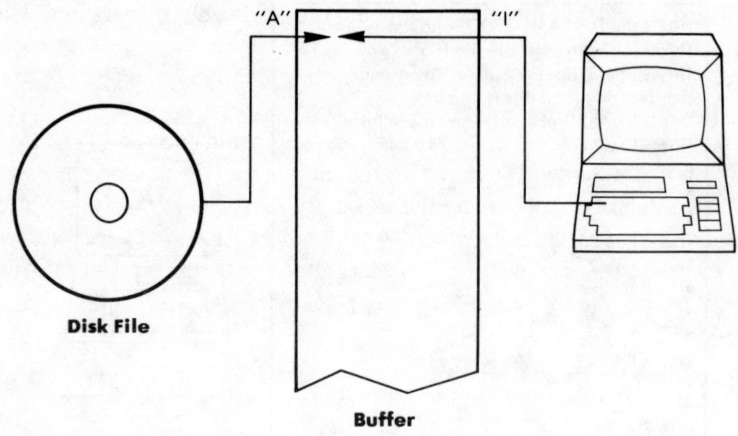

Figure 4.7: Putting Lines Into the Buffer

Before

1: This is the file SAMPLE.TXT, and this is line 1.
2: This is logically line 2 in the file.
3: This is line 3, but the buffer may number
4: it differently (and this is line 4).
5: This is line 5. There are many more lines.
6: This is a newly-inserted line.
7: This is another added line.

*2W↲

After

This is the file SAMPLE.TXT, and this is line 1.
This is logically line 2 in the file.

Temporary file SAMPLE.$$$
on disk

becomes

1: This is line 3, but the buffer may number
2: it differently (and this is line 4).
3: This is line 5. There are many more lines.
4: This is a newly-inserted line.
5: This is another added line.

Buffer

Figure 4.8: Saving the Buffer on the Disk

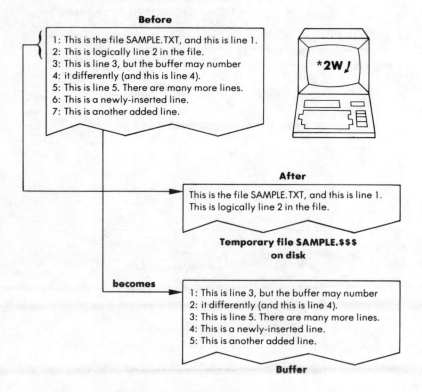

The example in Figure 4.8 shows a write operation of two lines. The lines in the final edit buffer move up to the beginning, releasing more space to append more lines. The next example shows an append operation of the next twenty lines.

After modifying the text in the buffer, you could end the ED session (and write the rest of the buffer to the output file) by using the E command, as shown in the example in Figure 4.9. The E command also copies the *rest* of the source file — the lines not appended to the buffer — to the temporary output file. Note that the temporary output file contains the lines of text in their proper order.

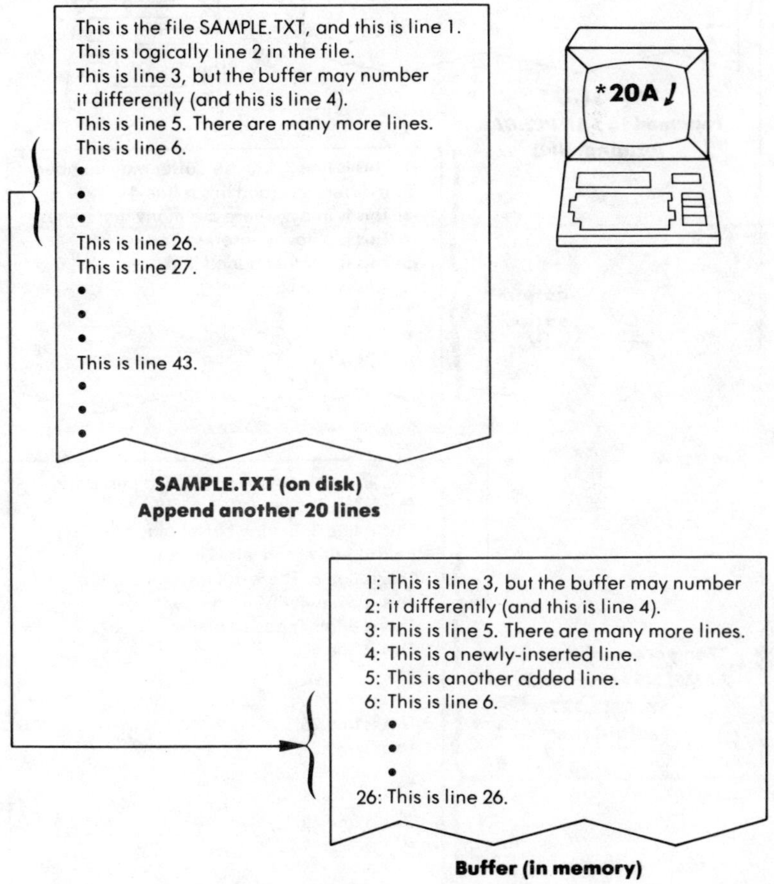
This is the file SAMPLE.TXT, and this is line 1.
This is logically line 2 in the file.
This is line 3, but the buffer may number
it differently (and this is line 4).
This is line 5. There are many more lines.
This is line 6.
This is line 26.
This is line 27.
This is line 43.
*20A
SAMPLE.TXT (on disk)
Append another 20 lines
1: This is line 3, but the buffer may number
2: it differently (and this is line 4).
3: This is line 5. There are many more lines.
4: This is a newly-inserted line.
5: This is another added line.
6: This is line 6.
26: This is line 26.
Buffer (in memory)

Figure 4.9: Appending 20 Lines to the Buffer

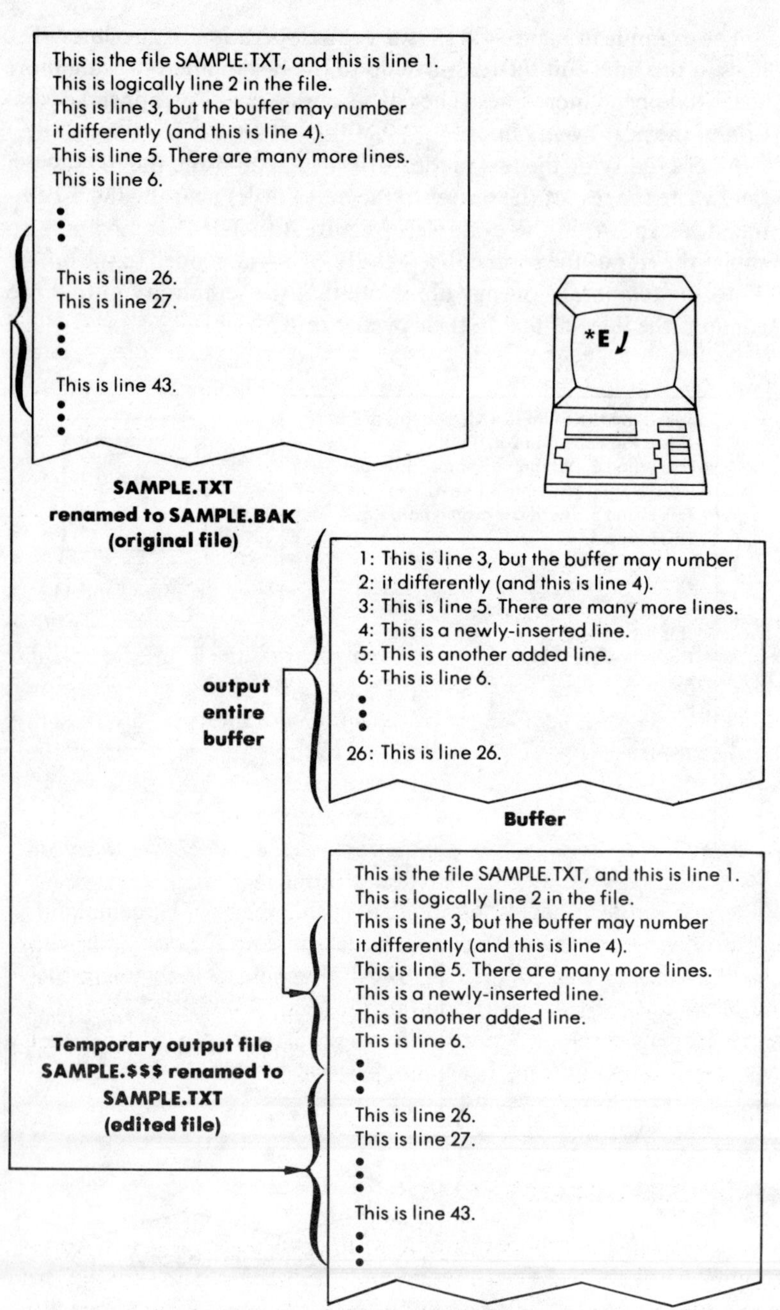
This is the file SAMPLE.TXT, and this is line 1.
This is logically line 2 in the file.
This is line 3, but the buffer may number
it differently (and this is line 4).
This is line 5. There are many more lines.
This is line 6.
This is line 26.
This is line 27.
This is line 43.
SAMPLE.TXT
renamed to SAMPLE.BAK
(original file)
*E
1: This is line 3, but the buffer may number
2: it differently (and this is line 4).
3: This is line 5. There are many more lines.
4: This is a newly-inserted line.
5: This is another added line.
6: This is line 6.
26: This is line 26.
output
entire
buffer
Buffer
This is the file SAMPLE.TXT, and this is line 1.
This is logically line 2 in the file.
This is line 3, but the buffer may number
it differently (and this is line 4).
This is line 5. There are many more lines.
This is a newly-inserted line.
This is another added line.
This is line 6.
This is line 26.
This is line 27.
This is line 43.
Temporary output file
SAMPLE.$$$ renamed to
SAMPLE.TXT
(edited file)

Figure 4.10: Finishing an Edit Session

As soon as the edit buffer is properly copied into the temporary output file, which is called SAMPLE.$$$, ED does two things: it renames the original SAMPLE.TXT to SAMPLE.BAK, and it renames SAMPLE.$$$ to SAMPLE.TXT. By doing this, ED creates a backup copy of the original SAMPLE.TXT (called SAMPLE.BAK), and renames the newly modified SAMPLE.$$$ to SAMPLE.TXT. (See Figure 4.10.) That is why it appears that ED modifies the file SAMPLE.TXT—actually, ED modifies the text in the edit buffer and uses SAMPLE.TXT as a backup and SAMPLE.$$$ as the future version of SAMPLE.TXT. NOTE: when you execute ED on a file, ED automatically deletes any 'BAK' file associated with the text file (in preparation for the new 'BAK' file that ED creates). The 'O' and 'Q' commands do not prevent this action, so be careful.

FILE MANAGEMENT

When you give ED a filename, it looks for the file; if ED does not find it, ED creates it. This file is called the "source" file, in CP/M's documentation. When you append text to the edit buffer from the source file (using the A command), ED copies the text lines from the top of the file into the buffer, counting the number of lines you specified in the A command. When you write lines to the temporary output file created by ED (filename.$$$), you free up space in the buffer in order to append more lines of text from the source file. As you write to the output file, lines are appended so that they stay in the same order (you can write specific lines to the output file in order to change that order). When you finish editing, or terminate ED using the E (or H) command, ED automatically renames the original file (the source file) to a file with a BAK extension (e.g., SAMPLE.BAK) to denote it as a backup file, and D renames the temporary output file (e.g., SAMPLE.$$$) to the name of your original (source) file (e.g., SAMPLE.TXT), so that your text file contains the newly-modified text.

ACCIDENTAL TERMINATION

If you terminate ED accidentally, without using the E (or H) command (i.e., there is a system error, or you inadvertently hit ↑C to reboot the system, or the power is cut off), the temporary output file (e.g., SAMPLE.$$$) will still remain with that filename, and your original source file (e.g., SAMPLE.TXT) would still be the old copy. The $$$ file would only have text you had already written to it (so it might not be useful), the edit buffer would be lost, and the original file would be the unedited version (i.e., before you invoked ED). NOTE: use the Q (quit) command to do this on purpose.

You can merge text lines from another text file with the text already in the edit buffer by using the R command, discussed later in this chapter (the other file is not modified in any way).

A SESSION WITH THE EDITOR

To create a new text file, first think of a name (a name that is not already used with another extension). We will use QUOTE.TXT as an example. Execute the ED command and create QUOTE.TXT by typing:

```
A > ED QUOTE.TXT ↲
```

In this example, we are in drive A; therefore, QUOTE.TXT will be in drive A. We are in drive A because the ED program (ED.COM) is in drive A. The example in Chapter 1 showed how you can execute ED from another drive by prefixing the drive letter and colon before the filename ED. You can also execute ED from drive A and put QUOTE.TXT on drive B by prefixing 'B:' to 'QUOTE.TXT'.

ED will display the message 'NEWFILE' if it is creating a new file. When ED is ready for an ED command, it will display the ED '*' prompt. You can now type any ED command. To insert new text from the keyboard, you should use the I command. The I command starts inserting text immediately after the CP (character pointer). Since you have not explicitly moved the CP (with an ED command), the CP is at the beginning of the buffer. To start inserting new text, type:

To actually insert text, you type the text as you would on a typewriter. To stop inserting text, you hold down CTRL while pressing the Z key (↑Z).

When you type 'I ↲', ED moves the cursor (the blinking pointer on the screen, or whatever symbol your terminal display uses) to the next blank line. You can now type text, which will automatically be inserted into the edit buffer as you transmit each line. *Each line must end with a* RETURN (as with a typewriter)—RETURN (represented with a ↲ in this book) transmits the line to the edit buffer. The line then becomes a *line in the buffer* (identified by a line number). If you want to type "a line in the buffer" that is actually longer than a line you can type at your terminal, use the combination of CTRL and E (↑E) to move the cursor to the next line on your screen without transmitting the line to the edit buffer. When you finally do hit RETURN, the entire line is transmitted to the buffer. Long lines cannot exceed 128 characters.

We will start the example from the beginning again. Note that you can use the keyboard editing keys RUBOUT (DELETE), ↑U (delete the line), ↑E (return the "carriage" without transmitting the line), and ↑R (retype the last line) in both the old and new versions of ED. You can use ↑H (backspace and delete a character) and ↑X (backspace to beginning of line) in only the new version of ED.

Here is our example again, from the start:

```
A> ED QUOTE.TEXT ↲
NEW FILE
*I ↲
"We have not ceased from exploration"
wrote T.S. Eliot.
 ↑Z
*
```

We use the combination CTRL and Z to stop inserting text (↑Z). We now have two lines of text—the first is the quotation, and the second is 'wrote T.S. Eliot'.

If you wish, you can use the U command before the I command, and anything you type is automatically converted to UPPER case (although as you type the text, it appears to be in upper and lower case). To turn off this automatic UPPER case translating, use the -U command (negative U).

Now that we have text in the buffer, we can display it. First, we have to move the CP (character pointer) back to the beginning of the buffer, since the I command inserted text and moved the CP. Here is an illustration showing the text and the position of CP in the buffer:

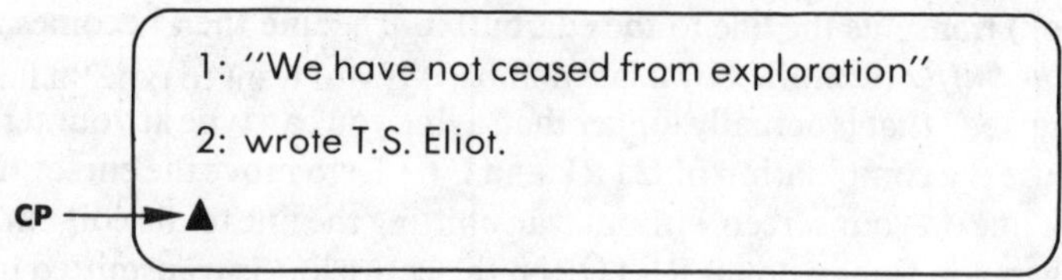

Figure 4.11: The CP is at the End of the Buffer

The manual for ED explains that the CP is *between* two characters. This is difficult to visualize and to use, so we changed our description to make it easier. The CP is an "imaginary" object, a reference pointer to use with ED commands. When you refer to Digital Research's documentation, bear in mind that their descriptions are based on CP being between two characters, and our descriptions are based on CP pointing to the rightmost of those two characters. The illustration in Figure 4.12 should clarify this:

Figure 4.12: Showing the CP's Position

Digital Research says that CP is *before* the first character of a buffer when moved to the beginning, and we say that CP is *at* the first character of a buffer when moved to the beginning.

DISPLAYING TEXT IN THE BUFFER

We will use the T command to display the text in the buffer. The format of the T command is:

±nT

where n can be zero, or any number, or a number (#) sign. This is illustrated in Figure 4.13. If n is zero, T will display the current line up to

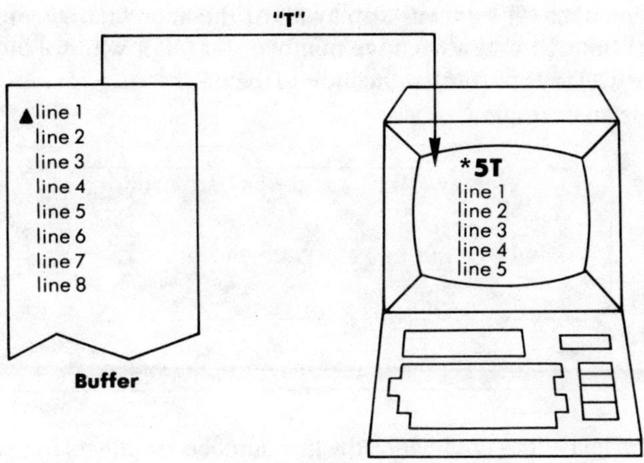

Figure 4.13: Displaying Text

(but not including) the CP (the current line is the line with CP in it). If you do not specify n, 1 is assumed. If n is 1 (or if it is assumed to be 1), the current line is displayed from the CP to the end of the line. If n is a positive number, T will display n number of lines from the CP (current line) on; if n is a negative number, T will display lines before the CP (and not including the CP). If you use the number (#) sign, T will substitute '65535' (maximum number of lines allowed in the buffer), i.e., the entire buffer will be displayed. You can type the entire buffer by moving CP to the beginning of the buffer (by using the B command, shown in Figure 4.14) and using a number (#) sign with T; other-

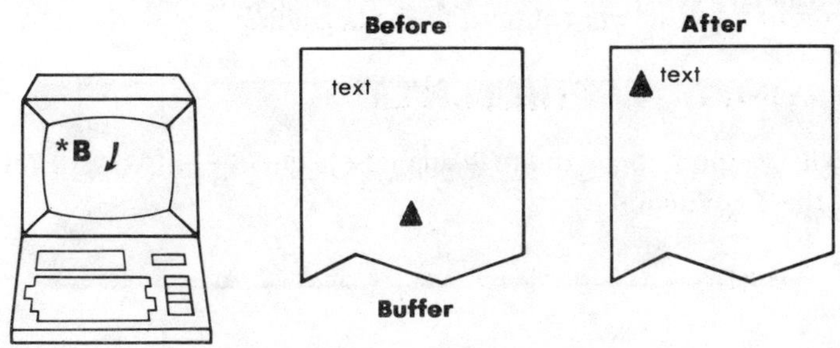

Figure 4.14: Moving the Cursor

wise, a number (#) sign will display all of the lines *following* (and including) the CP, and a negative number (– #) sign will display all of the lines previous to (but *not* including) the CP.

Here is an example:

```
   *-2T
1: "We have not ceased from exploration"
2: wrote T.S. Eliot.
 : *
```

If your display does not include the line numbers (numbers followed by the colon), try executing the V command (version 1.4 of CP/M or later):

```
   *V
 : *
```

The ':' tells you that the CP is at the beginning of line 3; however, line 3 has no text yet, so the CP is actually pointing to the end of line 2 (after the 'Carriage Return' sequence).

The command '-2T' above tells ED to display only the two lines before the one containing the CP (i.e., the current line, which is line 3).

In CP/M versions 1.4 or later, you can specify the actual line number in a T command to display that line. For example, if you just wanted to display line 1, you would type '1:T' as a command:

```
2: *1:T
1: "We have not ceased from exploration"
1:
```

Note that the command '1:' with 'T' moved the CP to line 1 (current line is now line 1). You can specify a line number as a command to move the CP to that line. For example:

```
1: *2:↲
2: *
```

A simple T command will display the current line:

```
2: *T↲
2: wrote T.S. Eliot.
2: *
```

An easy way to display the entire buffer is to execute two commands: the B command to move the CP to the beginning of the buffer, and the T command with a number (#) sign to display the entire buffer. Note that you can put both commands on the same command line and execute them:

```
1: *B#T↲
1: "We have not ceased from exploration"
2: wrote T.S. Eliot.
1: *
```

In the above examples, the CP pointed to the first character in the line. You can move the CP in the current line by using the C command:

±nC

C will move the CP +n characters forward, or −n characters backward. For example, if the CP is at the beginning of line 1, and you type this command:

1: "We have not ceased from exploration,"
2: wrote T.S. Eliot.

CP

```
1: *5C
1: *
```

The CP would be pointing to the sixth character ('a', since a quote counts as one character) in line 1. The command 'T' would display the line from the CP to the end (including the CP):

```
1: *T
ave not ceased from exploration"
1: *
```

The command '0T' would display line 1 from the beginning up to but *not* including the CP:

```
1: *0T
"We h
1: *
```

SAVING THE FILE AND ENDING THE ED SESSION

At this point, you should learn how to save the contents of the buffer and leave ED. The easiest way to save and exit ED at the same time is to use the E command:

```
1: *E
```

Wherever you are in the buffer, this command will empty the buffer (and the rest of the source file, if you had not appended the entire source file) into the temporary output file and rename the output file to the name of your source (original) file. If you started with an empty QUOTE.TXT and added the text as shown in the previous examples, you should end up with a QUOTE.TXT containing a line by T.S. Eliot, and a QUOTE.BAK that is empty (a backup of the file before you edited it).

APPENDING LINES TO THE BUFFER (EDITING AN EXISTING FILE)

When you have an existing text file, and you execute ED to edit it, the A command then has to be executed to bring text lines into the edit buffer. Otherwise, there will be no text in the buffer except the text that you insert by using ED's I command. You might want to insert new text *before* the first line of your existing text file—by using the I command to insert new text before appending the existing file's text to the buffer with the A command; however, you can easily do this *after* the old text is in the buffer. So, you will want to use the A command first to see the old text. The A command adds ("appends") lines to the end of the buffer.

The A command's format is:

```
nA
```

The command A will append n lines of text from the original (source) text file. If you do not specify n, A appends only one line. If you use a number (#) sign instead of n, A will bring the entire source file (up to 65535 lines) into the edit buffer. Since most text files are not that large, you can use the form '#A' to bring in any file that would probably fit in the edit buffer. If you specify a zero for n, the A command will append to fill *half* of the buffer (useful for large files). Use the form '0A' in conjunction with '0W' to append and write-out half of the buffer (discussed in this chapter in "Writing Lines Out to the File").

If you append only a portion of your source (original) file to the buffer, your *next* A command would start appending from the source file where the last A left off. You would easily append ten lines, change some text, write out the ten lines to the temporary output file (with the W command discussed later), and append more lines from the source file. Or, if you have enough room in the buffer, you could append more lines from the source file to the end of the existing lines in the buffer.

Here is a simple example, using QUOTE.TXT as a source file:

```
A>ED QUOTE.TXT ↵
  *V↵  (if using version 1.4, not needed in version 2.2)
 :*A↵  (appends only one line)
1:*2A↵  (appends next two lines, but there is only one
         more line in the file anyway)
2:*B#T↵  (go to beginning and display all lines)
1:"We have not ceased from exploration"
2:wrote T.S. Eliot.
1:*
```

Since there are only two lines in QUOTE.TXT, a simple '#A' command would suffice to bring in all of the lines.

MOVING AROUND IN THE BUFFER

With text in the buffer, you can move around at will and change any text, as well as insert new text anywhere. You can also locate and substitute pieces of text, and append other lines of text from a special *library source* file (discussed later).

If you are following the examples and editing QUOTE.TXT, you should now go the bottom of the buffer and insert more text. The -B (negative B) command is used to move to the end of the last line, as in this example:

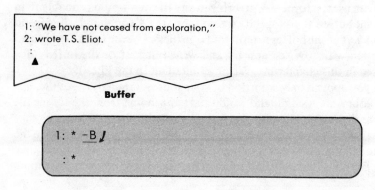

```
1: "We have not ceased from exploration,"
2: wrote T.S. Eliot.
 :
 ▲
```

Buffer

```
1: * -B↵
 : *
```

The "end of the last line is actually a 'Carriage Return', which in ASCII code is a combination of RETURN and LINE FEED: two characters that perform the operation of returning the carriage and generating a new line. Therefore, the "end" of the last line is actually the beginning of the next new line; however, the next new line's number is not displayed until you insert characters using the I command. You can insert characters that will form the new line. For example:

```
1: "We have not ceased from exploration"
2: wrote T.S. Eliot.
3: "And the end of all our exploring,
4: will be to arrive where we started,
5: and know the place for the first time."
 :
 ▲
```

Buffer

```
 : *I ↵
3: "And the end of all our exploring, ↵
4: will be to arrive where we started, ↵
5: and know the place for the first time." ↵
6: ↑ Z ↵
 : *
```

Now you can display the entire buffer by using the B and T commands:

```
 : *B#T ↵
1: "We have not ceased from exploration"
2: wrote T.S. Eliot.
3: "And the end of all our exploring,
4: will be to arrive where we started,
5: and know the place for the first time."
1: *
```

The easiest way to move to another line is to use line numbers. If you have version 2.2 of CP/M, ED will automatically display line numbers. If you have version 1.4, this feature is turned off; turn it on by executing the ED command V (-V turns it off again). If you have a version earlier than 1.4, you are out of luck—you cannot display line numbers and must use the L command to move to another line.

To select a line, type the line number followed by a colon as an ED command:

```
1: *2:
2: *
```

To select a *range* of lines, type the first line number, followed by *two* colons and the second line number, as in this example (the T command can also be used to display the range of lines):

```
1: "We have not ceased from exploration"
2: wrote T.S. Eliot.
3: "And the end of all our exploring,
4: will be to arrive where we started,
5: and know the place for the first time.
```

Buffer

```
2: *3::5T
3: "And the end of all our exploring,
4: will be to arrive where we started,
5: and know the place for the first time."
3: *
```

When you specify a single line, the CP is moved to the beginning of that line. When you specify a range of lines, the CP is moved to the beginning of the first line in the range, and ED counts the number of lines in the range (in this case, three), and applies that number to the T command (i.e., '3T') to display the range. The CP remains on line 3.

You can also move up and down lines by using the L command. The format for the L command is:

±nL

The L command will move the CP +n lines forward or -n lines backward in the buffer, and put the CP at the beginning of the line selected. Here is an example:

```
3: *1L↵
4: *-2L↵
2: *
```

The form '0L' (where n is zero) moves the CP to the beginning of the current line.

You can use line numbers to select a range of lines that begin at the current line by preceding the ending line number with a colon:

```
2: *:5T↵
2: wrote T.S. Eliot.
3: "And the end of all our exploring,
4: will be to arrive where we started,
5: and know the place for the first time."
```

CHANGING, INSERTING AND DELETING TEXT

Text in a line is changed by moving the CP to the text and deleting existing text and inserting new text. You can also find a group of characters and substitute another group, as discussed in the next section.

When you delete a line of text, the line numbers reflect the deletion and change accordingly, as in this example:

```
2:*1::5T↵
1:"We have not ceased from exploration"
2:wrote T. S. Eliot.
3:"And the end of all our exploring,
4:will be to arrive where we started,
5:and know the place for the first time."
1:2:↵
2:K↵
2:*1::4T↵
1:"We have not ceased from exploration"
2:"And the end of all our exploring,
3:will be to arrive where we started,
4:and know the place for the first time."
1:*
```

The K command above deletes line 2, and the other lines "move up" to use the space. The opposite occurs when you insert a line — the other lines "move down" to accommodate the newly-inserted line.

The format of the K command is:

+nK

The K command will delete ("kill") the current line if no n is specified. Otherwise, the K command will delete either +n or −n lines from the current line. If you supply a number (#) sign for n, K deletes 65535 lines following (and including) the current line (+#K), or 65535 lines behind (and not including) the current line (-#K). Use these forms to clear out unwanted lines from your buffer, but remember — you cannot bring back those lines (unless they already exist in the source or backup file).

To delete *characters* (not entire lines), you use the D command:

+*n*D

The D command deletes (erases) the character pointed to by the CP (character pointer) if no n is specified. Otherwise, the D command deletes +n characters following (and including) the CP, or −n characters behind (and *not* including) the CP.

Here is an example: we will change the word 'from' to 'ROM' (and then back to 'from'). We will do it the hard way — moving the CP by using the C command, deleting 'from' by using the D command, and inserting 'ROM' by using the I command:

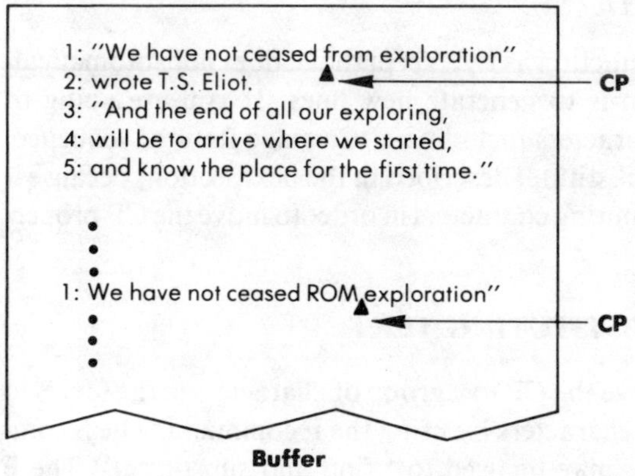

Buffer

```
1: *1::4T↵
1: "We have not ceased from exploration"
2: "And the end of all our exploring,
3: will be to arrive where we started,
4: and know the place for the first time."
1: *T↵
1: "We have not ceased from exploration"
1: *20C↵
1: *4DIROM↑ Z0LT↵
1: "We have not ceased ROM exploration"
1: *
```

In this example, we move the CP to the 21st character by using the command '20C'. Counting the character pointed to by CP, we delete 4 characters using the D command. Then we use the I command to insert 'ROM' (terminated by Z)—note that the I command inserts before the CP and moves the CP. The D command deletes the CP character and also moves the CP. We use the L command to move the CP to the beginning of the line, and we use the T command to display the line.

This is a new form of the I command:

```
Iinsertions ↑Z
```

It performs the same function as I ↲ except that it does not automatically insert carriage returns to generate new lines. If you are going to change a group of characters including a 'Carriage Return' sequence, use the S command (substitute) described in the next section, because it is much easier than counting characters in order to move the CP properly.

FINDING AND SUBSTITUTING TEXT

An easier way to move the CP to a group of characters in the text is to "find" that group of characters by using the F command. The S command, discussed next, may be used to "find and substitute." The F command is a primitive version of the S command, and will be described first.

An example will show the format for the F command. We will execute F to find 'ROM' in line 1:

```
1:*FROM↲
1:*
```

The illustration shows where the CP is at this moment:

```
"We have not ceased ROM ▲ exploration"
                        CP
```

The F command moves the CP to the character immediately following the last character found, in order to make it easier to use the D command (to delete the characters found). We will move CP back to the beginning of the line, and execute the F command along with the D and

I commands in the next example:

```
1:0L↲
1:*FROM ↑Z-3DIfrom ↑Z0LT↲
1:"We have not ceased from exploration"
1:*
```

-3 characters from the CP (i.e., 'MOR'). The CP is now in position for us to use the I command to insert "from." The '0LT' command combination moves the CP to the beginning of the line and displays the line.

Note that you can end an F command with a RETURN if you are not going to include another command on the same line.

The F command can also begin with a number (i.e., nF where n is a positive number) that will tell it to find n occurrences of the group of characters. For example, if you type the command '5Fthis ↲', the command will not stop or move the CP until it finds the fifth occurrence of 'this'. The F command can search the text that is in the buffer; in order to search the *entire source file*, you have to use the N command (discussed in "Advanced ED Operations").

If you are trying to find a group of characters including the Carriage Return sequence, you can substitute a special key combination, ↑L, to represent the sequence of RETURN and LINE FEED. In our example with the S command, we will demonstrate the use of ↑L.

The S (substitute) command is the one most often used to find and substitute groups of characters. The S command combines the actions of the F, D, and I commands shown earlier. The format for the S command is:

$$\text{nSoldtext}\uparrow\text{Znewtext}\begin{Bmatrix}\uparrow Z\\ \downarrow\end{Bmatrix}$$

The S command searches the buffer for the group of characters *oldtext* and substitutes the group of characters *newtext*. You can use ↑Z or RETURN to end the *newtext* string (use ↑Z if you want to add another command to the S command). You can execute this substitution *n* number of times, and it will execute until it reaches the *n*th time, or until it reaches the end of the buffer.

For example, if you typed the command "#SPeking ZBeijing ↲", it would substitute the word "Beijing" for "Peking" throughout the text in the buffer (the number sign (#) represents 65535 times).

We will use the S command to alter our example and change the text from prose to poetry. First, we will correct the end of the first line and the beginning of the second line in one S substitution:

```
1:*2T↲
1:"We have not ceased from exploration"
2:"And the end of all our exploring,
1:*S" ↑L" ↑Z/ ↑L ↑ZB2T↲
1:"We have not ceased from exploration/
2:And the end of all our exploring,
1:*
```

In the above example, we use the S command to find the group of characters starting with unquote, and ending with a quote on the next line (↑L stands for a Carriage Return), and substitute a slash followed by a Carriage Return. We then execute the combination 'B2T' to move the CP to the beginning of the buffer and display the next two lines.

Our next example will substitute a slash (/) for a comma (,) in two lines:

```
1:*2::4T↲
2:And the end of all our exploring,
3:will be to arrive where we started,
4:and know the place for the first time."
4:*2:↲
2:*2S,↑Z/↑ZB4T↲
1:"We have not ceased from exploration/
2:And the end of all our exploring/
3:will be to arrive where we started/
4:and know the place for the first time."
1:*
```

In this example, we first move the CP to the beginning of line 2 ('2:'), and then perform the substitution ('/' for ','). Then we move the CP to the beginning of the buffer and display four lines (B4T).

We need to put only the first characters of lines 3 and 4 into upper case:

```
1:*3:↲
3:*DIW↑Z1LDIA↑ZB4T↲
1:"We have not ceased from exploration/
2:And the end of all our exploring/
3:Will be to arrive where we started/
4:And know the place for the first time."
1:*
```

In this example, we move the CP to the beginning of line 3 and delete the first character (D command deletes 'w'). Then we insert (I command) a capital W. We move the CP to the next line (1L command), delete the first character (D command deletes 'a'), and insert a capital A. Finally, we move the CP to the beginning and display four lines.

WRITING LINES OUT TO THE FILE

Normally, you would end your ED session by using the E or H commands. Each performs a write operation on the entire buffer; i.e., it *writes* the lines of text to the temporary output file. Both commands also copy the rest of the source file (i.e., the lines that were not appended to the buffer) to the output file, and rename the files so that you end up with the newly-modified text in the source file. The E command also terminates ED; whereas the H command keeps you in ED and prepares the new source file for further editing.

If you just want to write lines to the output file without copying the entire buffer or the rest of the source file, use the W (write) command. The W command takes the following form:

```
nW
```

The W command writes the next n lines from the current line (including the current line) to the output file. The output file is the temporary file with '$$$' as an extension. If you do not specify n, the current line is written out to the file.

To illustrate the W command, we will add more lines to our example and write several lines out to the temporary output file:

```
1:*-BI↵
5:↵
6:                    — wrote T.S. Eliot ↵
7: ↑Z
6:B#T↵
1:"We have not ceased from exploration/
2:And the end of all our exploring/
3:Will be to arrive where we started/
4:And know the place for the first time."
5:
6:                    — wrote T.S. Eliot
1:*3W↵
1:#T↵
1:And know the place for the first time."
2:
3:                    — wrote T.S. Eliot
1:*#W↵
 :*
```

In this example, we first add new text to the bottom ('-BI' commands) of the buffer (use a RETURN to make a blank line, and an I to insert a tab space). Then we display the entire buffer with the CP at the beginning of the buffer ('B#T' commands). We then output the next three lines, including the current line (lines 1, 2, and 3). These lines are now in QUOTE.$$$, the temporary output file. The remaining lines of the buffer are now renumbered. The last command ('#W') outputs the next 65535 lines including the current line, which outputs the remainder of the buffer. The buffer is empty, and ED displays no line number (':*').

We still have to save the *rest* of the source file (if there were any unappended lines) and *rename* the temporary output file QUOTE.$$$ to QUOTE.TXT (and rename the old QUOTE.TXT to QUOTE.BAK). The E and H commands will do these operations automatically.

A special form of the W command goes with the '0A' form of the A command — '0W' (where *n* is zero) will write-out half of the buffer, and '0A' will append to fill half of the buffer. The number of lines that equal half of the buffer depends upon the length of your text lines and the size of your system. These forms are mostly used to "pull in half a buffer, push out half, pull in another half, etc."

If you want to rearrange lines in the buffer, or interweave lines from another file, then you must use special commands (described in "Advanced Operations") to bring lines from files to the buffer, and *then* write the finished version out to a file by using the W command (or, save the entire buffer and the remainder of the source file with the E or H commands).

ADVANCED ED OPERATIONS

Searching Through the Source File

You can use the N command to do a "find" (F command) on the buffer *and* the rest of the source file. The N command operates in the same manner as the F command but does not stop at the end of the buffer — it performs an automatic append and continues to append lines from the source file until it finds the group of characters that you specified in the command.

The format for the N command is:

nNtext { ↑Z / ↵ }

NOTE: braces { } denote an option between two commands. The N command searches for the *n*th occurrence of *text* in the lines following the CP in the buffer; if it does not find the *n*th occurrence, it will append lines from the source file into the buffer until it does. You can end your *text* string with ↑Z if you are going to add another command; otherwise, you can use RETURN.

The N command will put the CP after the last character of the *n*th occurrence of *text*, just like in F commands.

Inserting Text From a Library Source File

A "Library Source File" is a convenient term in Digital Research's documentation for any file with a 'LIB' extension (e.g., SAMPLE.LIB). You can use a "library source file" as an alternate source file—a file with text that you want to insert into the buffer to merge with lines from the original source file. To do this, you must first have a file with a 'LIB' extension that already has the text in it.

The format for the R command is:

```
Rfilename
```

The R command inserts the lines from the LIB file that you specify in *filename*. It will insert the lines at the current position of the CP in a way similar to the I command. R will insert the entire 'LIB' file until it finds the end-of-file (↑Z) marker.

Transferring Lines To and Inserting Lines from a Temporary File

If you have version 1.4 or a successive version of CP/M, you can use the new X command to transfer lines from the buffer to a temporary "holding" file, and you can use the R command to insert the lines into the buffer from this "holding" file. The "holding" file is named X$$$$$$.LIB and only exists while the ED program is running. Any normal termination of ED will delete the file, but if you terminate ED with a ↑C (warm boot), the file will still be there (however, once you execute ED again, the file is deleted).

The format of the X command is:

```
nX
```

The X command transfers (copies) the next n lines from the current line to the temporary file X$$$$$$.LIB. The lines in the buffer will remain there: they are only copied to the temporary file. If you wish, you can use the K command to delete the lines after copying them. The transferred lines accumulate in the temporary file in the order in which they are copied by successive X commands. Using this command, new text may be built in successive blocks.

The lines can be retrieved by using the R command in the form 'R' without the *filename*. All of the transferred lines are then inserted following the CP (similar to the I command). However, the R command does not empty the temporary file, it simply copies the lines. You can retrieve them again and again (useful for repetitious lines). You can empty the temporary file (i.e., delete it) by executing the form '0X' (where n is zero) of the X command.

If you want to preserve the temporary file X$$$$$$.LIB, use ↑C to abort ED, and immediately rename the file (to get rid of the LIB extension) so that it won't be destroyed when you execute ED again.

Juxtaposition

The J command is used to juxtapose three groups of characters in a text. It finds a group of text, juxtaposes a second group, and deletes the characters following this pair until it finds yet a third group of text, effectively juxtaposing all three groups of text.

The format for the J command is:

```
nJstring1↑Zstring2↑Zstring3  { ↑Z }
                             { ↵  }
```

The J command starts searching from the CP in the buffer for the first occurrence of 'string1.' If it finds 'string1,' the J command inserts string 2 immediately following 'string1', and moves the CP to the end of 'string2'. The J command then looks for 'string3'; if it finds 'string3', the J command deletes all characters between 'string2' and 'string3', and leaves the CP pointing to the first character of string3. If the J command does not find 'string3', it doesn't delete anything. The J command does this n number of times, or until it runs out of lines in the buffer.

One use of the J command is to shorten lines of text. Pick a group of characters that will be the end of the line to be shortened. They will be the 'string1'. The concept is to juxtapose them to the Carriage Return sequence, represented by ↑L ('string3'). This result is achieved by inserting a blank or null 'string2'.

Repeating a Set of Commands

You can string together several ED commands into one "command" that can then be executed repeatedly. The M command (for "macro") takes the following form:

```
                      ↑Z
nMstringofcommands  {    }
                      ↵
```

Group your commands into 'stringofcommands', preceeded by 'M', and M will execute the commands n times, if n is greater than one. If n is zero or one, the 'stringofcommands' are executed repeatedly until an error occurs (like reaching the end of the buffer).

Here is an example that changes all occurrences of 'Peking' to 'Beijing' within the current buffer, and dispatches each line that is changed:

```
MSPeking↑ZBeijing↑Z0TT
```

ED'S ERROR CONDITIONS

When an error occurs within the ED program, ED displays the last character it saw before the error, and one of the following error indicators:

?	Don't recognize the command, what is it?
>	The buffer is full. Use one of the commands D, K, S, W, E, or H to remove characters. Or, your string with F, N, or S is too long.
#	Cannot execute the command that many times (as in an F command reaching the end of a buffer).
0	Cannot open the LIB file in an R command (check to see if the LIB file exists, or if you used the right filename).

Figure 4.15: ED's Error Messages

Newer versions of CP/M display 'BREAK x AT c' where x is one of the error symbols, and c is the ED command that was executing.

Occasionally, the system behind ED (i.e., CP/M or MP/M) detects a system error condition (such as a disk error). Depending upon the condition, you can usually terminate ED by doing a ↑C (warm start), but you must first retrieve the original copy of the source file. For example, if CP/M detects a CRC (cyclic redundancy check) error, it will display:

```
PERM ERR DISK d
```

where d is your current disk drive. You can choose to ignore the error by typing any character at your terminal (however, you should check your buffer for mistakes), or you can perform a warm boot (↑C) or a cold boot (reboot the system) and retrieve the BAK file (file with the BAK extension, e.g., QUOTE.BAK).

CP/M Version 2.2 Enhancements Summary

In CP/M version 2.2, ED assumes that the line numbering option is always on. To eliminate the line numbers, type: – V. (Of course, this mode can be reinstated with : V.)

When the insert mode is used (I), the usual CP/M control characters may all be used: DEL, ↑C, ↑E, ↑H, ↑J, ↑M, ↑R, ↑U, ↑X. They are described in Appendix D.

Finally, ED respects the file attributes of version 2.2. For example, a read/only file may be examined, but not changed. If this file must be modified, then its read/only status must first be changed to R/W, by using a STAT command.

SUMMARY

In this chapter, you have learned how to use an editor, ED. ED is a general text editor that allows you to modify text with just a few key strokes. ED is used most often to create a simple file, such as a program (if no other specialized editor is available). Although ED's commands are less convenient than a specialized word processor, it can be used to type letters or documents.

ED is a convenient tool for correcting and modifying existing files. (In particular, ED can be used to "clean up" a System Diskette that has erroneous or spurious characters due to mishandling.) ED can also be used to substitute new words or lines into a file. Summaries of ED's control characters and commands are presented in Appendices D and E.

In this chapter, you have not only learned how to use ED, the editor, but you have learned to use many commands, control characters and other conventions. You have also learned how to operate on files, and have followed transfers of text between disk, memory and CRT. This knowledge will help you understand the operation of most other programs on the computer.

5

INSIDE CP/M (AND MP/M)

INTRODUCTION

This chapter will describe the internal operation of the CP/M operating system. You will want to read this chapter if you are interested in learning about the ways in which an operating system works, or plan to modify or use some of CP/M's routines. However, if you only wish to use CP/M to accomplish a specific task, the information presented in this chapter is not necessary.

This chapter will be of greatest value to a systems programmer, or any person already familiar with programming who wants to understand how CP/M operates. Since a book on CP/M would not be complete without this information, this chapter is presented for these specific readers. If you want to know "what is happening under the hood," read on.

We will first present a simplified overview of CP/M's operation, by introducing its logical components, their roles, and the way they interact with each other. After that the *memory allocation,* i.e., the way in which these software modules are spread over the memory will be described, as well as the organization of the file system. Then, each of CP/M's three modules will be presented in detail along with the commands that are provided to use their capabilities. Another section will discuss the problems encountered when adapting CP/M to new hardware configurations and an example of CP/M alterations to make the system behave as a menu-driven system, will be shown. Finally, a special section will be devoted to MP/M.

AN OVERVIEW OF CP/M's OPERATION

Flow of Control

CP/M has three functional modules. They are called *CCP* (Console Command Processor, *BIOS* (Basic Input/Output System), and *BDOS* (Basic Disk Operating System). (See Figure 5.1.)

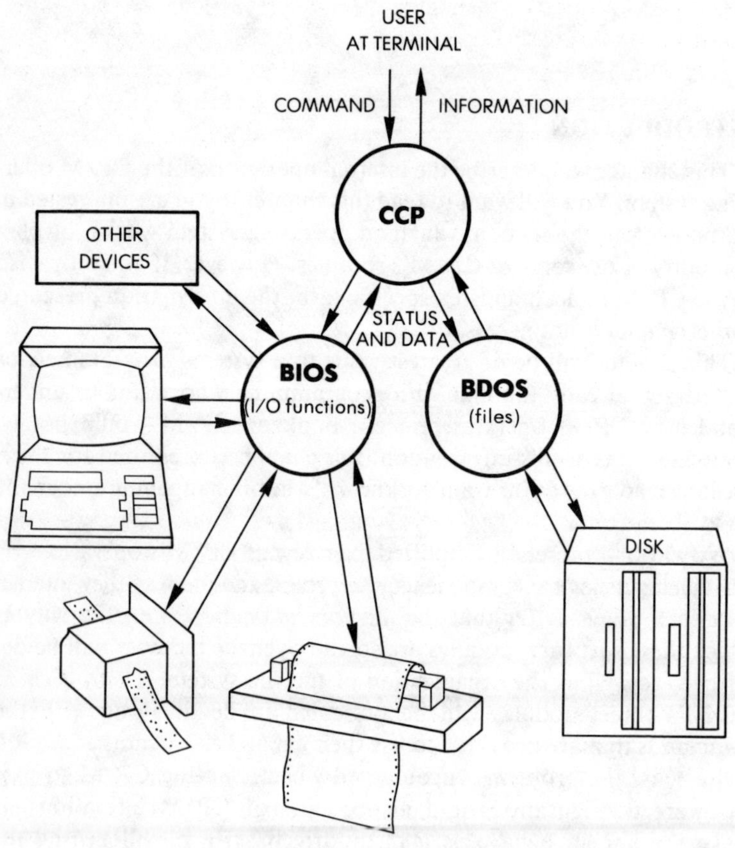

Figure 5.1: Flow of Control

The function of CCP is to communicate with the user and to interpret the commands typed at the keyboard. CCP is primarily a *command interpreter* and uses the resources provided by the other two modules, BIOS and BDOS. This is only a simplified description since we will later see that CCP, in fact, also does internal processing. Conceptually, CCP can be viewed as the "intelligent part" of the operating system, while the other two modules are service modules.

BIOS includes a collection of *peripheral drivers,* i.e., routines in charge of communicating with the various devices connected to the system. BIOS' function is to send or receive status and data information between a device and CCP's debugger. BIOS is called by CCP, with specific parameters specifying the service required. This is illustrated in Figure 5.1.

BDOS is in charge of managing the disk files. It includes a number of utility routines that will perform the required functions on the disk. Like any good disk-operating system, BDOS's purpose is to make the file management invisible (or "transparent") to the user. BDOS will go through all of the chores required to locate the various blocks of information spread over the surface of the diskette, verify the validity of the access and the integrity of the data, and efficiently allocate and release storage.

Memory Allocation

CP/M partitions the available memory into four zones, as shown in Figure 5.2. The top of the memory is reserved for the CP/M routines proper, i.e., for CCP, BDOS, and BIOS, as shown in Figure 5.2. A few locations at the bottom of memory are reserved for the system. These are the first 256 memory locations, i.e., *page 0* (described in more detail later). Finally, the largest part of memory, between location 0100 hexadecimal and CBASE (called TPA) is available for program execution. This standard memory allocation loads programs at 100H in S-100 bus computers such as Cromemco, Imsai, Altair, and North Star. However, in the case of other computers (e.g., the TRS 80 and Heath H8) with pre-stored programs in ROM in low memory, the programs start at 4300H.

The TPA or *Transient Program Area* is the name used in CP/M documentation for any program to be executed. CP/M assumes that the system has 16, 32, 48, or 64K. In a 16K system the base of CCP, called CBASE, is at memory address 2900 (hexadecimal). For each

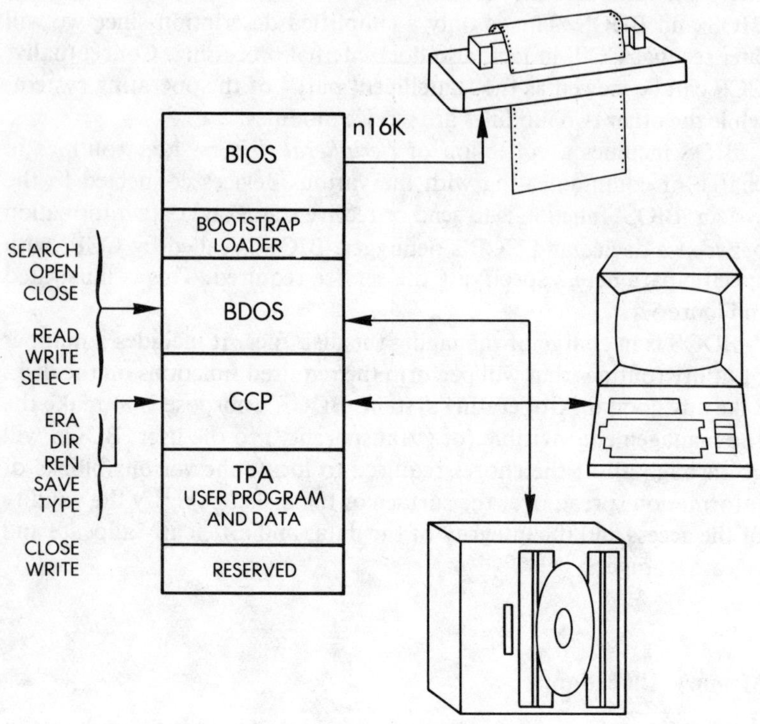

Figure 5.2: CP/M Memory Map

16K added to the system, this address is incremented by 4000 (hexadecimal). This means that every 16K of memory added to the system extends the TPA by that amount.

It will be seen later that a user program may use almost all of memory by overlaying CCP or other areas of memory belonging to CP/M routines. This will be discussed later in more detail. However, this means that when the program finishes execution, it should bring CP/M back into memory before exiting.

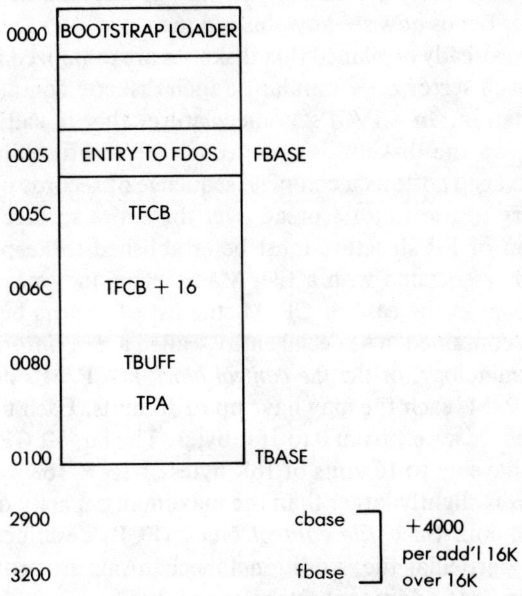

Figure 5.3: Standard CP/M Map

DETAILED DESCRIPTION

The File System

One of the primary functions of any *disk operating system* (DOS) is to provide effective and convenient management of disk-based files. An understanding of the overall organization of the file system is, therefore, required to understand the operation of the disk operating system proper (BDOS for CP/M) as well as the operation of CCP, which constructs and manipulates file descriptors. All of the file processing is done between CCP and BDOS, and the BIOS portion of CP/M does not have to worry about the explicit nature of a file. BIOS will essentially transmit and receive simple data streams. Let us examine the CP/M file structure.

A *file* is a logical unit that contains text, data, or programs. The disk operating system's task is to implement this logical facility with the physical resources provided by the storage medium, i.e., the diskette in our case. Let us now see how this is done.

We have already explained that diskettes are organized in tracks and sectors. Each sector on a standard 8 inch diskette contains 128 bytes of information. In CP/M's nomenclature, this is called a *record.* Every file on the diskette is a collection of records. Since it is not possible to keep a file as a complete sequence of records on the disk, it is necessary to use sectors spread over the entire surface of the disk. Some form of list structure must be established to keep track of all the records associated with a file. Many techniques may be used for this purpose. In the case of CP/M, the list of sectors belonging to a disk file is contained in a special entity, called a *descriptor* in computer science terminology, or the *file control block* in CP/M's nomenclature.

With CP/M, each file may have up to 16 units. Each unit has from 0 to 128 records, i.e., from 0 to 16K bytes. The largest CP/M file may therefore have up to 16 units of 16K bytes or 16 × 16K = up to 256K bytes. This is slightly larger than the maximum capacity of a standard 8 inch diskette. Each *file control block* (FCB) describes up to 16K bytes of a particular file. Additional mechanisms are provided to link together up to 15 additional extensions of the file.

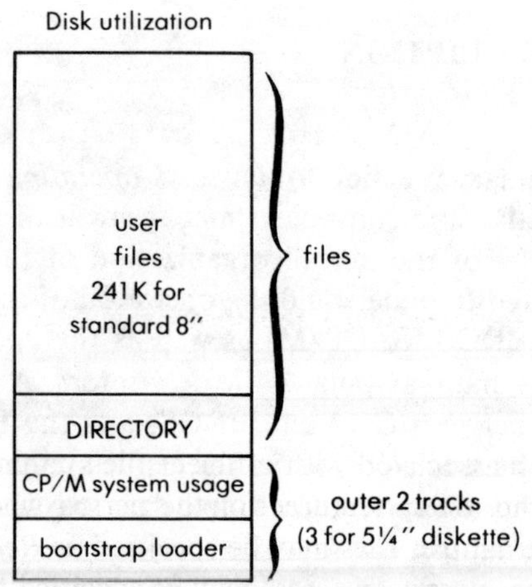

Figure 5.4: Disk Space Utilization

The actual utilization of disk space is shown in Figure 5.4. The outer two tracks of the diskettes are used to store the CP/M system. The rest of the disk is used to store the files and file directory.

The file control block itself uses 33 bytes and is stored in a directory area of the diskette reserved for that purpose. (See Figure 5.4.) Whenever the file is active, i.e., accessed through CP/M, its FCB is brought into the transient program area so that it can be accessed quickly and conveniently by the operating system.

We have accomplished our task: that of mapping a logical file onto the sectors available on a standard diskette. This was done by keeping a directory of the blocks, allocated to the file, in a special location called FCB.

A basic requirement of any good operating system is that the user be able to designate a file by using a *symbolic name* (users find it a nuisance to have to refer to files by numbers). CP/M provides this facility, along with an additional safeguard that also requires the user to specify the *type* of the file. Therefore, a mechanism must be provided for locating an *actual* file when its *logical* name is provided, by looking at the file directory until a match is found between the name provided by the user and the directory's entry. This association between an actual file and its name is performed within the FCB. The other essential part of the file control block (FCB) is the name of the file. This is shown in Figure 5.5.

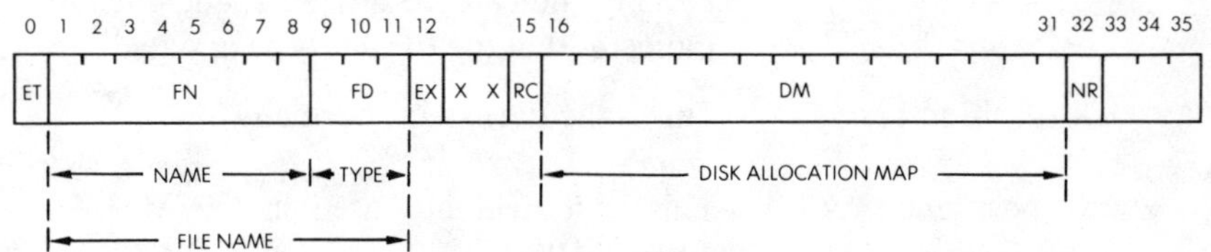

Figure 5.5: The File Control Block

The next task associated with efficient file system design is to provide security and safety features for the period when files are being accessed. For example, files may be specified as *Read-Only* or *Read-and-Write.* Also, *password* access may be specified for a file, or a file may be *executable* but not *readable,* and equipped with several protection devices that prevent unauthorized access or execution. CP/M version 1.4 provides virtually no such safeguards, but it has reserved several bytes in the FCB (File Control Block) to incorporate this safeguard. CP/M version 2.2 now provides four file attributes: R/O, R/W, SYS, and DIR.

Finally, a number of bytes are required for system bookkeeping functions. They are shown in Figure 5.5. In particular, location NR in position 32 contains the next record number to read or write.

Let us review the fields of the File Control Block shown in Figure 5.5. It contains eight fields which are, from right to left:

ET (position 0):	This is the entry type. It is normally 0, and not used in CP/M 1.4. It is the drive code in CP/M version 2.2 or MP/M.
FN (positions 1-8):	This is the file name containing up to eight characters. Any character not supplied by the user will be entered as an ASCII blank.
FD (positions 9-11):	This is the file type. It has one to three alphanumeric characters and is similarly completed with ASCII blanks if necessary. Whenever the directory of a diskette is listed, the file name and file type are displayed or typed. In CP/M version 2.2, two bits indicate the attribute, and one bit indicates that the file has been updated.
EX (position 12):	This is the file extent, normally 0.
XX (positions 13 & 14):	This is a field not used in CP/M 1.4, normally 0.
RC (position 15):	This is the record count. A file module may have from 0 to 128 records (up to 16K bytes). It is called the current extent size.
DM (positions 16-31):	The disk allocation map keeps track of the actual disk sectors used by this file module.

NR (position 32):	This contains the next record number to read or write, normally 0, and called CR in CP/M version 2.2. R0-1-2 (positions 33-35) is used only by CP/M version 2.2 for random accesses and represents the optional record number (0 to 64K).

System Operation

Under the CP/M operating system, each machine language program is installed or loaded within the transient program area (shown in Figure 5.2). In "standard CP/M," it starts execution at address 100H. In CP/M terminology, the program is called a "transient" and may use the operating system resources by executing a JMP to address 05H. This address is the gateway to the operating system. It is a single fixed entry point independent of the actual memory size and results in a transfer of control to the CP/M. The actual CP/M routines are resident in the high end of memory, (as shown in Figure 5.2). The call to the operating system must be accompanied by a parameter specifying the service requested. This parameter is passed as a function number and is contained in the C register of the 8080 or the Z80. Twenty-seven codes are provided by CP/M 1.4 (36 for CP/M 2.2) to access the various I/O devices, including the disk files.

CP/M Execution

From the CP/M user's point of view, the system works in the following manner: the CCP (Console Command Processor) displays the system prompt, and waits for a command. The actual transmissions are handled by the BIOS (Basic Input/Output System), and the command line ends up in CCP's buffer.

When CCP receives the command (and associated filenames), it executes the command immediately if the command is built-in (i.e., residing permanently in the system's portion of the computer memory). If the command is not built-in, CCP assumes that the command is a transient program with a filename of type "COM" (e.g., PIP.COM), and asks BDOS to find the file and read a copy of it into the TPA (Transient Program Area), the unused portion of the computer memory (i.e., not already used by the CP/M system components). CCP then constructs a File Control Block for the file(s) to be acted upon by the command (or program).

If there is more than one filename, the CCP constructs a File Control Block for each file, but assumes that the new program in the TPA (i.e., the transient command) will handle finding and accessing the files. The CCP only looks for the first file by calling BDOS and asking for a copy of the file.

The CCP then terminates, thus freeing space in the computer memory: the transient program can now overlay the space used by CCP.

From the system point of view, all files look the same. BDOS finds the file by looking at the File Control Block created by the CCP. This FCB is half-empty and only contains the filename. Each file on the diskette has its own FCB (a copy of the last one created by the CCP), so BDOS simply matches the filename from CCP's FCB with filenames in the files' FCBs.

When BDOS finds the correct file, it supplies more information for the File Control Block (FCB) that CCP created. Whenever the program accesses that particular file, DBOS changes some of the information in the File Control Block. When the program closes the file, BDOS makes a final change and then copies the FCB in the computer memory (along with the file's updated information) onto the diskette, updating both the file and the file's copy of the FCB.

The BDOS assumes that all files are the same, identified by filenames. The CCP looks at the first word that is typed (after displaying the system prompt) and assumes that it is either a built-in command or a command (program) that resides on a diskette with a filename that is the name of the command, including the "COM" extension (e.g., PIP.COM, LOAD.COM, etc.). If the first word is not a built-in command, and CCP does not find a file of type COM with a name matching the first word, CCP redisplays the word that was typed and follows it with a question mark.

If a 'COM' extension is put on a file that is not a proper program, and the name of that file is then typed as a command, the CCP will actually try to execute the file as if it were a program.

The CCP also looks at any associated filenames that might be typed with the command, but it does not judge them or decide how to use them. As soon as the command (or program) starts executing, the command (program) itself decides what to do with the associated files. For example, the ASM command is a transient program that only works on files with the extension 'ASM'. The LOAD command is another transient program that expects to have a file of type 'HEX' to load. The LOAD command produces a 'COM' file from a 'HEX' machine language program file.

To communicate with the devices (peripherals), the system uses a "message carrier," the BIOS. The BIOS performs simple operations like "read a character from the terminal keyboard" and "write a character to the printer." To the systems programmer and installer, the BIOS is the part of the system that must be modified to suit the hardware environment. Digital Research supplies a BIOS that will work on an Intel MDS-800 with standard devices that connect to the MDS-800 (corresponding to the Intellec MDS hardware environment peripheral definitions). To operate this version of CP/M in another hardware environment, the system programmer only has to alter the BIOS module.

FDOS AND CCP OPERATIONS

General Organization

CP/M's memory map (after it is loaded into the computer's main memory) is shown in Figure 5.6. The main entry point to FDOS is at

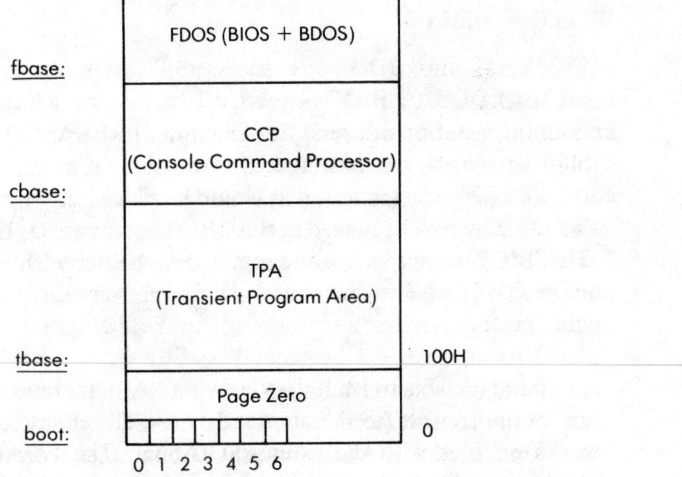

Figure 5.6: Entry to Actual fbase Address (Size of Available TPA + CCP Space). FDOS is a Jump to fbase.

location *boot* + 0005H in "page zero," the area of main memory that the system reserves for system values. The location *boot* starts machine code instructions that perform a system restart (warm boot); therefore, transient programs need only to jump to *boot* to call back the CCP to resume CP/M operations. The exact values for *boot, tbase, cbase* and *fbase* depend upon the version of CP/M, but the addresses are always used—a user program (a transient program) or a transient command fills from *tbase* up to *cbase,* and possibly up to *fbase* if it will overwrite the CCP.

When the CCP receives a command line, it looks for a COM file to match the name of the command, unless the command is built-in, in which case it executes immediately. The CCP also builds File Control Blocks for any filenames that also appear in the command line. After the CCP is finished, the COM file's memory image is brought into the TPA (maybe even overwriting the CCP), where it can access the FDOS operations.

The FDOS is divided into the two parts that have already been introduced: the BIOS, which controls all peripherals and transmissions, and the BDOS, which searches disks for files and manages the File Control Block for each file in order to provide random access. Let us now examine both parts in more detail.

BIOS Operations

The BIOS and BDOS are accessed through the principal entry point for FDOS. A BIOS is specified by passing a function number and an information address. For example, if the ASCII character 'B' should be sent to the terminal, the function number for the "write console" operation (function 2) would be placed in register C, and the value of 'B' would be placed in the CPI register pair D, E.

The BIOS operations are summarized below with each function number. (It is wise to check with Digital Research for enhancements or changes):

1. Read console (terminal). Returns an ASCII character.
2. Write console (terminal). Sends an ASCII character.
3. Read reader. Returns an ASCII character from the "reader" device (RDR:).
4. Write punch. Sends an ASCII character to the "punch" device (PUN:).

5. Write list. Sends an ASCII character to the "list" device (LST:).
6. Direct console input/output (CP/M version 2.2 and MP/M only). Send 'FF' to receive character or status, or send a character to the console.
7. Get I/O status. Return byte with status of device.
8. Set I/O status. Send byte with status to device.
9. Print buffer. Send entire string (starting with address and ending in '$').
10. Read buffer. Send address of read buffer and return with filled buffer.
11. Interrogate console ready. If the least significant bit of the byte is 1, then console character is ready.

File Control Blocks

When BDOS creates a file, it also constructs a file control block for the file with information including the file's name and allocation of memory. Each file control block can describe 16K bytes, which is 128 records of 128 bytes each; this unit is called an "extent." Up to 256K bytes can be addressed with one file control block by using automatic CP/M mechanisms.

The file control blocks are stored with the files on diskette, and the BDOS brings them into main memory before the files are actually accessed (BDOS "open file" and "make file" operations). BDOS and the transient program continually update the file control blocks while the transient program executes. When the transient program executes BDOS's close file operations, BDOS records the final versions of the file control blocks on diskette. Thus, all file updating of individual files occurs in the computer's main memory, with unaltered original files remaining on the disk.

The CCP constructs transient file control blocks for the filenames in a command line, and leaves most of the information blank for the transient command (program) to provide. The CCP compares the filename found in the command line (stored in a read buffer for CCP inspection) to filenames found by BDOS in file control blocks in order to retrieve the proper memory allocation information (i.e., to find extents of a file). The CCP always translates lower case characters in the command line to UPPER CASE to conform with CP/M filename conventions.

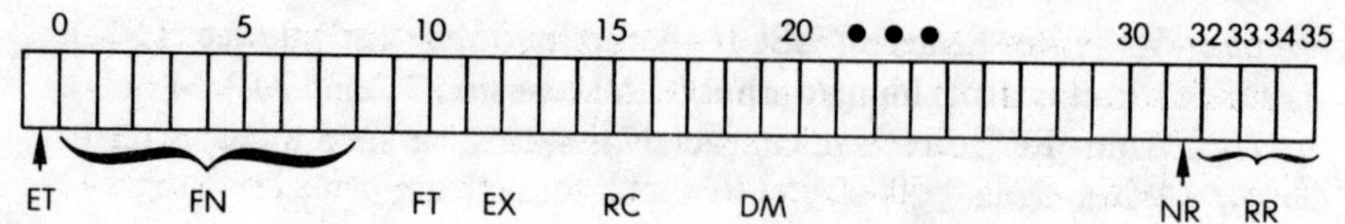

Field	Positions	Information
ET	0	Entry type (assumed zero in CP/M 1.4, set to "drive code" in CP/M 2.2 and MP/M).
FN	1-8	Filename padded with blanks (ASCII characters).
FT	9-11	File type, sometimes called filename extension (also padded with blanks).
EX	12	File extent, normally set to zero.
	13-14	Reserved for system use.
RC	15	Record count, or current extent size (0 to 128 records).
DM	16-31	Disk allocation map, filled in and used by CP/M.
NR	32	Next record number to read or write (current record number in CP/M version 2.2).
RR	33-35	Optional random record number (CP/M version 2.2 and MP/M only) in the range 0-65535.

Figure 5.7: Field Positions Information

BDOS Operations

BDOS can also be accessed by using the FDOS entry and passing a function number and an information address (the entry point to FDOS is *boot* + 0005H). For example, if a read on a disk file must be performed, the program should send the function number for a disk read (20 or 33), along with the address of the file control block for the file you want to read. The BDOS would perform the function and then return with either a successful completion indicator, or an error indicator (indicating that the read was not successful).

The BDOS operations and their function numbers are summarized below. (Again, check with Digital Research for enhancements or changes.)

12. Lift Disk Head (version 1.4). The function lifts the head from current disk. Return version number (version 2.2 and MP/M). This returns the version number of your CP/M system to provide version-independent programming.
13. Reset disk system. This function initializes BDOS, resets read/write state for all disks, selects drive A and sets the default DMA address to *boot* + 0080H (used by programs to change disks without requiring a ↑C from the terminal or a system restart).
14. Select disk. You designate (1 for A, 2 for B, 3 for C, etc.) a disk drive as the current drive for subsequent file operations.
15. Open file. Send a file control block address, and BDOS will find a matching file control block in the directory area of the disk, and return with the proper directory code indicating that the proper information was copied to the file control block. This allows subsequent file access.
16. Close file. Send the address of a file control block, and BDOS will record the new directory information in the file control block on the disk (the reverse of an open file function, with the same codes returned).
17. Search for file. Send the address of the file control block that contains a filename, and BDOS will look for the first match of that filename and return the address of the file control block on disk that matches the one set up by CCP (or the program).
18. Search for next occurrence. Use this function *after* function 17 to find the next occurrence of a match for the filename, and return with the address of the next file control block on disk.
19. Delete file. Send the address of the file control block that contains a filename, and BDOS will delete that file from the disk.
20. Read sequentially. If the file has been opened or activated by a make function, this function will read the next 128 bytes (record) into memory at the current DMA address, and return an indicator for a successful read, an end of file, or unwritten data during random access.
21. Write sequentially. If the file has been opened or activated by a make function, this function will write 128 bytes starting at the

current DMA address to the file named by the file control block. This function will overwrite existing data in the file (if any).

22. Make file. Similar to the open file function, this function creates a new file as well as opening it. Send the address of a file control block with a new filename, and this function will create the file and initialize its file control block (in main memory as well as on disk) as an empty file. You must make sure that you are not creating a duplicate of a file on the same disk, and rendering them both inaccessible. Try using the delete function first on the new filename.
23. Rename file. Send address of the file control block, and BDOS will rename the filename area of the block and record it on disk.
24. Return log-in vector. This function determines which disk drives are "on-line."
25. Return current disk (version 2.2 and MP/M only). This function returns a number corresponding to the letter (A, B, C, etc.) of the disk drive that is currently selected.
26. Set DMA address. This function sets the Direct Memory Address (address where the file pointer stopped after a read or write operation) to another value to find data records elsewhere in memory. A cold start, warm start, or a disk reset will set the DMA to *boot* + 0080H.
27. Get address of allocation vector. The system maintains an allocation vector in the main memory for each on-line drive. This function returns the address of the vector for the current drive. Various programs (like STAT) use this vector to determine the amount of remaining storage space.
28. Write-protect disk. This function provides temporary write protection. Any attempt to write to the disk (without an intervening cold or warm start) will generate an error message.
29. Get read/only vector. This function returns a vector that indicates which drives are write protected; i.e., that have the read/only bit set.
30. Set file attributes. This function allows you to set or clear indicators attached to files that provide read/only and system attributes.
31. Get disk parameter block address. This function returns the BIOS disk parameter block address, and is useful for computing space and changing values of disk parameters when the disk environment changes.

32. Get or set user code. You can use this function to find out or change the user code currently active (user areas are in version 2.2 and MP/M only).
33. Read randomly. This function uses the RR field of the file control block to select a record number and read the record. It returns with the DMA pointing to the desired record, and the record number is *not* advanced as with sequential read operations.
34. Write randomly. This function is initiated in the same manner as a random read operation, except that it writes the data to the disk from the current DMA. If the file's space has not yet been allocated, the operation allocates before writing. The record number is *not* advanced.
35. Compute file size. Send this function a file control block address, and it returns the record address of the "logical record" following the end of file (virtual file size). You can append data to an existing file by using this information to set the random record position before performing a series of random write operations. The virtual size corresponds to the physical size if the file was written sequentially; otherwise, the file may have unallocated holes as a result of random write operations.
36. Set random record position. This function returns the random record position after a series of sequential read or write operations. It is useful for switching from sequential to random file operations, or for initial sequential scanning of the file before random read or write operations.

INSTALLING AND ALTERING CP/M

CP/M is always tailored to a specific input/output (and memory) configuration. Digital Research distributes a form of CP/M that works instantly on Intel's MDS-800 microcomputer development system. Other hardware and software vendors supply versions of CP/M that work on other hardware systems. Most likely, you will be buying a version of CP/M that automatically works without alterations. However, if you have a CP/M version, and you wish to tailor it to a new hardware environment because of new input/output devices you will need to "patch" the BIOS portion of CP/M; if you have MP/M, you will need to "patch" the BIOS and the XIOS portions. Patching the BIOS means inserting the new input/output routines required by your specific devices. This is not a difficult task, but it is device- and installation-dependent. For this reason, specific instructions cannot be presented here. Refer to the applicable version of Digital Research's *CP/M Alteration Guide.*

If you are bringing up a new CP/M version from scratch, the problem is more complex. If your system already has the rudimentary elements for program development and execution, you can write your own routines (called GETSYS and PUTSYS) to read the "system" from a diskette into the computer's memory and write back a patched version of the system onto a new diskette to be used as the System Diskette. Otherwise, you must use another system to generate the new diskette to be used with your system.

If you have a version of CP/M up and running, you can easily write assembly language programs to perform special tasks; you could also make use of SYSGEN.COM and MOVCPM.COM to help alter CP/M so that you don't have to write your own GETSYS and PUTSYS programs. However, your version of SYSGEN.COM might not work with your type of disk or diskette (minidiskettes, hard disks, and others). You might have to alter CP/M first before you can use SYSGEN.COM.

Digital Research provides minimal versions of GETSYS and PUTSYS programs in the documentation that they provide (*CP/M Alteration Guide* or *MP/M User's Guide*). To begin, you must write a GETSYS program to read the first two tracks of the supplied system diskette (the first two tracks' files are not displayed by DIR, but consist of the system itself). You can find the BIOS portion of the system and change it (called "patching" the program). You can save the altered system on diskette by writing a PUTSYS program. Finally, you can write a version of GETSYS, a "bootstrap" program, and place it on track 0, sector 1 using your PUTSYS program. After testing it, you should have a properly working system that automatically starts when you "cold start" your computer.

If your are using a CP/M system to alter a CP/M system for another hardware environment, and the disk media is compatible, then you can use shortcuts to create your new system diskette: MOVCPM (MOVCPM.COM), and SYSGEN (SYSGEN.COM). This is called a "second level system regeneration" in Digital Research's documentation.

You can combine a memory reconfiguration (MOVCPM) and a diskette initialization (PUTSYS) by using MOVCPM instead of GETSYS to read in the existing system, and SYSGEN instead of PUTSYS to place the altered version on your new system diskette.

MOVCPM is the transient command MOVCPM.COM, and you

have to supply arguments:

```
MOVCPM bb *
```

where bb is the number of kilobytes (e.g., 32k, 64k, 20k) for the new memory image of the system. You supply an asterisk (*) to tell MOVCPM to leave this memory image in memory (the TPA). You could also supply an asterisk to replace bb, and MOVCPM will calculate the largest amount of memory it can dedicate to the new system. The MOVCPM command is described in more detail in the next part of this section.

Here is an example of a MOVCPM operation:

```
A > MOVCPM 32 * ↵
CONSTRUCTING 32K CP/M VERS x.x
READY FOR "SYSGEN" OR
"SAVE 34 CPM32.COM"
A >
```

As the display suggests, the new 32K system is in the TPA, ready for your next operation, which should either be a SYSGEN or a SAVE. Since you want to alter the BIOS portion of the system, you will also want to SAVE a version of it (calling it 'CPM32.COM' for a 32K system, if you wish). Once it is SAVEd, you can load it into memory again using DDT (CP/M's debugger program), and alter the BIOS portion.

If you plan to make major alterations (or alterations at another time), it would be easier to create your own BIOS, since you also have to create your own bootstrap program (you can call them 'CBIOS' and 'BOOT' if you wish). You would use the ED program (CP/M's editor program) to create CBIOS.ASM and BOOT.ASM, and use the ASM program (CP/M's assembler) or another assembler to create CBIOS.HEX and BOOT.HEX, which could be loaded by using LOAD to create CBIOS.COM and BOOT.COM—actual programs that can be tested before you merge them with your new system.

When you have the new CPMbb.COM (where bb is the memory size you used with MOVCPM) system in memory using DDT, you can merge CBIOS.COM and BOOT.COM with it, or alter these portions while testing it, and finally use SYSGEN to put the altered system onto the first two tracks of your new system diskette. Here is an example:

```
A >SYSGEN ↲
SYSGEN VERSION xx.xx
SOURCE DRIVE NAME (OR RETURN TO SKIP) ↲
```

(Respond with a RETURN to skip SYSGEN's read operation, since you already have the altered system in memory.)

```
DESTINATION DRIVE NAME (OR RETURN TO REBOOT) B
```

(This assumes the new system diskette is in drive B.)

```
DESTINATION ON DRIVE B, THEN TYPE RETURN ↲
FUNCTION COMPLETE
DESTINATION DRIVE NAME (OR RETURN TO REBOOT) ↲
A >PIP B:=A:*.*[V] ↲
•••
```

(Copying messages)

```
•••
A >
```

If you have a copy of CP/M as a .COM file on the disk, you may use a shortcut:

```
A > SYSGEN CPM.COM↲
    SYSGEN VERSION 2.2
    DESTINATION DRIVE NAME (OR RETURN TO REBOOT):
    (etc, . . .)
```

You should follow the instructions provided in Digital Research's *CP/M Version 2.2 Alteration Guide,* to alter the BIOS, and create GETSYS, PUTSYS and BOOT programs.

RECONFIGURING (ADJUSTING MEMORY SIZE) USING MOVCPM

Frequently, the size of a system is increased or reduced (memory boards removed). CP/M must be altered accordingly. The MOVCPM program (MOVCPM.COM) allows the user to simply reconfigure the CP/M system for any memory size.

The MOVCPM program can be executed as a command with optional arguments:

$$\text{MOVCPM}\left\{\begin{matrix} * \\ \\ \text{bb} \end{matrix}\right\}*$$

The optional bb argument tells MOVCPM how much memory it should manage in the new CP/M system; if you don't specify bb, or if you specify an asterisk (*) instead of bb, MOVCPM will configure the new system to manage *all* of the available RAM memory of your host computer (RAM is "random access memory"). In most cases, you will want CP/M to manage (and take advantage of) all of the available RAM memory.

The optional second asterisk (*), if you supply it, will tell MOVCPM to keep the newly configured system in memory (the TPA) in preparation for a SYSGEN or a SAVE. In most cases, you would want to save this new system, or write it out to a diskette by using SYSGEN. If you don't supply the second asterisk (*), MOVCPM will boot this new system without permanently recording it.

Here are a few examples:

A >MOVCPM ↲	This command relocates the CP/M system to take advantage of all of the RAM memory (starting at 100H, the beginning of the TPA) in the host computer, and then execute the system without recording it on diskette.

A >MOVCPM 32 ↵	This command relocates CP/M to manage 32K memory, and executes the system without recording it.
A >MOVCPM 32 * ↵	This command relocates CP/M to manage 32K memory, and leaves the memory image of the system in memory (the TPA) in preparation for a SYSGEN or SAVE.
A >MOVCPM * * ↵	This command relocates CP/M to manage all of the host computer's RAM memory (starting at 100H), and leaves the memory image of the system in memory in preparation for a SYSGEN or SAVE.

The last two forms use the second asterisk (*) to leave the new version of the system in memory so that you can either SAVE the contents of memory in a disk file, or SYSGEN the system in memory to write it out to the first two tracks of the diskette (to create a system diskette). When either "MOVCPM * *↵ " or 'MOVCPM bb *↵ ' is executed, the message READY FOR "SYSGEN" or "SAVE bb CPMbb.COM" is displayed upon completion of the MOVCPM program (bb is the number of kilobytes).

The command line you supply could contain a "menu" program that provides access to other programs by chaining to the programs depending on which program the user picks out of the "menu." Everytime a program finishes, or after every cold or warm start, the menu would then be displayed again, and the user would make another selection. When using this version of the system, the user would not be able to execute CP/M commands, since after every program execution or interruption, the system would automatically execute the menu program again.

To insert your own command line for automatic execution, bring the system into memory by using MOVCPM or SYSGEN, and SAVE it. Once you have a SAVEd memory image of the system, you can use DDT to insert the patch. The location for the patch should start at address 0980H; using DDT's D command, you can display the contents of memory at that location:

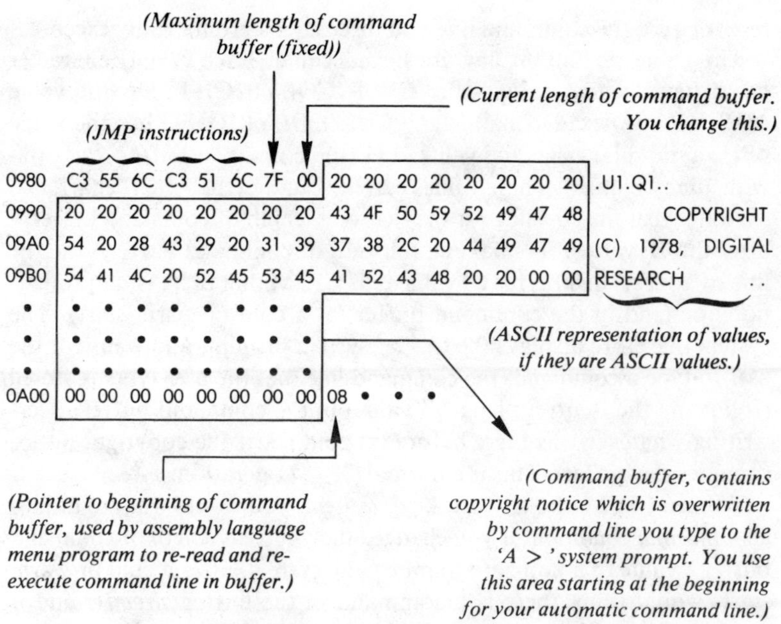
(Maximum length of command buffer (fixed))
(Current length of command buffer. You change this.)
(JMP instructions)
0980 C3 55 6C C3 51 6C 7F 00 20 20 20 20 20 20 20 20 .U1.Q1..
0990 20 20 20 20 20 20 20 20 43 4F 50 59 52 49 47 48 COPYRIGHT
09A0 54 20 28 43 29 20 31 39 37 38 2C 20 44 49 47 49 (C) 1978, DIGITAL
09B0 54 41 4C 20 52 45 53 45 41 52 43 48 20 20 00 00 RESEARCH ..
0A00 00 00 00 00 00 00 00 00 08
(ASCII representation of values, if they are ASCII values.)
(Pointer to beginning of command buffer, used by assembly language menu program to re-read and re-execute command line in buffer.)
(Command buffer, contains copyright notice which is overwritten by command line you type to the 'A > ' system prompt. You use this area starting at the beginning for your automatic command line.)

Figure 5.8: Displaying the Contents of Memory

A CP/M ALTERATION EXAMPLE: A MENU SYSTEM

This example is provided to show you how to use CP/M resources. One valuable home and business application is a "turn-key" system that immediately starts executing programs when you do a cold start (e.g., after hitting the RESET button, the system automatically executes a program that in turn chains to other programs to perform system housekeeping or control operations). Another useful tool for business or home environments) is a *menu program* (mentioned previously), which gives the user a choice of programs to execute; this menu program would be automatically executed in a "turn-key" system to keep system programs protected.

You can provide both by modifying special locations in the CP/M system—the locations usually filled by the command that you type when you get the system prompt. They are at the base of the CCP (Console Command Processor), and you modify those locations by using DDT (or any other debugger, such as SID). Essentially, you insert a command line into those locations and you insert a flag to tell CP/M to execute the command line, instead of displaying the system prompt. Then, whenever the user performs a cold or warm start (system reset or ↑C), the command line you inserted is automatically executed.

The values in the display are hexadecimal. Each ASCII character has a hexadecimal value—the 'C' of 'COPYRIGHT' has the value 43H ('H' for hexadecimal), the 'O' of 'COPYRIGHT' has the value 4FH, and a blank has the value 20H (the command buffer starts out with many blanks). These values can be found in the ASCII chart.

Notice that the 00 value for the "current length of command buffer," after the 7F value for "maximum length of command buffer," on the line of address 0980. This 00 value tells CP/M that there is, at present, no command in the command buffer (at a cold or warm start). The system therefore displays the 'A >' system prompt, and waits for the user to type a command; the command line that the user types is stored (following the "current length" value) in the command buffer, overwriting whatever was there before (at cold start, the copyright notice occupies the buffer). This is a normal CP/M operation.

To turn CP/M into a "turn-key" system, you would want to induce an *abnormal* condition: if you changed the "current length of command buffer" value to a non-zero number, the system, after a cold or warm start, would think there is a command in the buffer *already,* and it would execute the command. Following completion or interruption (or warm start or cold start), the system would return again to this value, and think that there is already a command in the buffer. In short, the system would never get around to displaying the 'A >' system prompt!

You would, of course, have to provide a command line for the command buffer, overwriting the copyright notice (you could also move the copyright notice to the end of the command buffer). You can use up to and including location 0A07H, but you absolutely cannot modify locations above it. Location 0A08H contains the pointer to the beginning of the command buffer, which you will need if you write a menu program in assembly language.

To insert the command line, type in DDT's 'S' command, (as described in the documentation for DDT supplied by Digital Research), using hexadecimal values for the ASCII characters of the command line. This command line should end with the value 00, and you should count all of the characters (including blanks) of your command line up to but not including the final 00, and put this character count into the location for the "current length of the command buffer," to tell CP/M how long your command line is.

An easy way to implement a menu system is to use BASIC. Most BASICs have the CHAIN program statement, so that one BASIC program can chain to another, and the other can chain back to the menu program. This menu program can be written in BASIC, and the BASIC language interpreter would take care of the command buffer to execute BASIC programs (i.e., you would not need to use the pointer to the beginning of the command buffer in location 0A08H). CBASIC2 (Software Systems) or Microsoft BASIC (MBASIC.COM, by Microsoft Consumer Products) could be used, since both of them allow you to execute a BASIC program as part of the CP/M command line in order to execute the BASIC.

For example, Microsoft BASIC is supplied as MBASIC.COM, a command you can execute by itself to "bring up" Microsoft BASIC (execute the BASIC interpreter) or you can also execute Microsoft BASIC *with an argument* that is the name of a BASIC program, as in this example:

```
A >MBASIC PROG
```

In this example, MBASIC is the BASIC interpreter program which in turn executes the BASIC program PROG.BAS ('.BAS' extension is expected on filenames for Microsoft BASIC programs).

If you write a BASIC program MENU.BAS, you could use it in the following command line:

```
MBASIC MENU
```

You could insert this command line into the command buffer. The current length of the command buffer would be 11, so you would put the value 0B (hexadecimal) in the location for the "current length of the command buffer," and you would then insert the command line "MBASIC MENU" into the command buffer as shown in Figure 5.9.

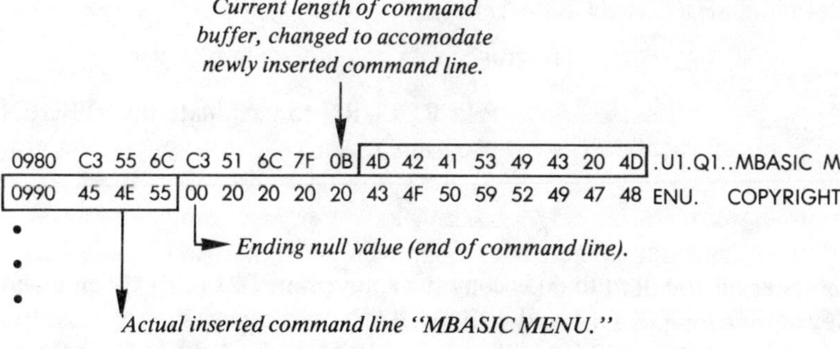

Current length of command buffer, changed to accomodate newly inserted command line.
0980 C3 55 6C C3 51 6C 7F 0B 4D 42 41 53 49 43 20 4D .U1.Q1..MBASIC M
0990 45 4E 55 00 20 20 20 20 43 4F 50 59 52 49 47 48 ENU. COPYRIGHT
Ending null value (end of command line).
Actual inserted command line "MBASIC MENU."

Figure 5.9: Memory Shows the Line Inserted

When you finish applying the "patch" above, you should execute DDT's G0 command to terminate DDT. Without doing anything to destroy the contents of the TPA, use the SAVE command to save the new version of your system:

A > SAVE 34 AUTOCPM.COM ↲

(Call your new version something like 'AUTOCPM.COM' to distinguish it from other versions of your system.)

If you are using CP/M version 1.4, you should *first* do the following SYSGEN operation to put the newly modified system on the first two tracks of your new system diskette, *then* do the above SAVE operation (because version 1.4's SAVE command destroys the contents of the TPA). If you're using version 2.2 of CP/M, you can safely use the SAVE command first (to save a memory image of your new system), and then use SYSGEN to put the new system on the first two tracks of your new system diskette:

A > SYSGEN ↲

SOURCE DRIVE NAME (OR RETURN TO SKIP) ↲

(Hit RETURN to skip, since the newly modified system is already in memory.)

DESTINATION DRIVE NAME (OR RETURN TO REBOOT) B

(This assumes your new system diskette is in drive B.)

DESTINATION IN DRIVE B, THEN TYPE RETURN ↲

FUNCTION COMPLETE

DESTINATION DRIVE NAME (OR RETURN TO REBOOT) ↲

(Hit RETURN to terminate the SYSGEN program.)

A >

Now all you need to do is copy the appropriate files (CP/M command files, MBASIC.COM and MENU.BAS) to the new system diskette. Upon cold start, CP/M will execute MBASIC, and the MENU.BAA, instead of supplying the usual system prompt. Your MENU.BAA must be capable of providing access (via CHAIN or SWAP statements) to other BASIC programs.

If you wanted to write your menu program in assembly language, the program would have to be smart enough to reconstruct another command line in the command buffer to branch to other programs. This program would use the "pointer to the beginning of the command buffer" in location 0A08H to tell the system to go back and read (and execute) the reconstructed command line.

MP/M

Installing and Altering MP/M

To install an MP/M multi-user system, you need a CP/M system, because the MP/M loader (MPMLDR.COM) needs to have a version of CP/M's BIOS included (LDRBIOS.COM). MP/M can be executed ("brought up") from CP/M by executing MPMLDR.COM, which loads the MP/M system (MPM.SYS) into memory from the diskette (similar to SYSGEN.COM, which loads a CP/M system into memory). From CP/M, you must first *generate* your MP/M system by using the program GENSYS.COM, which is provided with MP/M, and will run in CP/M.

The GENSYS program asks several questions, and then uses the information you supply to build MPM.SYS. The MPMLDR program then loads MPM.SYS into memory, and relocates it automatically.

To answer all of the questions for GENSYS, you need to know what kind of system you want, whether you want "banked memory" or not, and what "resident system processes" you desire ("resident system processes" are described in the next section). Here is a sample run of GENSYS:

```
A>GENSYS ↵

MP/M 1.0 SYSTEM GENERATION

TOP PAGE OF MEMORY = 0 ↵

NUMBER OF CONSOLES = 2 ↵

BREAKPOINT RST # = 5 ↵

ALLOCATE USER STACKS FOR SYSTEM CALLS (Y/N) ?Y

MEMORY SEGMENT BASES, (FF TERMINATES LIST)
```

: 00,0 ↲

: 00,1 ↲

: 00,2 ↲

: FF ↲

Select Resident System Processes: (Y/N) Y

TIME	?Y ↲
SCHED	?Y ↲
ATTACH	?Y ↲
SPOOL	?Y ↲
MPMSTAT	?Y ↲

A >

The answers above are described here:

Top page of memory: You enter the hexadecimal address of the top page of your system's RAM memory. If you enter a zero, the MP/M loader determines the size of memory at load time by finding the top page of RAM memory.

Number of consoles: You enter the number of consoles to be hooked up to your system; each console takes up 256 bytes of memory. MP/M version 1.0 supports up to 16 consoles.

Breakpoint RST #: You enter the breakpoint restart number to be used by DDT or SID (debugger programs). Restart zero is not allowed; neither are the restarts used by the MP/M system. Consult the MP/M documentation supplied by Digital Research.

Allocate user stacks for system calls: Answer 'Y' for yes if you intend to use CP/M '.COM' files as commands in your MP/M system. MP/M requires more stack space than CP/M.

Memory segment bases: You can specify one to eight user memory segments with the same address space but with different bank numbers, as described in the MP/M documentation. The first memory location you specify should be your first actual RAM location (if you have

ROM starting at 0000H). The bank number follows the location, separated by a comma. This list is terminated with 'FF'.

Select resident system processes: Answer 'Y' for yes to each program that you want to be "resident" instead of "relocatable" or "transient." Resident processes are programs that reside within the operating system, and are not displayed in a directory display (much like CP/M's built-in commands).

If this routine looks complicated, that's because it is! MP/M is a brand new concept for microcomputers—shared multi-user systems have not yet proliferated in the low-end microcomputer marketplace. Typical of "advanced ideas," this one is far too complicated for normal microcomputer operations. Obviously, this generation process will become easier to perform in subsequent releases of MP/M. (Most of this information can be found in an easily updatable form in Digital Research's *User's Guide to MP/M.*)

Once you have generated MPM.SYS, you can use MPMLDR.COM to load it into memory and execute it. MPMLDR.COM requires no answers—simply execute it as a command.

MP/M is designed to run on an Intel MDS-800 microcomputer development system, but it has a portion called XIOS (Extended BIOS) that you can alter for other hardware environments. In addition to rewriting the XIOS portion, you must also customize the MPMLDR.COM program to load MPM.SYS and execute it. Note that MPMLDR.COM uses the standard CP/M BIOS (called LDRBIOS) to relocate and execute the MP/M system; therefore, at the least you need a version of CP/M's BIOS (you can write your own, or modify an existing one). Using your modified BIOS (LDRBIOS), patch the BIOS portion of MPMLDR.COM and place it back on diskette using SYSGEN.COM (if you can't use SYSGEN.COM, you need to write GETSYS and PUTSYS programs, as described in MP/M's documentation, and in the previous section of this chapter). To perform this patch, read into memory MPMLDR.COM using DDT or SID (debugger programs), and either perform the change manually, or merge your LDRBIOS.HEX with it. When you are finished, SAVE the contents as MPMLDR.COM, and execute MPMLDR.COM to initiate MP/M from a running CP/M.

To customize your XIOS portion of MP/M, follow the detailed instructions in the MP/M documentation provided by Digital Research. Use the GENMOD program to produce the XIOS.SPR (system page relocatable) file from two concatenated HEX files.

MP/M Operation

MP/M is comprised of several components: The XIOS (BIOS and extended IOS) to interface with the hardware environment (which can be altered), the BDOS and XDOS (Basic and extended disk operation) to perform file operations, and the CLI/TMP (Command Line Interpreter and Terminal Message Process) to handle console input/output.

CP/M is a "sequential" system, with only one program running at any one time. MP/M, however, has to accomodate many programs running "at the same time," and sharing the same resources: the CPU (computer), the disk media, consoles, and line printers. MP/M is a "priority driven" system, which means that the process (running program) with the highest priority gets the CPU. A process holds its resource until it is finished with it, it issues a system call, it is interrupted, or the real-time clock ticks once (optional). The ensuing contest for resources is called *"dispatching."*

The "dispatcher" looks at the process's "*descriptor*" to determine its priority and to decide whether it should run ahead of other processes. The dispatcher also uses the process descriptor to store temporary information about the process, and the state it was in when it was interrupted.

When all processes have equal priority, the dispatcher executes them in a "first in—first out" order. *Queues* are used to synchronize processes by having one process send a message at a certain time during its run, while another waits at the queue for the message. The waiting process is suspended until the message arrives.

A *queue* is a waiting list, organized as a special file that can be opened and closed and fed information sequentially. A queue can be used to temporarily receive information to transfer to another program that writes the information onto the disk. Queues are also used to spool files to the line printer, and to provide exclusive use of a resource by a process. For example, if one process set up a queue that only held information when the line printer was not busy, and another process had to first receive information from the queue before accessing the line printer, then that mechanism would provide exclusive use of a shared resource. The second process would wait until it received the message that the line printer was free.

MP/M provides another way to synchronize processes by employing *flags* set by one process and examined by another process. Flags provide a method of synchronization and process interruption that is independent of additional hardware interrupt devices and software interrupt mechanisms.

As an option, a real-time clock (that can be reset) may be used to provide accurate time of day measurement, and system timing in order to schedule processes, or for the execution of disk programs. It also provides the ability to delay the execution of a process.

There are no "built-in" commands for MP/M; all "commands" are either transient '.COM' programs, page relocatable '.PRL' programs, or resident system processes created from '.RSP' programs at system generation (GENSYS execution). Transient programs require use of the "absolute TPA" area of memory, and they require extra stack space; most programs should be made "relocatable" so that they can occupy virtually *any* space available in memory, and still execute properly. Most relocatable programs employ *macros* that are many instructions rolled into one, and you need MAC (Macro-Assembler program sold separately by Digital Research) to assemble programs. The program GENMOD, supplied with MP/M, converts two concatenated '.HEX' files into a page relocatable file with a '.PRL' extension. This '.PRL' program executes properly if you use ORG statements correctly, as described in the *MP/M User's Guide* from Digital Research.

GENMOD accepts a file that contains two concatenated '.HEX' files offset from each other by 100 hexadecimal bytes. The format of the GENMOD command is:

```
GENMOD file.hex file.prl $bbbb
```

The argument file.hex must be a filename including the '.HEX' extension of a file with two concatenated '.HEX' files offset by 100H bytes. The argument file.prl must be a filename including the '.PRL' extension for the new page relocatable program. The optional $bbbb argument provides additional memory beyond the explicit code space allotted, in order to provide extra space for buffers. If your program needs the extra memory, supply a dollar ($) sign followed by four hexadecimal digits. Here is an example:

```
1A >GENMOD B:FINAL.HEX PERFORM.PRL $1000 ↵
```

This command will convert FINAL.HEX on drive B to PERFORM.PRL on the current drive, and allot an extra 1000H bytes of memory to the program.

You can also create your own resident system process using GENMOD by substituting a file.rsp argument for file.prl. A resident system process starts out as a ".RSP" program; when you generate MP/M using GENSYS, you have the option of incorporating all '.RSP' files within the system as resident system processes. The '.RSP' files supplied include MPMSTAT, SPOOL, system time (TOD) and scheduler (SCHED). You can create your own '.RSP' file, provided that you make it page relocatable, the first two bytes of the file for the address of BDOS/XDOS are reserved, and your process descriptor is built according to the instructions provided with MP/M's documentation.

MP/M handles each console by employing a process called the TMP (Terminal Message Process). When a command line is typed, the TMP sends it to the CLI (Command Line Interpreter) where it is parsed and scrutinized. The CLI is actually a more advanced CCP (Console Command Processor) used by CP/M. The CLI takes the first word of the command line and tries to open a queue by that name, assuming first that it is simply a request to put a message into a queue (since the CLI also handles that operation). If there is no queue by that name, CLI first looks for a '.PRL' file by that name; if there is a queue by that name, the rest of the command line is copied into the queue as a message. If the CLI finds a '.PRL' file by that name, it makes a request for relocatable memory in which to load and run the program; then, it loads and runs the program. If the CLI does not find a '.PRL' file, it looks for a '.COM' file; if it finds a '.COM' file, it makes a request for absolute TPA memory, and loads and executes the program. If the program contains file specifications or is followed by filenames in the command line, the CLI also creates file control blocks (as the CCP does in CP/M systems).

At the console, you can "detach" a running program (i.e., the program's output does not appear at the terminal, and the terminal is free) in order to execute other programs by using ↑D. When you hit ↑D again, the next process waiting for the console (the process with higher priority) will return. You can also use the ATTACH program to attach a console to a specific program. Here is an example:

```
1A> ATTACH PROG1 ↵
                              (PROG1 takes over console)
```

A program can only be attached to the console it was detached from. You can use the MPMSTAT resident process (if generated with your system), or the MPMSTAT.RSP program (if renamed to MPMSTAT.PRL) to provide a display of processes in the system:

```
1A> MPMSTAT
          ***** MPM 1.0 STATUS DISPLAY *****

Ready Process(es):
MPMSTAT     cli     Idle
```

(The ready processes are those that are ready to run and are waiting for CPU time. The first one has the higher priority, and is running at the moment.)

```
Process(es) DQing:
[Sched]      Sched
[ATTACH]     ATTACH
[SPOOL]      Spool
```

(These processes are waiting for messages from the queues that are in brackets. They are arranged from higher to lower priority.)

```
Process(es) NQing:
```

(Usually similar to the above display, this display shows that there are no processes at this time writing to queues.)

```
Delayed Process(es):
```

(There are no processes delayed at this time. A delayed process is one that is waiting for a specified amount of clock ticks on the system time unit.)

```
Polling Process(es):
    PIP
```

(The PIP process is polling the console device.)

```
Swapped Process(es):
```

(Swapping is not implemented in version 1.0 of MP/M.)

Process(es) Flag Waiting:
01 - Tick
02 - Clock

(These are processes that set and alter flags to syncronize other processes.)

Flag(s) Set:
03

(The "one minute interval" flag is set.)

Queue(s):
tod SCHED ATTACH STOPSPLR SPOOL MPMSTAT
Cliq Parseq ListMQ DiskMQ

(These are all the queues in the system. Queues in all upper case letters can be sent messages from the CLI, or from the console via the CLI. For example, the SPOOL queue can receive filenames by typing 'SPOOL', followed by filenames at the console.)

Process(es) Attached to Consoles:
[0] - MPMSTAT
[1] - PIP

(The processes attached to consoles are listed by console number and process name.)

Process(es) Waiting for Consoles:
[0] - TMP0 DIR
[1] - TMP1

(These processes are waiting for the consoles they were detached from; for example, TMP0 is waiting for console 0, and DIR is waiting for TMP0 to finish with console 0. Since TMP0 is the console message process, DIR will wait until a ↑D (or ATTACH) is executed).)

```
Memory Allocation:
Base = 0000H      Size = 4000H      Allocated to PIP 1
Base = 4000H      Size = 2000H      *  Free  *
Base = 6000H      Size = 1100H      Allocated to DIR 0
```

(This display shows the base, size, and owner of memory segments, along with the owner's originating console number in brackets. Unallocated segments are free to be used.)

SUMMARY

The internal operations of CP/M and MP/M have been explained in this chapter. The principles of these operations are not complex, and should be understood in order to modify CP/M.

We have now learned all of the resources available with CP/M and MP/M. However, this does not automatically mean that the user has sufficient training to successfully and effectively use the computer: practice is required.

As you practice, you will appreciate the value of the practical recommendations presented in the following chapter.

```
Memory Segments:
Base = 0000H     Size = 2000H     Allocated to PIP I
Base = 2000H     Size = [illegible]00H     * [illegible]
Base = [illegible]00H     [illegible] = [illegible]00H     Allocated to [illegible]
```

[illegible]

SUMMARY

The internal operations of CP/M and MP/M have been explained in this chapter. The principles of these operations are not complex and should be understood in order to modify CP/M.

We have now described all of the resources available with CP/M and MP/M. However, this does not automatically mean that one can use the [illegible] training, in successfully and effectively [illegible] the computer, practice is required.

As you practice, you will appreciate the value of the practical recommendations presented in the following chapter.

6

REFERENCE GUIDE TO CP/M AND MP/M COMMANDS AND PROGRAMS

INTRODUCTION

This chapter is a quick reference guide to CP/M and MP/M commands and utility programs (introduced in Chapters 1 through 4). This guide is organized so that the user can look up the key-word of a command or program. These key-words are presented in alphabetical order.

We will now describe the format used in this chapter. The following is a sample of a descriptor that appears next to every command:

- • CP/M version 1.4
- ∘ CP/M version 2.2
- ∘ MP/M version 1.0

Looking at the above sample, the black dot next to CP/M version 1.4 tells you that the command or program applies to that particular version of CP/M. The open dot appearing beside CP/M version 2.2 and MP/M version 1.0 tells you the example does not apply to them. Many commands and programs apply to all three systems.

After the purpose of each command or program is described, its nature is indicated in parenthesis: i.e., built-in command, '.COM' file, '.PRL' file, or resident process (MP/M).

Next, a concise format is shown that demonstrates the possible *arguments* used when the command or program is executed. This typestyle indicates that an argument is required (e.g., filename), while this *typestyle* indicates that an argument is optional (e.g., *filename*). The braces { } indicate a choice, where at least one of the arguments is required (unless one of the arguments is optional within the braces).

In some cases, one part of an argument is optional, while another part is required (e.g., *d:*filename (where *d:* is optional and filename is required)). In any case, read the descriptions of the argument below the formats.

Some general assumptions are made throughout this guide. For example, the assumption is made that a filename argument, whether optional or required, can have within it an optional drive letter (e.g., B:FILE) that specifies an alternate disk drive from the current one. This is always the case unless the argument is defined to exclude drive specifiers. In cases where drive specifiers are shown as part of the argument, you should read the instructions for that particular argument.

Another general assumption is that all '.COM' files can be executed if they are on a disk (on the current or alternate disk drive), as well as all '.PRL' files. For example, to execute SAMPLE.COM, you would type 'SAMPLE ↲'. If SAMPLE.COM existed on drive B and you were in drive A, then you could type 'B:SAMPLE ↲' to execute it.

Finally, everything that you would type into the system is underlined. The ↲ symbol is for the Carriage Return (RETURN or CR key), and the ↑ symbol, combined with a letter such as C (i.e., ↑C), stands for the Control (CTRL) key used simultaneously with the letter key.

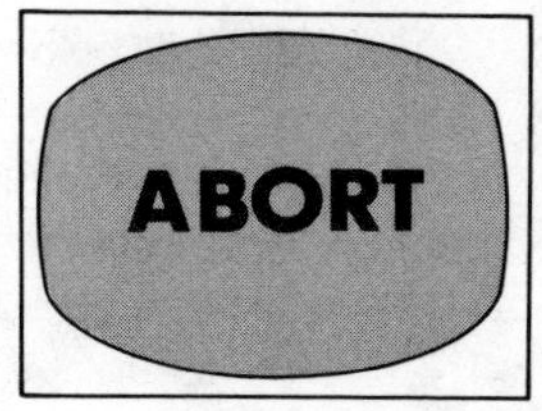

∘ CP/M version 1.4
∘ CP/M version 2.2
• MP/M version 1.0

Abort a running program

(ABORT.COM or ABORT.PRL)

FORMATS:

1. ABORT programname
2. ABORT programname consolenumber

ARGUMENTS:

programname The name of the running program to be aborted.

consolenumber Number of the console from which the program has been initiated. Must be specified if that console is another one than the console at which the ABORT is specified.

DESCRIPTION:

This command halts execution of the specified program. It should be used with care since any user may abort any program started at any console.

HOW TO USE IT:

If the program was started from your console, simply specify ABORT followed by the program name. If the program was started from another console, use the second format and specify the console number.

EXAMPLES:

0A> ABORT COMPUTE↵

(COMPUTE was started at this console.)

2A> ABORT TEST 1↵

(TEST was started at console 1.)

- CP/M version 1.4
- CP/M version 2.2
- MP/M version 1.0

Assemble a file

(ASM.COM) supplied with CP/M (or MP/M)

FORMATS:

1. ASM filename
2. ASM filename.*shp*

ARGUMENTS:

filename — The name of an '.ASM' source file (text file) that contains assembly language instructions as ASCII text. ASM looks for 'filename.ASM'; the '.ASM' extension does not have to be specified in filename.

.shp — The optional parameters for ASM, that consist of three letters preceded by a period. The s must be the letter of the drive (A, B, . . ., P) containing the source '.ASM' file, if not on the current drive. The h must be either the letter of the drive (A, B, . . ., P) to receive the '.HEX' file created by ASM, or 'Z' to tell ASM to skip the function of creating the '.HEX' file (described below). The p must be either the letter of the drive (A, B, . . ., P) to receive the '.PRN' file created by ASM, or 'X' to send the '.PRN' file to the terminal display, or 'Z' to tell ASM to skip the function of creating the '.PRN' file (described below).

DESCRIPTION:

The assembler program (ASM.COM) turns an assembly language source file (written in 8080 or Z-80 code) into a machine code file of type '.HEX' that can subsequently be LOADed (using the LOAD command) into the system as a transient command (executable program). ASM also creates a listing file with a '.PRN' extension that contains the assembly language source lines with error flags and hexadecimal notation (machine code) generated by ASM.

HOW TO USE IT:

Use format 1 if the '.ASM' source file is on the current disk and you want to create the '.HEX' and '.PRN' files also on the current disk drive. Otherwise, you must use format 2, and explicitly specify s as the drive for the source file, h as the drive to receive the '.HEX' file, and p as the drive to receive the '.PRN' file. If you want ASM to assemble the file and only create the '.PRN' file (i.e., skip the '.HEX' file), then specify a 'Z' for h. If you want ASM to only create the'.HEX' file when it assembles the source file, then specify a 'Z' for p (to skip the '.PRN' file). If you want ASM to send the '.PRN' file to the terminal display only (and not save a copy on disk), then specify an 'X' for p.

In both format cases, ASM translates ("assembles") the assembly language source lines into Intel hexadecimal notation to denote machine code (binary code). If ASM finds errors in the source file, it displays the line in error and an error code.

EXAMPLES:

```
A> ASM PROG ↲
```

(Execute ASM on the file PROG.ASM in the current drive.)

```
A> ASM DOTHIS.ABZ ↲
```

(Execute ASM on the file DOTHIS.ASM in drive A; put the new file DOTHIS.HEX on drive B, and skip the creation of DOTHIS.PRN.)

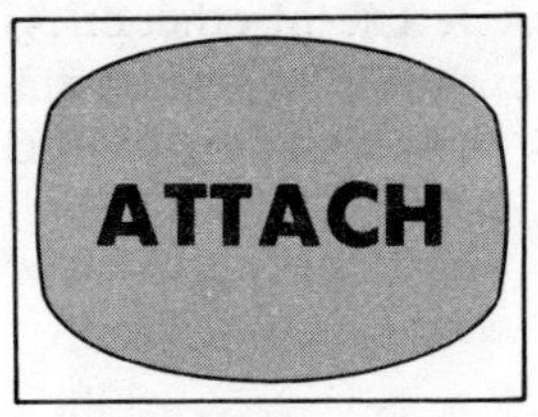

- ○ CP/M version 1.4
- ○ CP/M version 2.2
- • MP/M version 1.0

Attach a console to a detached program

(Resident process or ATTACH.PRL)

FORMAT:

ATTACH progname

ARGUMENT:

progname — The filename for a program that was detached from the console currently executing ATTACH.

DESCRIPTION:

The ATTACH program attaches a detached program to the console. The detached program, however, must have been detached from the same console (terminal). You can detach a program from a console by hitting ↑D while the program is running. A process that is waiting for the console automatically attaches itself when you detach a process.

HOW TO USE IT:

ATTACH can be executed as a command along with the progname argument, if you have ATTACH as a resident system process generated with the MP/M system, or if you have ATTACH.PRL accessible on a disk.

EXAMPLE:

```
1A> ATTACH PROG1.PRL ↲
```

(PROG1.PRL takes over console.)

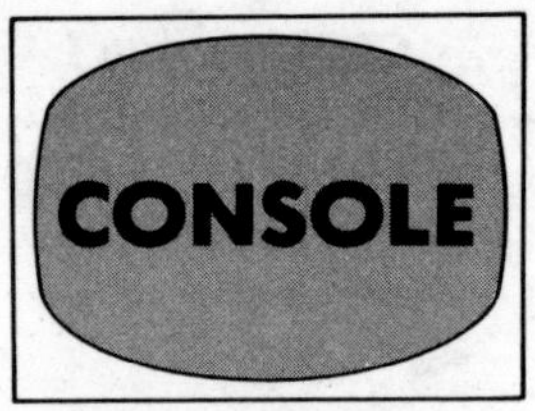

- ◦ CP/M version 1.4
- ◦ CP/M version 2.2
- • MP/M version 1.0

Display the console (terminal) number currently executing CONSOLE command

(CONSOLE.COM or CONSOLE.PRL)

FORMAT:

```
CONSOLE
```

DESCRIPTION:

When the CONSOLE commmand is typed at a terminal, it returns with the console number of the terminal being used. This could be helpful in determining which console (terminal) has detached programs waiting for it, as shown in an MPMSTAT display.

EXAMPLE:

```
0A> CONSOLE ↲
Console = 1
0A>
```

(The console currently being used is console 1, the second console (after console 0.)

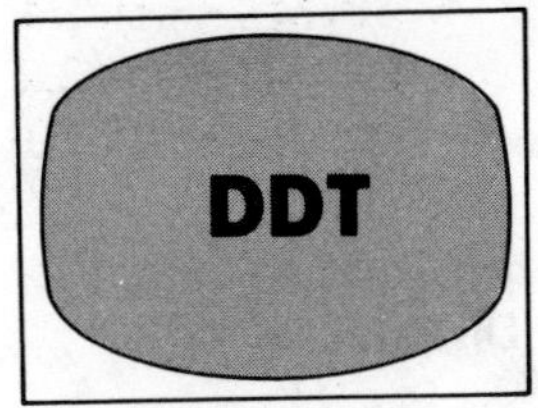

- CP/M version 1.4
- CP/M version 2.2
- MP/M version 1.0

Debug—Execute the debugger program to load, alter, and test programs

(DDT.COM or DDT.PRL)

FORMAT:

DDT *filename*

ARGUMENT:

filename Optional argument for the name of a '.COM' or '.HEX' file; you must also specify its extension.

DESCRIPTION:

DDT replaces the CCP in memory and loads filename into the TPA; if no filename is specified, DDT occupies the TPA and waits for a file to be input into memory. DDT also displays the NEXT address (address after the last address in the program being debugged) and the PC (program counter). DDT has its own commands for inserting values, displaying memory locations, saving comments, setting break-points, and other debugging functions.

HOW TO USE IT:

To execute DDT, it must exist as a program on an accessible disk (i.e., as DDT.COM or DDT.PRL in MP/M systems). To terminate DDT properly, use the G0 command.

EXAMPLE:

A> <u>DDT PIP.COM</u> ↵

NOTE: For additional information, refer to the *CP/M Dynamic Debugging Tool (DDT) User's Guide* supplied by Digital Research.

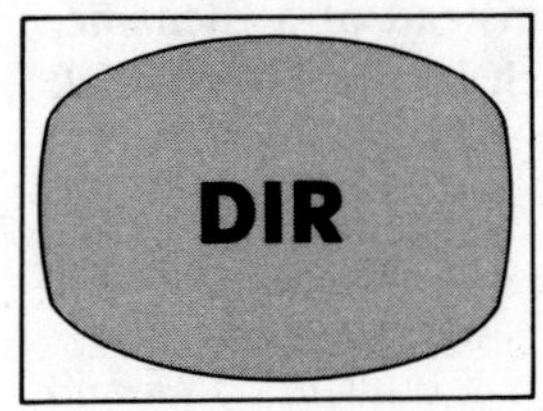

- CP/M version 1.4
- CP/M version 2.2
- MP/M version 1.0

Directory—Display a list of filenames in the current disk drive's directory

(Built-in command in CP/M, DIR.COM or DIR.PRL in MP/M)

FORMAT:

```
        ⎧filename ⎫
DIR     ⎨         ⎬
        ⎩filematch⎭
```

ARGUMENTS:

filename Optional argument to tell DIR to find only the file named by filename.

filematch Optional replacement for filename to tell DIR to find several files and list their names. Both filename and filematch can have drive specifiers.

DESCRIPTION:

If a filename or filematch is not specified, DIR assumes that what is wanted is a list of all of the filenames in the current drive's directory (only files with the $DIR attribute, not files with the $SYS attribute). Note, however, that DIR only displays the files in the current user area, in CP/M version 2.2 and MP/M.

If a filename is supplied, DIR displays only that file, if it is in the current disk drive, and in the current user area. If a drive specifier is supplied (i.e., A:, B:, C:, . . ., P:), DIR looks in that specified drive, in the current user area.

If a filename match (filematch) is supplied instead of a filename, DIR looks for all files that match the filematch in the current disk drive (or drive specified), and in the current user area.

HOW TO USE IT:

In CP/M version 1.4 and version 2.2, DIR is a built-in command (i.e., part of the operating system), and can be executed from any disk drive and user area. In MP/M, DIR can either be supplied as DIR.COM or DIR.PRL. DIR.COM or DIR.PRL must exist in the current drive unless you specify another drive as a prefix to DIR. It must also be in the current user area in order to be executed in an MP/M system. NOTE: DIR's display in version 1.4 is vertical only, while version 2.2 (and MP/M) displays have horizontal rows and vertical columns.

EXAMPLES:

```
A> DIR ↲

ASM.COM     DUMP.COM     ED.COM      PIP.COM
LOAD.COM    PROG.HEX     BASIC.COM
STAT.COM    SAMPLE.TXT   FILE.TXT
TONE.TXT    SYSGEN.COM   32CPM.COM
GAME1.INT   GAME1.BAS    GAME2.INT
GAME2.BAS   SOURCE.BAS   TEST.SYS
•
•
•
```

(CP/M version 2.2 display of all files with the $DIR attribute in drive A, user 0.)

```
B> DIR *.TXT ↲

SAMPLE.TXT
PROG.TXT
POEM.TXT
NAME.TXT
BOOK.TXT
ONE.TXT
LETTER.TXT
FILE.TXT
```

(CP/M version 1.4 display of all files in drive B with '.TXT' extensions.)

- ◦ CP/M version 1.4
- ◦ CP/M version 2.2
- • MP/M version 1.0

Reset (change) disk in a multi-user system

(DSKRESET.COM or DSKRESET.PRL)

FORMAT:

DSKRESET

DESCRIPTION:

When DSKRESET is executed, it sends a message to the other terminals hooked up to the system: "Confirm reset disk system (Y/N)?" If any terminal responds with an "N" for no, then the disk reset request is denied. If all terminals respond with a "Y" for yes, then the user may change the disk (diskette). It is important that the user indicate to other users that he or she is going to change a disk or diskette, since other users might still be in the process of updating or accessing files on the disk.

EXAMPLE:

```
0A> DSKRESET ↲

Confirm reset disk system (Y/N) ? Y
```

(This message appears at every terminal hooked up to the system.)

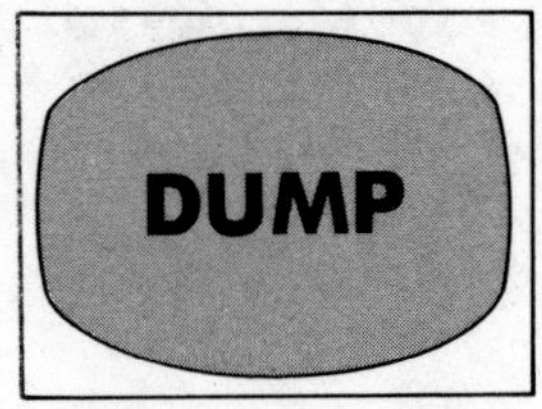

- CP/M version 1.4
- CP/M version 2.2
- MP/M version 1.0

Dump file to terminal
Display the contents of a disk file in hexadecimal form

FORMAT:

DUMP filename

ARGUMENTS:

filename The name (including extension) of any disk file.

DESCRIPTION:

DUMP displays in hexadecimal notation the contents of any disk file on the terminal screen, listing sixteen bytes at a time, with each line's absolute byte address on the left.

HOW TO USE IT:

Execute the DUMP program (DUMP.COM) as a command, supplying a filename with its extension. If DUMP.COM is not on the current drive, specify a drive letter to precede the command.

EXAMPLES:

A> DUMP SCRATCH.HEX ↲

A> DUMP B:NONAME.COM ↲

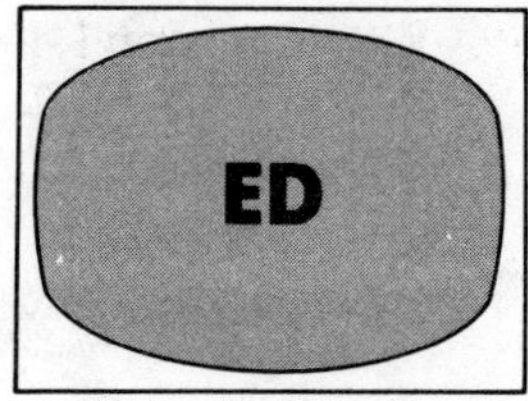

- CP/M version 1.4
- CP/M version 2.2
- MP/M version 1.0

Edit a file

(ED.COM or ED.PRL)

FORMAT:

ED filename

ARGUMENT:

filename — Name of a file to be edited; must be a text file (or other type of ASCII file). You must also supply the extension.

DESCRIPTION:

The ED program creates an edit buffer and allows the user to modify text in this buffer. First, ED deletes any '.BAK' file that matches filename's primary name (e.g., SAMPLE.BAK for SAMPLE.TXT). Then, it allows the user to append text to the buffer to modify the text. Text can be output to a temporary file while other text is modified in the buffer. Text from "library" files can be inserted. When ED is terminated with the E command, ED updates the source file and creates a backup file of the original source file.

HOW TO USE IT:

You must have ED.COM or ED.PRL on an accessible disk (diskette). Chapter 4 describes how to use ED. There is an additional summary of ED commands in Appendices D and E.

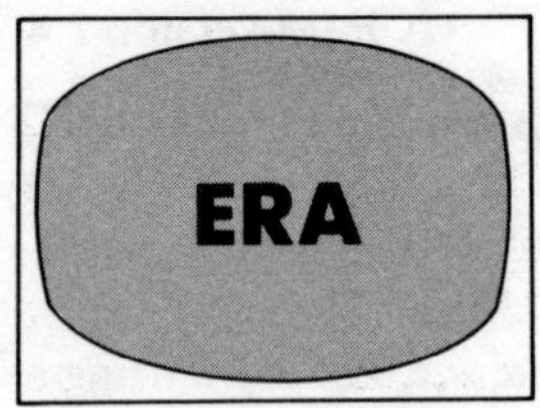

- CP/M version 1.4
- CP/M version 2.2
- MP/M version 1.0

Erase one or more files from disk or diskette

(Built-in command in CP/M, ERA.COM or ERA.PRL in MP/M)

FORMAT:

```
     (filename )
ERA  {         }
     (filematch)
```

ARGUMENTS:

filename — A filename argument must be given with ERA to tell it to erase a certain file. A filename must include the file's extension, and it can also include a drive specifier.

filematch — A filename match can be supplied for a filename (as described in Chapter 2) to tell ERA to erase several files at once. The filematch '*.*' with ERA will erase all of the files in the current drive in version 1.4, or all of the files in the current drive and user area but not other user areas, in version 2.2 and MP/M.

DESCRIPTION:

The ERA command erases any file that is supplied as a filename argument, unless the file is read-only (has the $R/O attribute), or the current disk (or disk specified) is read-only. If ERA does not find the file, it displays the message "No File". ERA, in CP/M version 2.2 and MP/M, only erases files in the current user area. You can erase files in an alternate drive by specifying the drive as part of the filename or filematch (e.g., 'ERA B:FILE1.*' erases all instances of FILE1 with any extensions that exist in the current user area in drive B).

HOW TO USE IT:

ERA is a built-in command in CP/M version 1.4 and version 2.2 that you can execute from any drive. In MP/M, ERA is supplied as ERA.COM or ERA.PRL (command file for absolute memory, or relocatable file for relocatable memory). ERA.COM or ERA.PRL must exist in the current drive, or be referred to from another drive using a drive specifier (e.g., B:ERA).

To erase an entire disk in CP/M version 1.4, you only need to use the filematch '*.*' to match all the files on a disk. To erase an entire disk in CP/M version 2.2 and MP/M, you must write a program that will fill up the disk with nonsense data, or you must use the form 'ERA*.*' in each user area, making sure that there are no read-only files (with the $R/O attribute) left undeleted.

EXAMPLES:

A> ERA SAMPLE.TXT ↵

(This command erases file SAMPLE.TXT in drive A.)

A> ERA B:JUMP.TXT ↵

(This command erases file JUMP.TXT in drive B.)

0A> ERA *.* ↵

(This is an MP/M example, where ERA erases all files in user area 0 of drive A.)

A> ERA *.HEX ↵

(This command will erase all files that have '.HEX' extensions in drive A.)

- ◦ CP/M version 1.4
- ◦ CP/M version 2.2
- • MP/M version 1.0

Erase one or more files from disk or diskette

(ERAQ.COM or ERAQ.PRL in MP/M)

FORMAT:

```
ERA filematch
```

ARGUMENT:

filematch A filename match is supplied to tell ERAQ to erase several files one after the other.

DESCRIPTION:

The ERAQ command erases in turn all of the files that match the filematch argument, unless the file is read-only (has the $R/O attribute), or the specified disk is read-only. Unlike ERA, ERAQ requests the user to confirm before erasing each successive file.

HOW TO USE IT:

ERAQ is supplied under MP/M as ERAQ.COM or ERAQ.PRL (command file for absolute memory, or relocatable file for relocatable memory). ERAQ.COM or ERAQ.PRL must exist in the current drive, or be referred to from another drive using a drive specifier (e.g., B: ERAQ).

To erase a user area, use the filematch '*.*' to match all of the files in the current user area. To erase an entire disk, you must write a program that will fill up the disk with some data, or you must use the form 'ERAQ*.*' in each user area, making sure that there are no read-only files (with the $R/O attribute) left undeleted.

EXAMPLE:

```
0A> ERAQ PROG.* ↵
A: PROG TXT? Y
A: PROG INT? Y
```

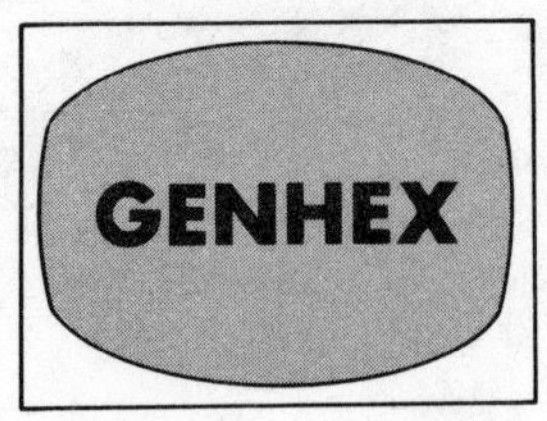

- ◦ CP/M version 1.4
- ◦ CP/M version 2.2
- • MP/M version 1.0

Transform a COM file into a HEX file

(GENHEX.COM or GENHEX.PRL)

FORMAT:

GENHEX programname.COM offset

ARGUMENTS:

programname The name of the program (must be a .COM type). May be preceded by a disk designator.

offset Offset for the .HEX file to be generated (hexadecimal).

DESCRIPTION:

This command generates a file of type HEX from a file of type COM and offsets the resulting file by a specified amount.

HOW TO USE IT:

This command is generally used to generate a page-relocatable (PRL type) file using a GENMOD command. In this case, the offset is either 0 or 0100 bytes (hexadecimal).

EXAMPLE:

1A> GENHEX ACTION.COM 100↵

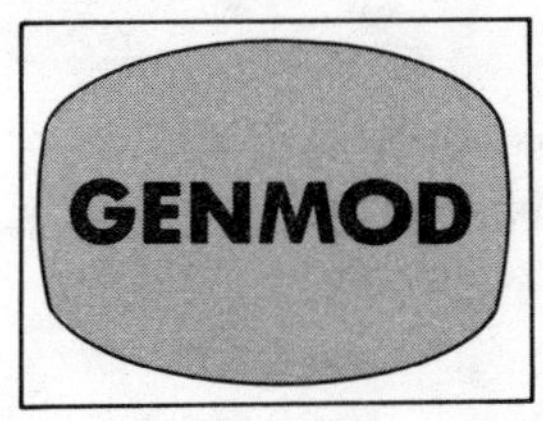

- ∘ CP/M version 1.4
- ∘ CP/M version 2.2
- • MP/M version 1.0

Generate a modified program.
Create a relocatable program from two concatenated '.HEX' files
(GENMOD.COM or GENMOD.PRL)

FORMAT:

GENMOD file.hex file.prl *$bbbb*

ARGUMENTS:

file.hex — This '.HEX' file must contain two concatenated '.HEX' files offset from each other by 100H bytes.

file.prl — This is the name of the '.PRL' file to be created. You could substitute a '.RSP' extension to create a resident system process.

$bbbb — This is an optional hexadecimal number of bytes of additional memory for the program.

DESCRIPTION:

The GENMOD program produces a relocatable program with a '.PRL' (or '.RSP') extension from two concatenated '.HEX' files offset by 100H. If *$bbbb* is supplied, GENMOD also allots the amount of additional memory for the program.

HOW TO USE IT:

GENMOD must exist on diskette as GENMOD.COM or GENMOD.PRL. GENMOD.COM can also be executed from CP/M version 2.2, but the '.PRL' file can only be executed under MP/M.

EXAMPLE:

```
1A> GENMOD FINAL.HEX PERFORM.PRL $1000
```

(This command produces the relocatable program PERFORM.PRL from the file FINAL.HEX (which is a concatenation of two '.HEX' files offset by 100H), with 1000H additional memory.)

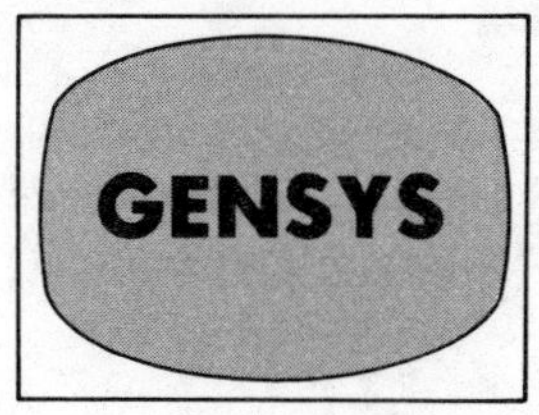

- CP/M version 1.4
- CP/M version 2.2
- MP/M version 1.0

Generate an MP/M system from CP/M

(GENSYS.COM)

FORMAT:

GENSYS

DESCRIPTION:

The GENSYS program asks several questions about the new system, then builds the file MPM.SYS to hold the system. The program MPMLDR.COM loads the system (MPM.SYS) into memory. GENSYS is used to generate new versions of the system. GENSYS also allows the user to incorporate resident processes with the system. GENSYS looks for files with '.RSP' extensions, and asks the user to select resident processes from a list.

HOW TO USE IT:

GENSYS.COM can be executed from a CP/M or MP/M system. You must answer questions with a value and a RETURN. For a more complete description of each question, see Chapter 5, "Installing and Altering MP/M."

EXAMPLE:

```
1A> GENSYS ↵

MP/M 1.0 System Generation

Top page of memory = C0 ↵
Number of consoles  = 2 ↵
Breakpoint RST #    = 5 ↵
Allocate user stacks for system calls (Y/N) Y ↵

Memory segment bases, (ff terminates list)
   : 00 ↵
   : 40 ↵
   : 60 ↵
   : ff ↵

Select Resident System Process: (Y/N)
TIME        ?Y ↵
SCHED       ?N ↵
ATTACH      ?Y ↵
SPOOL       ?Y ↵
```

- CP/M version 1.4
- CP/M version 2.2
- MP/M version 1.0

Load a file into executable memory
Converts a '.HEX' file into an executable command '.COM' file
(LOAD.COM)

FORMAT:

LOAD filename

ARGUMENT:

filename — The name of a file with a '.HEX' extension; the extension is not necessary.

DESCRIPTION:

The LOAD program takes a program that is in valid Intel "hexadecimal format" and converts it into a command file that can be executed (file with a '.COM' extension). The command file becomes filename.COM (the hexadecimal file is filename.HEX).

HOW TO USE IT:

To execute LOAD.COM, you must have it on an accessible disk. You can execute LOAD.COM from an alternate disk by specifying a drive letter prefix to the command. You use the '.COM' file created by LOAD as a transient command, to be loaded and executed in the TPA whenever you simply type the filename of filename.COM.

EXAMPLE:

A> LOAD SAMPLE ↵

(SAMPLE.HEX is converted to SAMPLE.COM.)

A> SAMPLE ↵

(You can now execute SAMPLE.COM.)

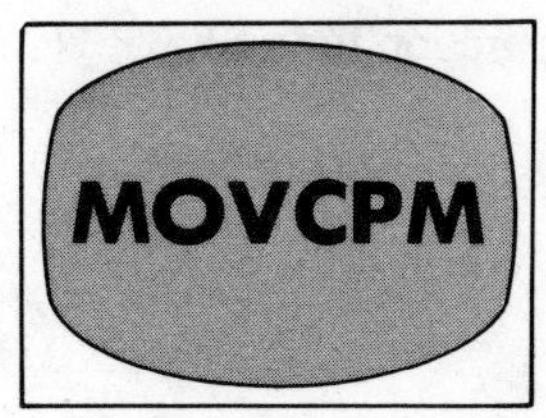

- CP/M version 1.4
- CP/M version 2.2
- MP/M version 1.0

Reconfigure a version of CP/M to fit another memory requirement

(MOVCPM.COM)

FORMAT:

```
MOVCPM  { * }  *
        { bb}
```

ARGUMENTS:

bb — Optional memory size, in decimal digits representing number of kilobytes (e.g., "32" for 32K system). If replaced with an asterisk (*), MOVCPM would calculate the total amount of RAM (random access memory) of the host computer, and build a CP/M for that size.

* — A second asterisk (*) after either bb or the first asterisk (*) tells MOVCPM to leave the new system in memory in preparation for a SYSGEN or SAVE operation. This argument is also optional. If it is not supplied, MOVCPM executes the new system without recording it on diskette (disk).

DESCRIPTION:

The MOVCPM program creates a memory image of the system and reconfigures it to match a given size in bb or the maximum size of the host system. If the second asterisk (*) is not supplied as in 'MOVCPM * * '; or bb is not followed with an asterisk as in 'MOVCPM 32 *', MOVCPM leaves the newly tailored system in the TPA in preparation for a SYSGEN or SAVE to record the version on diskette. If you do not supply the asterisk, then the new system will be executed but not premanently recorded.

HOW TO USE IT:

You can execute MOVCPM.COM if it exists on any accessible diskette or disk. It is most often used to prepare a new system for alterations for another hardware environment.

EXAMPLES:

```
A> MOVCPM 48 ↲
```

(This command constructs a 48K version of CP/M and executes it without storing it on diskette.)

```
A> MOVCPM 32 * ↲
```

(This command creates a 32K CP/M and leaves it in memory in preparation for a SYSGEN or SAVE operation.)

```
READY FOR "SYSGEN" OR
"SAVE 32 CPM32.COM"
A> MOVCPM * * ↲
```

(This command constructs a maximum memory version of CP/M and leaves it in memory, ready for a SYSGEN or SAVE.)

NOTE: for additional information see Chapter 5, "Installing and Altering CP/M."

- ◦ CP/M version 1.4
- ◦ CP/M version 2.2
- • MP/M version 1.0

MP/M loader
Load, relocate, and execute the MP/M system
(MPMLDR.COM)

FORMAT:

```
MPMLDR
```

DESCRIPTION:

The MPMLDR program loads the file MPM.SYS that contains the generated system, relocates it in memory, then executes it to bring up MP/M. MPMLDR also provides a display of the system parameters—the number of consoles, the breakpoint, the top of memory, and a memory segment table.

HOW TO USE IT:

You can execute MPMLDR.COM from MP/M or from CP/M. You can also bring it into the system from the first two tracks of a system diskette using a cold start loader program. For more information, see Chapter 5, "Installing and Altering MP/M."

EXAMPLE:

```
A> MPMLDR ↵

MP/M 1.0 Loader

Number of consoles = 2
Breakpoint RST #   = 5
Top of memory      = C0FFH
Memory Segment Table:

SYSTEM DAT C000H 0100
•
•
•
```

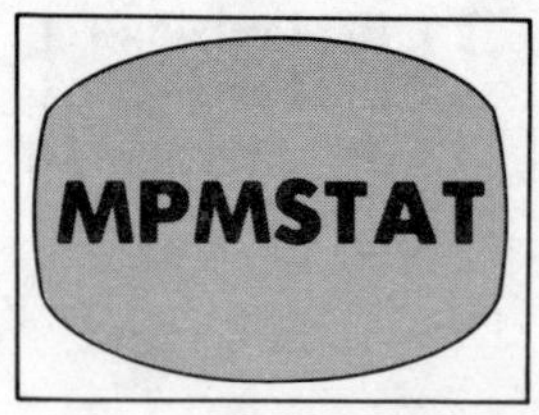

- ◦ CP/M version 1.4
- ◦ CP/M version 2.2
- • MP/M version 1.0

Display MP/M system status

(Resident process of MPMSTAT.PRL)

FORMAT:

```
MPMSTAT
```

DESCRIPTION:

MPMSTAT displays the names of processes waiting for CPU time, processes waiting for messages from queues, and processes waiting to send messages. It also displays delayed and polling processes, flags waiting, flags set, queues in operation, processes waiting for consoles, processes attached to consoles, as well as memory allocation for the entire system.

EXAMPLE:

```
1A> MPMSTAT ↲
```

Note: The output shows the status of the various processes. See page 104 for detailed example.

- CP/M version 1.4
- CP/M version 2.2
- MP/M version 1.0

Peripheral Interchange Program
Perform one or multiple copy operations
(PIP.COM)

FORMATS:

```
       ⎧d:newcopy⎫
1. PIP ⎨         ⎬   =d:oldcopy[p]
       ⎩d:       ⎭

2. PIP
   *d:newcopy=d:oldcopy[p]
   * . . .
   * . . .
   * ↵

      ⎧dev:      ⎫   ⎧dev:      ⎫     ⎧dev:      ⎫
3. PIP⎨          ⎬ = ⎨          ⎬[p], ⎨          ⎬,. . . [p]
      ⎩d:filename⎭   ⎩d:filename⎭     ⎩d:filename⎭

4. PIP d:=d:filematch[p]
```

ARGUMENTS:

{d:newcopy / d:} The user must choose, in formats 1 and 2, whether he/she wants the new copy to have the new name newcopy, or whether the new copy should have the same name but be on a different drive, drive d:.

*d:*oldcopy	In both forms 1 and 2, the name of the file being copied is required, but the drive specifier is not.
[p]	In all formats, the user can use a PIP parameter following the file to be affected by the parameter (optional).
dev: *d:*filename	In format 3, the user must choose between a dev: (device name, e.g., CON:) or a filename with optional d: drive specifier. This form can be used to send a file to a device, receive data from a device to a file, or send special device codes to a device.
d:=*d:*filematch	Both d: for destination and filematch for source is required; the d: on filematch is optional. Format 4 is used to copy several files onto another diskette using the same names for the files.

DESCRIPTION:

Format 1: If only d: is supplied and not newcopy, the new copy will have the same name as the old copy; however, the d: on the left must be different from the d: optional prefix on the right. If d: is omitted, oldcopy is assumed to be on the current diskette drive. If the user supplies newcopy, the new copy will have a new name, and the user can copy oldcopy to newcopy without drive specifications (without d: or *d:*).

Format 2: PIP expressions follow the same rules; however, if the user wants to perform several PIP operations, he/she can execute PIP and leave it in memory while the user provides PIP expressions to PIP's asterisk (*) prompt. PIP can be terminated by typing RETURN only. With some parameters, different actions occur when PIP is executed as a command (format 1) rather than as a program (format 2).

Format 3: In PIP commands or expressions, dev: (device names) can be used as well as d:filename (filenames). The user cannot copy from a receive-only device, and the user cannot send to a send-only device. The left side of the expression is always the destination (i.e., a receiving device or file), and the right side is always the source (i.e., the sending device or file being copied). The user can concatenate (join) source files into one destination file or device. The user can also use special device names listed in Appendix F.

Format 4: The user can copy several files onto another diskette by using a filematch (filename match) with optional drive specifier *d:*. Note that the drive specifier on the left side is required (d:), and that the new copies have the same name as the old ones, but are on another diskette. The user cannot have two files with the same name on the same diskette (in the same user area).

The device names allowed in PIP expressions are listed in Appendix F. The keywords used to perform special functions are listed in Appendix G.

HOW TO USE IT:

You can execute PIP.COM from any alternate drive by specifying the drive letter as a prefix to the command (e.g., "B:PIP ↵ "). You can also execute PIP, leave it in memory while you pull out the system diskette to insert one to be copied, and return to the system after re-inserting the system diskette and terminating PIP with a simple RETURN. Chapter 3 has complete descriptions of practically every PIP application.

EXAMPLES:

```
A> PIP B:=*.* ↵
```

(This command copies all of the files on the current drive to drive B.)

```
A> PIP ↵
*FILE2=TEST2 ↵
```

(This expression copies TEST2 and calls the copy FILE2.)

```
*LST:=FILE2 ↵
```

(This expression sends a copy of FILE2 to the LST: device.)

```
*PUN:=NUL:,PROG.ASM,EOF: ↵
```

(This expression sends 40 nulls to the PUN: device, along with the file PROG.ASM, and the end-of-file character.)

```
*B:=PROG.ASM ↵
```

(Create a copy of PROG.ASM on drive B with the same name.)

* ↲

A> PIP FILE2=FILE1[G2] ↲

(This works only in CP/M version 2.2, copying file FILE1 from user area 2 to FILE1 in the current user area on the same disk.)

NOTE: for additional information see Chapter 3 and Appendices F (PIP Device names), G (PIP Keywords), and H (PIP parameters).

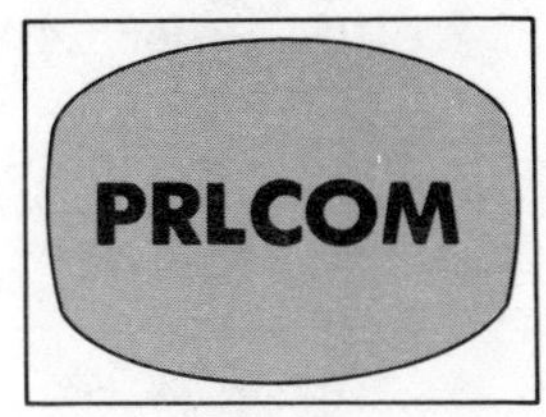

◦ CP/M version 1.4
◦ CP/M version 2.2
• MP/M version 1.0

Transform a PRL file into a COM file
(PRLCOM.COM or PRLCOM.PRL)

FORMAT:

PRLCOM programname1. PRL programname2. COM

ARGUMENTS:

programname1 The name of the source program (may be preceded by a disk unit designator).

programname2 The name of the destination program (may be preceded by a disk unit designator).

DESCRIPTION:

This command transforms a program of type PRL into a program of type COM. If the name of the resulting COM program is already used, the user is told and given the option to cancel the command.

HOW TO USE IT:

Whenever the user wants a program to reside in an absolute TPA rather than a relocatable memory segment, the result is achieved with PRLCOM, by making a program a COM file instead of a PRL file.

EXAMPLES:

1A> PRLCOM DOIT.PRL DOIT.COM ↲

or:

2A> PRLCOM DOIT.PRL B : NUNAME.COM ↲

- CP/M version 1.4
- CP/M version 2.2
- MP/M version 1.0

Rename a file

(Built-in command in CP/M, REN.COM or REN.PRL in MP/M)

FORMAT:

```
REN newname=oldname
```

ARGUMENTS:

newname and oldname	Required arguments for filenames including extensions; drive letter prefixes are not allowed.

DESCRIPTION:

The REN command (or program) renames oldname to newname; the user must include the entire filenames with extensions.

HOW TO USE IT:

In CP/M, REN is a built-in command that can be executed at any time. In MP/M, you have to have REN.COM or REN.PRL on an accessible disk.

EXAMPLE:

```
A> REN NEWTRIC.HEX-OLDDOG.HEX ↵
```

(This command renames the file OLDDOG.HEX to NEWTRIC.HEX.)

- CP/M version 1.4
- CP/M version 2.2
- MP/M version 1.0

Save contents of memory in a disk file

(Built-in command)

FORMAT:

SAVE p filename

ARGUMENTS:

p — The required number of ''pages'' (256-byte segments) to be saved, in decimal.

filename — The required name of the new disk file, with extension.

DESCRIPTION:

The SAVE command saves the contents of the TPA (scratchpad memory) starting at location 100H and up to p pages (256-byte segments) in filename, which can be subsequently debugged or executed (if the contents of the TPA was an executable program before it was saved).

In MP/M, this operation is implemented within the revised debugger programs DDT or SID.

HOW TO USE IT:

To calculate p, you must first use DDT to load the original program into memory and use the NEXT value. The NEXT address will be 1 higher than the last address of the program; however, to figure the number of pages, use this simple algorithm:

If NEXT's last two digits (hexadecimal) are 00, subtract 1H (e.g., 1C00H – 1H = 1BFFH). If the last two digits are not 00, leave the number alone. Now, take the first two digits, or the "high order bits" (e.g., '1B' from the value 1BFFH), and convert that hexadecimal value to decimal for the number of pages (p).

Since SAVE is built-in, you can execute it at any time.

NOTE: in version 1.4, the user cannot perform two consecutive SAVEs on the same contents of the TPA, because the first SAVE causes a directory operation that changes several areas of the TPA. In version 2.2, however, this problem has been fixed—the user can perform two consecutive SAVEs on the same TPA.

EXAMPLE:

```
A> DDT SAMPLE.COM ↵
NEXT  PC

1D00  00

- G0 ↵
```

(The value under NEXT is 1D00H. Subtract 1H, to get 1CFFH. Take the number 1CH and convert to decimal, to get 28.)

```
A> SAVE 28 COPY.COM ↵
```

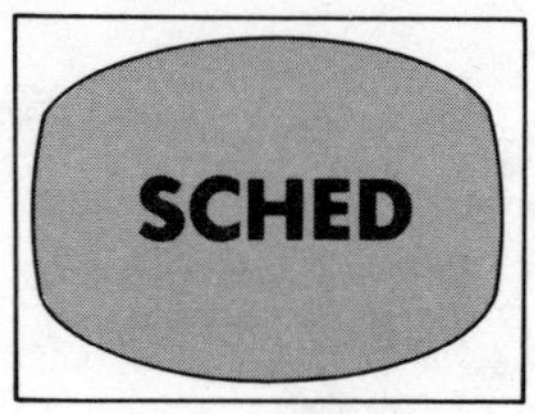

- ∘ CP/M version 1.4
- ∘ CP/M version 2.2
- • MP/M version 1.0

Schedule a program for execution at a later date and time

(Resident process or SCHED.PRL)

FORMAT:

SCHED mm/dd/yy hh:mm program

ARGUMENTS:

mm/dd/yy The required argument for date, where mm is the month (1 to 12), dd is the day (01 to 31), and yy is the last two digits of the year.

program The filename for a file with a '.COM' or '.PRL' extension; the extension does not have to be supplied.

DESCRIPTION:

The SCHED program, when executed, sits in the memory waiting for the time and date to match what was given as arguments. When it encounters that specific time and date, SCHED automatically executes the program that is specified.

HOW TO USE IT:

The SCHED program might exist as a '.PRL' file, or as a resident system process, and you must supply the proper arguments. Note that anyone can reset the time or date with a TOD command operation, so a certain amount of cooperation is needed to make SCHED reliable.

EXAMPLES:

0A> SCHED 12/31/80 23:59 EIGHTY ⏎

(This command schedules the program EIGHTY.COM (or EIGHTY.PRL) for execution on December 31st, 1980, at 11:59 PM.)

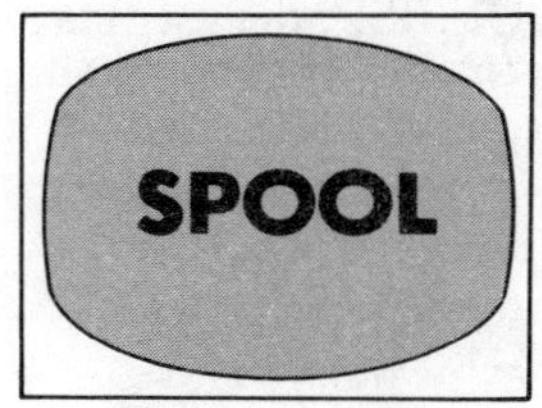

- ○ CP/M version 1.4
- ○ CP/M version 2.2
- • MP/M version 1.0

Send one or more files to the spool queue, usually for the line printer

(Resident process or SPOOL.PRL)

FORMAT:

SPOOL filename, *filename* . . .

ARGUMENTS:

filename and *filename*	The first filename is required, and the following filenames are optional additional files to be sent to the spool queue. The user must also specify filename extensions.

DESCRIPTION:

The SPOOL command sends the files one by one to the spool queue, where they wait in order until they are successfully handled by the LST: device (usually the line printer, although other devices can be assigned to the LST: device using STAT). The files must be ASCII text files (source files, edited files, listings, etc.).

HOW TO USE IT:

The SPOOL program should either be a '.PRL' file in the current disk drive, or a resident system process, which you can execute as a command providing at least one filename. Use the command STOPSPLR to cancel the spool queue operation.

NOTE: if SPOOL.PRL is used instead of SPOOL.RSP, the user may abort from another terminal. For example, if SPOOL.PRL was activated from terminal 3, it may be stopped by typing:

```
2B> STOPSPLR 3
```

EXAMPLE:

```
0A> SPOOL PROG.PRN,SAMPLE.TXT,NOVEL.JNC
```

(This command sends PROG.PRN, SAMPLE.TXT and NOVEL.JNC to the LST: device, which is usually a line printer or teletype device. The files wait in the spool queue until handled by the device.)

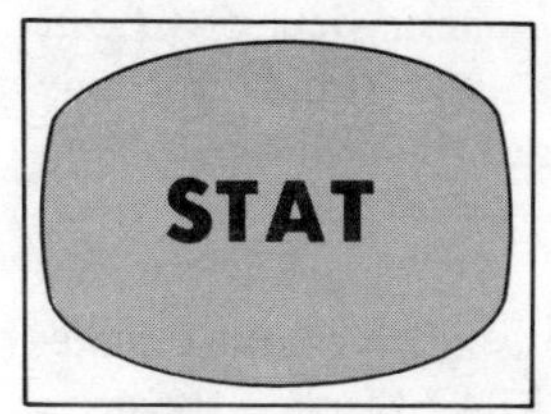

- CP/M version 1.4
- CP/M version 2.2
- MP/M version 1.0

Display status information, and assign devices

(STAT.COM or STAT.PRL)

FORMATS:

1. STAT {DEV: | VAL:}

2. STAT gen: =dev:,*gen:* =*dev:*,...

3. STAT *d:* =*R/O*

4. STAT *d:* {filename | filematch}

5. STAT *d:* {filename | filematch} {$S | $R/O | $R/W | $SYS | $DIR}

6. STAT *d:* {DSK: | USR:}

ARGUMENTS:

DEV: } VAL: } In format 1, DEV: produces the display of actual device assignments, while VAL: produces a display of potential device assignments (in CP/M version 2.2, VAL: also lists the possible STAT commands).

gen:=dev; In format 2, gen: stands for a generic device (CON:, PUN:, RDR:, or LST:), while dev: stands for any physical device that is appropriate for a device assignment to a generic device.

d:=R/O In format 3, d: = R/O (where d: is a drive letter) makes drive d: read-only; with only d:, STAT displays the drive status; with no argument STAT displays the current drive's status (i.e., read-only or read-write).

d:{filename | filematch} In format 4, the user could supply d:filename (d: is optional) to display the status (size in records and bytes, number of extents, etc.) of a specific file, or the user could supply d:filematch to display several files at once.

$S
$R/O
$SYS
$R/W
$DIR

When using the arguments for format 4, format 5 allows CP/M version 2.2 and MP/M users only to use the $S parameter to display more size information for a file or group of files and to use the $R/O, $R/W, $SYS and $DIR parameters to set file attributes. The $R/O (read-only) attribute prevents overwriting or deleting the file; it is cancelled by the $R/W (read-write) attribute. The $SYS (system) attribute "hides" the file from the DIR command; it is cancelled by the $DIR (directory) attribute.

d:DSK:
USR:

In CP/M version 2.2 and MP/M only, format 6 displays disk characteristics with DSK: (the current disk, or the optionally alternate d; drive). To display the current and active user areas, use USR:.

DESCRIPTION:

STAT provides statistical information about files and disks (diskettes), and assigns physical devices to generic device names (to be used with PIP). STAT also makes a disk read-only (format 3), a file read-only (format 5) in CP/M version 2.2 and MP/M, and displays the current user area, as well as all active user areas.

HOW TO USE IT:

To display statistical information, simply execute STAT.COM (or STAT.PRL) in one of its various formats. To assign devices, you should use format 2. Generic device names are CON: (console device), RDR: (reader device), PUN: (punch device), and LST: (list device), while physical devices are listed with PIP in Chapter 3.

EXAMPLES:

Using CP/M version 2.2:

```
A> STAT PIP.COM $S ↲

Size      Recs     Bytes     Ext     Acc
  55        55       12K       1     R/O      A:PIP.COM

A> STAT SAMPLE.COM $R/O ↲

A> STAT B: ↲

BYTES REMAINING ON B:  192K
B:      R/O
A>
```

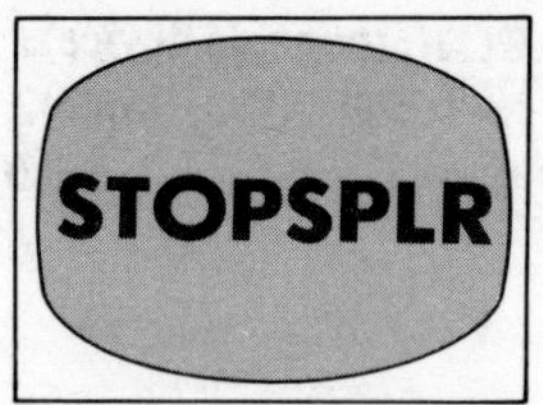

- ◦ CP/M version 1.4
- ◦ CP/M version 2.2
- • MP/M version 1.0

Cancel a spool queue operation and empty the spool queue

(Resident process or STOPSPLR.PRL)

FORMAT:

```
STOPSPLR
```

DESCRIPTION:

The command STOPSPLR stops a SPOOL operation in progress and empties the spool queue. (See the SPOOL command.)

EXAMPLE:

```
0A> STOPSPLR ↵
```

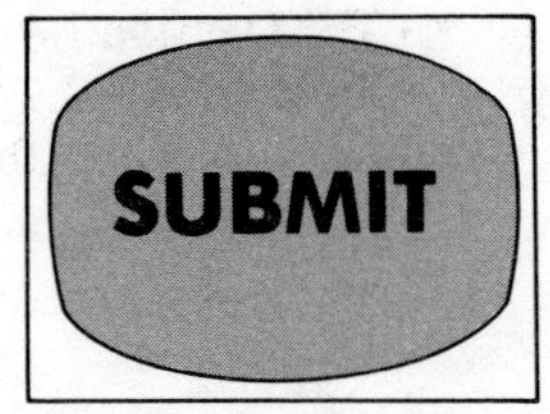

- CP/M version 1.4
- CP/M version 2.2
- MP/M version 1.0

Execute a batch of commands
(SUBMIT.COM or SUBMIT.PRL)

FORMAT:

SUBMIT filename *v1 v2 v3 . . .*

ARGUMENTS:

filename — The required name of a text file of command lines, expected to have a '.SUB' extension; '.SUB' is not supplied in the filename argument.

v1 v2 v3 . . . — The optional values to be plugged into variables in the submit file. Variables take the form $1, $2, $3, etc., and v1 substitutes for $1, v2 substitutes for $2, etc.

DESCRIPTION:

The SUBMIT program accepts the file filename.SUB and builds the file $$$.SUB, which is executed after a warm start (after the SUBMIT program terminates). The $$$.SUB file's command lines are executed until the file is exhausted. To build the $$$.SUB file, SUBMIT substitutes v1 for $1 in the '.SUB' file, v2 for $2, etc. Submitted files are only acted upon when they appear in drive A.

HOW TO USE IT:

Create a '.SUB' file, using ED, that contains command lines with arguments expressed as variables ($1, $2, etc.). Execute the batch of commands by executing SUBMIT.COM on the '.SUB' file.

EXAMPLE:

Suppose the file SMALL.SUB contained these lines of text:

```
DIR $1.*
PIP $2:=$1.BAK
ERA $1.BAK
```

If the user submitted this file using this SUBMIT command:

```
A> SUBMIT SMALL PROG B ↵
```

The user would get the following command lines in $$$.SUB:

```
DIR PROG.*
PIP B:=PROG.BAK
ERA PROG.BAK
```

When SUBMIT finished substituting to build $$$.SUB, the system would execute the contents of $$$.SUB.

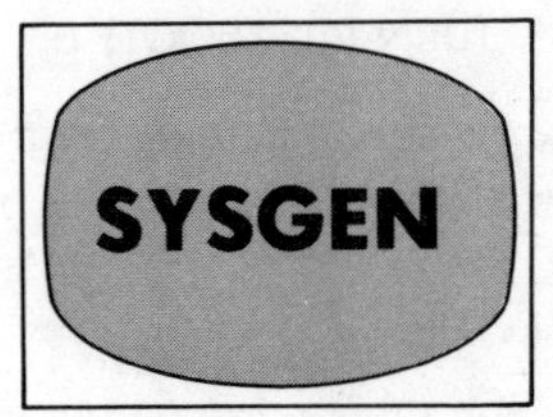

- CP/M version 1.4
- CP/M version 2.2
- MP/M version 1.0

Generate a copy of CP/M
Bring the system into memory and/or make a copy of the system diskette
(SYSGEN.COM)

FORMAT:

SYSGEN

DESCRIPTION:

The SYSGEN program initializes a system diskette (writes the first two tracks of the diskette with the system). SYSGEN also brings the system into memory, and executes it.

HOW TO USE IT:

Execute the SYSGEN.COM program:

A> SYSGEN ↵

SYSGEN VERSION xx.xx

SOURCE DRIVE NAME (OR RETURN TO SKIP) A

(Respond with the letter of the drive where the system is located, unless you want to skip the system read operation if the system is already in memory due to a MOVCPM operation.)

SOURCE ON A, THEN TYPE RETURN ↵

FUNCTION COMPLETE

(System read operation is complete. The system is now in main memory.)

DESTINATION DRIVE NAME (OR RETURN TO REBOOT) B

(Respond with the letter of the drive holding the new system diskette to be initialized, or hit RETURN to execute the system in memory.)

DESTINATION ON B, THEN TYPE RETURN ↲

FUNCTION COMPLETE

(System is written to the new system diskette, which is now usable.)

DESTINATION DRIVE NAME (OR RETURN TO REBOOT) ↲

A>

(Hit RETURN to terminate SYSGEN.)

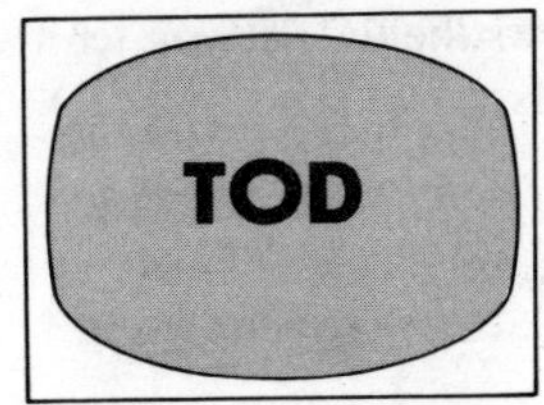

- ◦ CP/M version 1.4
- ◦ CP/M version 2.2
- • MP/M version 1.0

Time of Day
Display or set the time and date
(Resident Process or TOD.PRL)

FORMAT:

TOD *mm/dd/yy hh:mm:ss*

ARGUMENTS:

mm/dd/yy This is required only when setting the date, where mm is the month, dd is the day and yy is the last two digits of the year.

hh:mm:ss This is required when setting time or date, where hh is the hour (0 to 24), mm is the minute (00 to 59), and ss is the second (00 to 59).

DESCRIPTION:

In an MP/M system, the user can display the current time and date (including the day) by executing TOD without any arguments. If the date and time are supplied as arguments, TOD will first prompt the user with a message "Strike a key to set time," and the user can then hit any key when he/she is ready.

HOW TO USE IT:

The TOD program could exist in your current disk drive as a file with a '.PRL' (page relocatable) extension, or it could be a resident system process (command) loaded with the rest of the system when the system was generated. You should cooperate with other users in a multi-user system, since the computer only knows the time as you set it, and other users might have scheduled programs to run using SCHED.

EXAMPLES:

```
0A> TOD↲

Sat   12/29/79 02:37:21

0A> TOD   12/29/79 02:38:00↲

Strike a key to set time
Sat 12/29/79 02:38:00
```

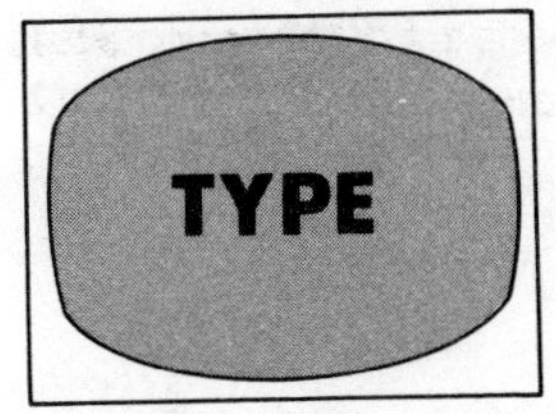

- CP/M version 1.4
- CP/M version 2.2
- MP/M version 1.0

Display contents of a file on the console (terminal) display screen

(Built-in command in CP/M, TYPE.COM or TYPE.PRL in MP/M)

FORMAT:

```
        (filename )
TYPE    {          }
        (filematch)
```

ARGUMENTS:

filename filematch	The user must supply either a specific filename with extension, or a filename match (filematch) to display several files.

DESCRIPTION:

The TYPE command displays the contents of any file, but the user will only be able to read the contents of an ASCII text file (source file, '.PRN' file, or listing file).

HOW TO USE IT:

TYPE in CP/M is a built-in command that you can execute at any time. In MP/M, it is supplied as either TYPE.COM (transient command) or TYPE.PRL (relocatable program).

EXAMPLES:

A> TYPE SMALL.SUB ↵

A> TYPE *.TXT ↵

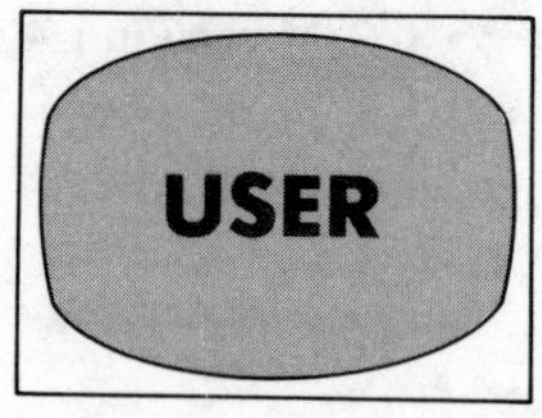

- ○ CP/M version 1.4
- ○ CP/M version 2.2
- • MP/M version 1.0

Change current user area,
or display user area in an MP/M system
(USER.COM or USER.PRL)

FORMAT:

1. USER *n* *(MP/M only)*

2. USER n

ARGUMENT:

n — Required argument n in CP/M version 2.2, and optional argument n in MP/M, stands for the user area number (zero to fifteen.)

DESCRIPTION:

Format 1 displays the current user number if no n is supplied; if n is supplied, USER changes the user area to user area n. Format 2 only allows changing, and not displaying, the user area. Format 2 changes the user area to user area n.

HOW TO USE IT:

The USER program is supplied either as USER.COM or USER.PRL.

EXAMPLE:

```
A> USER 3
A>
```

- ◦ CP/M version 1.4
- • CP/M version 2.2
- • MP/M version 1.0

Extended SUBMIT facility to provide input to programs executed in the submit file

(XSUB.COM)

FORMAT:

XSUB

DESCRIPTION:

When XSUB is placed at the beginning of a '.'SUB' file (or if XSUB is executed as a command), it relocates to the area directly below the CCP in order to process the command lines of the '.SUB' file and thereby provides buffered console input to the programs executed within the submit operation. Programs that read buffered console input get their input directly from the '.SUB' file.

HOW TO USE IT:

Insert 'XSUB' as the first command line of the '.SUB' file, and submit the file to the SUBMIT program. XSUB remains active until the next cold start, and the '.SUB' file is processed until it is exhausted.

EXAMPLE:

```
file NEW.SUB:      XSUB
                   DDT
                   I$1.HEX
                   R
                   G0
                   SAVE 1 $2.COM

A> SUBMIT NEW THIS THAT ↵
```

('THIS' substitutes for $1, and 'THAT' substitutes for $2; the XSUB program provides DDT with the DDT command lines 'ITHIS.HEX', 'R', and 'G0', and the XSUB provides the CCP with 'SAVE 1 THAT.COM'. XSUB remains active until a cold start).

7

PRACTICAL HINTS

INTRODUCTION

Now that you have acquired a good working knowledge of CP/M and its resources, here are some practical hints to improve your effectiveness in using the CP/M system. This chapter suggests ways to prevent some of the problems that can occur while using a CP/M system. A variety of recommendations and solutions are offered.

The prevention of problems is important when using a computer system. Very simple, obvious mistakes made by the user can cause very serious, major errors in the program. Discipline on the part of the user is, therefore, essential.

USER DISCIPLINE

Always make a copy of any new program or diskette being used for the first time, in the event that the original may be damaged accidentally. When inserting a new diskette on which you intend to write, execute a CTRL-C to log it in the system. From time to time, execute a STAT or a DIR command to verify your directory and the space remaining on the diskette.

At the end of a session where a long file has been manipulated, it is recommended that the user create a copy of this file on a fresh diskette. Sectors will be copied sequentially, and the new copy will be loaded much faster than the original file by any application program. The original file should be retained as the backup version.

The computer room should be kept organized to encourage user discipline. (A list of typical supplies is shown in the Appendix section of this book.) All user documentation, blank diskettes, and user programs should be available. The startup procedure for the system should be clearly posted, in addition to the precautions to be used for that system.

HANDLING DISKETTES

Respect the magnetic and physical integrity of diskettes. When handling diskettes:

— Do not put any magnetic object in contact with or in close proximity to a diskette. Examples of magnetic objects include transformers (telephones), screwdrivers (most are magnetized after a while), and any other metallic objects that could have become magnetized.

— Always store diskettes in their dust covers. Do not expose them to contamination by dust, smoke or other particles. In particular, do not scratch, touch, or attempt to clean the disk surface.

— Always label disks properly; indicate the date and the contents. A practical hint is to generate a listing of the directory for each disk, cut it out and then paste it on the disk cover so that the disk contents can be inspected at a glance.

— Keep a copy of any important diskettes in a separate location so that you do not risk losing all of your information at once.

— Do not bend, fold, spindle or mutilate diskettes.

— Do not expose diskettes to heat or direct sunlight.

— Always write on the diskette with a felt-tipped pen. Do not use a sharp pen, as this damages the diskette inside.

— Be sure that a diskette is not fully inserted in the disk drive at the time that the power is turned on or off.

— Make back-up copies of all essential information regularly.

Diskettes should be carefully protected from contamination by dust. This is particularly important in a dry environment where special care must be taken. Dust accumulates a static charge which makes the dust, as well as other particles, stick to the surface of the diskette.

Several precautions should be taken:

— Never place diskettes close to a source of dust. In particular, this applies to warehouses, stockrooms, dental work areas (near the grinding of dental plaster), classrooms (with chalk dust), and industrial environments.

— Keep the environment reasonably dust-free by frequently using a vacuum cleaner and keeping the tops of desks and cabinets wiped clean. If necessary, place a filter on the heating system or surface, or install an electrostatic air cleaner for the room.

— Try to prevent the buildup of static electricity in the room. A special antistatic spray may be used on the carpeting. The most effective solution, however, is to use a humidifier.

— Of course, it is also important to always keep the diskettes inside their covers.

THE PRINTER

Most quality printers will work very reliably for months or even years without breaking down. However, they must be treated with respect, or rather in a very orderly manner. All mechanical adjustments must be correct, without exception. If the user does not learn the purposes for all of the levers and make the correct adjustments, the printer may never operate correctly.

An example of a lever that should be checked is the "paper width" lever (labeled A through E on IBM typewriters). If a thin paper is used in the printer, and the lever is (accidentally) left on D or E (the settings for heavier paper), the printer may malfunction in an unpredictable manner. It may appear that there is a software interface problem, whereas, in fact, a simple paper width lever adjustment needs to be made. Setting the lever on "A" will correct the problem.

LISTINGS

Listings may require a significant amount of time, since the printer is usually the slowest input/output device connected to the computer. It is often convenient for the operator to walk away while the listing is in progress. However, it is strongly recommended that the operator check frequently on the correct operation of the printer. This is especially important at the beginning of a listing, when the paper could possibly jam in the printer (especially if self-adhesive labels are being used). Also, if "silk" ribbons are being used, they will stop abruptly at the end of the roll, rather than cause the characters to fade away progressively. As a result, part of a file listing could be totally blank. Unless the highest printing quality is required, plain ribbons are recommended.

When printing labels, it is important that the operator be present at all times. This is because any malfunction—including a mechanical malfunction of the printer—might result either in skipping a line or the jamming of labels. Either one of these occurrences would require a restart of the operation and could also result in physical damage to the printer (in the case of a jam).

Whenever a problem occurs during a listing, the listing must be restarted. The most frequent case consists of attempting to restart the listing halfway into a file. If the file is long, the safest procedure is to use PIP or ED (described in Chapter 3 and 4) to select the portion that needs to be printed out of the initial file. If the file is of moderate length, however, a quick and convenient solution consists of listing the file at high speed on the CRT display, then turning the printer on at the right moment with a CTRL-P, if the printing program allows the user to do so. TYPE allows this, but other specialized printing programs may not.

If the printer does not work when the system is turned on, check all physical settings on the printer. (It might be in local mode, for example.) Also, if several CP/M versions are being used on your installation, verify that your CP/M disk corresponds to the type of printer actually being used—a common mistake.

When doing long listings, it is possible for the operator to specify the listing of multiple files and walk away from the printer for an extended period of time (using a PRN assignment, for example).

Finally, for faster listings, use PIP rather than TYPE (use CON: = for a listing on the CRT and LST: = for a listing on the printer).

FILES

File Overflow

If the size of a file exceeds the capacity of a diskette, it will have to reside on two or more diskettes. In general, you should not just switch to a second diskette once the first one overflows. Try to order your file on the first diskette according to some useful criterion. For example, if your file is a name and address list, order it alphabetically or by zip code. If an alphabetical ordering is used, the first diskette will contain the names from A through L, and the second diskette will be used to store the names from M through Z. Each diskette will be approximately half-empty. This is a convenient partitioning of the diskette. As a result, it will still be possible, by using an appropriate program, to obtain a zip-sorted listing; however, there will be two separate zip sorts, one per diskette. They cannot be merged unless a hard disk is available, i.e., a disk with a large capacity.

Another possibility, once a file grows too large, is to separate it into subgroups. For example, if the file contains names and addresses of manufacturers and customers, these could be separated and placed on different diskettes.

Still another problem may occur. Assume you have a large file, say 170K, that you want to sort. Your sort program is on A, and A is fairly full: it has 120K of files. You will often not be able to sort, as many sorting programs require at least 170K of "workspace" on the disk in order to sort a 170K file.

The solution is simple: create a new system disk with only the SORT program on it, and use it. It will have enough space to sort. If the sort program still will not operate, you must cut your original file into two smaller ones by using an editor or other program that can extract part of your file (such as PIP).

Merging Files

Recall that PIP can be used to conveniently merge two or more files.

Wrong Word

A word or a code may need to be changed throughout the file. The editor program can accomplish this conveniently. See Chapter 4 for details.

Damaged File

Due to an operator's error or some system malfunction, a file could be damaged. This could have occurred when the operator typed control characters not allowed by the program, or because some type of failure occurred. However, as a result, the file will no longer load or execute. In many cases, if you are familiar with the structure of the file, i.e., the way that the file should look, and if the file contains text, it is possible to recover the file through appropriate surgery performed with the editor. The details are specific to the file being operated upon. Often, text files can be restored and salvaged. However, if the file is small, it is usually best to retype it rather than to attempt to save it, unless you are already familiar with such an operation.

When a file that was working correctly suddenly appears to be damaged or is misbehaving, an operator's error may be suspected. However, another frequent occurrence is a damaged system or program diskette. If the system diskette has been contaminated or damaged in any way, the information that it contains will have been altered and the system's behavior will become erratic. The usual programs may appear to execute normally. However, in fact, some of the commands do not work correctly and will damage existing files. Unfortunately, this will not be detected until a file has been significantly damaged. In this case, switch to a new system diskette and a new program diskette. Create a new file or use a backup copy of the old file. If this works, you should suspect that one of the previous diskettes had been damaged and discard it, or them.

USEFUL PROGRAMS

Editor

Chapter 4 showed that an editor is a powerful facility for operating on files and modifying them. ED provides such a facility. Other commercial editors are available that may be found to be more powerful or more convenient.

Track to Track Copier

A number of utility programs are also usually provided by the manufacturer of the computer system or the disk controller. A disk copier program will usually copy one disk from another, one track at a time. It is much faster than PIP when an entire diskette is being copied. A direct disk editor may also be available for performing changes on the diskette and examining it.

Erasing a Diskette

A diskette may need to be erased for one of two reasons: if the diskette simply needed to be erased and was not damaged, or if the diskette's directory was altered, rendering the diskette unusable (assuming that the diskette is still physically intact).

Erasing a "good" diskette may be accomplished by the command ERA*.*. Otherwise, in the case of a damaged directory, the diskette may be erased with an appropriate initialization program. Such a program, often called INIT, is provided by the computer or the disk controller's manufacturer, and is different for each computer system. INIT is a useful facility for erasing diskettes quickly.

Sequence of Commands

When executing a sequence of commands frequently, the SUBMIT file command may be created. The file consists of the sequence of commands that have to be executed in the computer and would be created under an editor such as ED. Then, by typing SUBMIT, followed by the name of the program, the sequence will be executed automatically. For example, if a given program is used frequently and requires the typing of a number of standard parameters before it can be used, the sequence can easily be typed into a file called START.SUB. The operator would only have to type the following in order to execute this program:

```
SUBMIT START ↵
```

STOP

When something is going wrong, you may want to stop everything. Do not pull the electrical cord out of the outlet. First, try CTRL-C. If it does not work, use RESET. Remember, however, that you will lose any information in the computer's memory. You will not damage the files. To stop the printer, you can physically turn it off.

MISCELLANEOUS HINTS

Remember that CP/M itself "does not take up any space" on your diskette. More exactly, two tracks are always "wasted" on an 8-inch diskette, whether you install CP/M or not. It is often convenient to put CP/M on most of your diskettes when they are blank. This way, you can boot from any diskette. Also you don't risk damaging files when disk swapping with PIP if you make the wrong move.

If you are in a duplicating mood, PIP is the next most useful program.

THE SEVEN COMMANDMENTS AFTER THE SYSTEM FAILS

Suspect the Operator First:

1. Check the mechanicals:
   — Are all switch positions correct? (Check systematically. No exceptions.)
   — Are fuses intact?
   — Are all cables attached with no loose or torn connections?
2. Did you give the correct command?
   — Turn everything off. Now, go turn the system on.
   — Repeat the command.

Suspect the Diskette:

3. Use a fresh diskette. (Often, the current diskette has been damaged through incorrect handling and will cause erratic system behavior.
   — Use a backup diskette. Do not use any program on your current diskette.
   — If no complete single backup exists, take the time to generate one.

Suspect the Software:

4. Make sure that you are using the correct programs:
   - The correct CP/M version if you have several.
   - The correct computer/interpreter for your application program. For example, CBASIC version 2 may be required.
   - The correct application program.

   Many application programs, word processors in particular, must be adapted to your terminal and printer. Unless this is done, some keys on the terminal may not work, and you may not be able to print.

Suspect the Hardware Last:

5. Check the mechanicals again, very thoroughly.
   - In particular, remove boards, clean the connections if necessary, and insert them back in place securely.
   - If the source of the malfunction can be attributed to a board, remove components from sockets, clean connections, and re-insert them.
6. Always try to identify the suspected malfunctioning device by exchanging it with a known good one: swap boards, swap printers, etc. This will give you positive proof and save much time.

   Never indict a device until you have tried swapping it with a known good one. A good deal of effort could otherwise be wasted.
7. From now on, use the correct prevention techniques, as explained in this book. In short:
   - Always be disciplined.
   - Don't use short cuts. Make no exceptions to the rules.

Finally, you will find a number of useful checklists in the Appendix section of this book. Remember that prevention comes first. User discipline is the essential key to successful computer utilization.

8

THE FUTURE

HISTORY OF CP/M

The CP/M operating system was created by Gary Kildall. While employed as a consultant for Intel Corporation, Gary Kildall wrote the first high-level language compiler produced by Intel, PL/M. Then, in 1974, he created his first version of a CP/M file system which was designed (at the time) to support a resident PL/M compiler.

CP/M made its initial commercial appearance in 1975 when the first licensing contracts were entered, but went relatively unnoticed for at least a year. During this time, the early versions of the editor (ED), the assembler (ASM), and the debugger (DDT) were developed. The first large-scale commercial user of this operating system was IMSAI (now defunct), which was licensed to distribute the CP/M version 1.3 that evolved into what IMSAI called IMDOS. CP/M has now evolved into CP/M version 2.2 (and successive versions), which is designed to take advantage of the larger storage capabilities of the hard disks now available. MP/M was designed to provide a multi-user time-sharing environment for multi-programming systems.

At this time, CP/M is probably one of the most frequently used operating systems on microcomputers. Although it can be criticized by operating systems users and designers who are familiar with more powerful time-sharing machines, it serves its purpose well, and has become a de-facto standard for many microcomputer users.

CP/M AND OTHER OPERATING SYSTEMS

Developing a *good* operating system has always represented a major investment. As a result, powerful time-sharing operating systems have been developed for only a few large computers. The most complex type of operating system is a time-sharing system with powerful scheduling and protection strategies. Although no consensus exists as to which time-sharing system is the best, the UNIX operating system is one that has gained a great deal of popularity in the 16-bit minicomputer field. A number of attempts are being made to implement UNIX on 16-bit microcomputers. However, the investment required to make these microcomputers fully compatible with a system like UNIX is very large, and the probability of complete success is limited.

One of the main advantages of CP/M (beyond convenience) is the fact that all CP/M-compatible software and files can now be shared by users. CP/M has the virtues of any standard operating system: compatibility. For this reason, CP/M will probably be used for a long time to come—as long as the processors on which it usually resides are being built.

EVOLUTION

Because improvements (and corrections) can always be made to any existing large program, CP/M and MP/M will continue to evolve. However, later versions of these two systems are usually compatible with previous ones. This means in practice, that most of the knowledge you may have acquired by reading this book should be applicable to any future versions of CP/M or MP/M that will be released. Additionally, by using and understanding CP/M, you will understand the functions of a "standard" operating system. Once these functions are understood, you should be capable of adapting easily to another operating system.

CONCLUSION

After reading this book, you should be proficient at using your CP/M-equipped computer. *The CP/M Handbook (With MP/M)* was designed to teach you how to use your system and to help you understand how it operates.

When learning how to use any program such as CP/M, remember that discipline is the key to trouble-free operation of a computer. By following proper procedures, errors and problems will be avoided. Particularly at the beginning, follow all of the rules presented in the text, strictly and without exception. As you become more experienced, you may be able to modify or ignore some of the rules. The correct use of a small computer and the peripherals is the subject of another book by the author.

When using this book, you can refer to any chapter to improve your understanding of a specific topic. With the exception of the first chapter, you do not need to memorize the entire contents of any chapter; you can simply learn about those features of interest to you. Then, the summaries in the Appendix section will prove to be quick references.

As you continue to use your computer system, you should learn about all of its resources. For example, even if you do not plan to use the editor now, you should try it. You will then be able to advance easily to using a word processing program, or to adapting or evaluating a new business program.

Once you have become familiar with all of the concepts and techniques presented in this book, you will be a competent computer user. You should then be capable of adapting quickly to other, similar programs or operating systems.

APPENDIX A

COMMON CP/M ERROR MESSAGES

There are three error conditions that are common to the system. These conditions are reported through the same general message:

BDOS ERR ON *d: error*

where *d* is a letter indicating the disk drive where the error occurred, and *error* is one of the following error messages:

BAD SECTOR

SELECT

READ ONLY

There is also a fourth error condition for CP/M version 2.2 where *error* would be the error message:

FILE R/O

(For descriptions of ASM, DDT, ED and other program errors, consult the documentation supplied with the relevant program.)

BAD SECTOR:

A "bad sector" error will occur if the disk controller cannot retrieve information from the diskette. This will occur when the diskette is worn (has a "bad sector"), or if the disk drive controller is malfunctioning. Another cause would be if the diskette was missing from the drive when you tried to access it. You may also get this error if you are trying to read files that were placed onto the diskette by a different controller than the one you are currently using. Even though disk controllers are said to be "IBM compatible", there might be small differences in record formats. For example, files written to diskettes using the Intel MDS-800 controller might be readable by another controller, but files written by another controller might produce the BAD SECTOR error when read by the MDS-800 controller. Also, if the information in a file has been damaged through diskette mishandling or by a damaged or erroneous program, this error will occur.

To try and recover from this error, you can either do a ↑C (CTRL-C to reboot the system), which aborts the program or file processing and returns you to the system, or you can choose to ignore the error and continue program execution and file processing by hitting RETURN, which tells the system to ignore the bad sector.

It might not be safe to ignore the error! If your program or file operation involves a directory write operation, you might destroy the integrity of your diskette by ignoring the error. Make sure that you have adequate backup copies.

SELECT:

This error occurs when you select a disk drive that does not exist. The value for *d* is the drive you selected, which is in error. The system automatically reboots when you hit any key on your terminal.

READ ONLY:

This error occurs when you try to write to a diskette that has been designated as a "read only" diskette through use of the STAT COMMAND (or by a program using the BDOS function). This error could also occur if you inserted a new diskette without performing a ↑C to reboot the system (and change the map to the diskette); you must perform a ↑C on any newly-inserted diskette in order to write to the new diskette (overwrite files, delete files, create files, or update files).

By hitting any key at your terminal, you can recover from this error condition and automatically perform a system reboot (↑C), which *also* changes the diskette to a read-write diskette (i.e., a diskette you can read or write to).

FILE R/O:

This error occurs only in newer versions of CP/M (CP/M version 2.2 and up), when you try to write (overwrite, update, or delete) a file that has the $R/O (read-only) attribute (assigned by STAT command or a user program). The $R/O attribute is described fully in Chapter 2, in the section on CP/M version 2.2 and MP/M.

To recover from this error, you can hit any key at your terminal. The operation involving the read-only file is aborted, and you have to change the $R/O attribute to $R/W in order to write to the file. Use STAT to change file attributes.

APPENDIX B

HEXADECIMAL CONVERSION TABLE

HEX	0	1	2	3	4	5	6	7	8	9	A	B	C	D	E	F	00	000
0	0	1	2	3	4	5	6	7	8	9	10	11	12	13	14	15	0	0
1	16	17	18	19	20	21	22	23	24	25	26	27	28	29	30	31	256	4096
2	32	33	34	35	36	37	38	39	40	41	42	43	44	45	46	47	512	8192
3	48	49	50	51	52	53	54	55	56	57	58	59	60	61	62	63	768	12288
4	64	65	66	67	68	69	70	71	72	73	74	75	76	77	78	79	1024	16384
5	80	81	82	83	84	85	86	87	88	89	90	91	92	93	94	95	1280	20480
6	96	97	98	99	100	101	102	103	104	105	106	107	108	109	110	111	1536	24576
7	112	113	114	115	116	117	118	119	120	121	122	123	124	125	126	127	1792	28672
8	128	129	130	131	132	133	134	135	136	137	138	139	140	141	142	143	2048	32768
9	144	145	146	147	148	149	150	151	152	153	154	155	156	157	158	159	2304	36864
A	160	161	162	163	164	165	166	167	168	169	170	171	172	173	174	175	2560	40960
B	176	177	178	179	180	181	182	183	184	185	186	187	188	189	190	191	2816	45056
C	192	193	194	195	196	197	198	199	200	201	202	203	204	205	206	207	3072	49152
D	208	209	210	211	212	213	214	215	216	217	218	219	220	221	222	223	3328	53248
E	224	225	226	227	228	229	230	231	232	233	234	235	236	237	238	239	3584	57344
F	240	241	242	243	244	245	246	247	248	249	250	251	252	253	254	255	3840	61440

APPENDIX C

ASCII CONVERSION TABLE

BIT NUMBERS															
b7 →								0	0	0	0	1	1	1	1
	b6 →							0	0	1	1	0	0	1	1
		b5 →						0	1	0	1	0	1	0	1
b7 ↓	b6 ↓	b5 ↓	b4 ↓	b3 ↓	b2 ↓	b1 ↓	HEX 1 / HEX 0	0	1	2	3	4	5	6	7
			0	0	0	0	0	NUL	DLE	SP	0	@	P	`	p
			0	0	0	1	1	SOH	DC1	!	1	A	Q	a	q
			0	0	1	0	2	STX	DC2	”	2	B	R	b	r
			0	0	1	1	3	ETX	DC3	#	3	C	S	c	s
			0	1	0	0	4	EOT	DC4	$	4	D	T	d	t
			0	1	0	1	5	ENQ	NAK	%	5	E	U	e	u
			0	1	1	0	6	ACK	SYN	&	6	F	V	f	v
			0	1	1	1	7	BEL	ETB	’	7	G	W	g	w
			1	0	0	0	8	BS	CAN	(	8	H	X	h	x
			1	0	0	1	9	HT	EM	)	9	I	Y	i	y
			1	0	1	0	10	LF	SUB	*	:	J	Z	j	z
			1	0	1	1	11	VT	ESC	+	;	K	[	k	{
			1	1	0	0	12	FF	FS	,	<	L	\	l	¦
			1	1	0	1	13	CR	GS	–	=	M	]	m	}
			1	1	1	0	14	SO	RS	.	>	N	^	n	~
			1	1	1	1	15	SI	US	/	?	O	_	o	DEL

THE ASCII SYMBOLS

NUL — Null
SOH — Start of Heading
STX — Start of Text
ETX — End of Text
EOT — End of Transmission
ENQ — Enquiry
ACK — Acknowledge
BEL — Bell
BS — Backspace
HT — Horizontal Tabulation
LF — Line Feed
VT — Vertical Tabulation
FF — Form Feed
CR — Carriage Return
SO — Shift Out
SI — Shift In
DLE — Data Link Escape
DC — Device Control
NAK — Negative Acknowledge
SYN — Synchronous Idle
ETB — End of Transmission Block
CAN — Cancel
EM — End of Medium
SUB — Substitute
ESC — Escape
FS — File Separator
GS — Group Separator
RS — Record Separator
US — Unit Separator
SP — Space (Black)
DEL — Delete

APPENDIX D

ED CONTROL CHARACTERS

Keys	Meaning
CTRL-C (↑C)	System restart (warm boot), restores system prompt.
CTRL-E (↑E)	Moves cursor to next line to continue command line (without executing or transmitting line).
*CTRL-H (↑H)	*Backspaces cursor to erase last character typed.
CTRL-I (↑I)	Moves cursor a "tab" space (7 columns long).
*CTRL-J (↑J)	*Performs a RETURN.
*CTRL-M (↑M)	*Performs a RETURN.
CTRL-L (↑L)	Replacement for Carriage Return sequence generated by RETURN in strings used with search and substitute commands.
*CTRL-R (↑R)	Retype current line (types a clean line).
CTRL-U (↑U)	Delete current line.
*CTRL-X (↑X)	*Backspace to beginning of current line and erase line.
**CTRL-D (↑D)	**Detach the current program from the terminal.
RETURN (↵)	Transmit (execute) the current line, or generate a Carriage Return to separate lines of text file.
RUBOUT or DELETE	Delete the last character typed (echoes the character).
CTRL-Z (↑Z)	Terminate the I command's inserting, or separate strings of text in search and substitutions, or place as marker at end of text file.
CTRL-P (↑P)	Echo everything typed or displayed at the lineprinter.
CTRL-S (↑S)	Temporarily halt a long display (strike any key to continue display).
BREAK	Discontinue execution of currently-executing ED command.

*CP/M 2.2

**MP/M

APPENDIX E

ED COMMANDS

Commands	Meaning
nA	Append *n* lines (or 1 line if no n) from the source file to the edit buffer. A "#" for n will append 65535 lines (fill the buffer), and a zero for n will append to fill half of the buffer (number of lines depends on size of your buffer and your system).
+/−nB	Move CP* to beginning if +B, or end if −B of the buffer.
+/−nC	Move CP forward (+) n characters or backward (−) n characters. The CP counts a "carriage return" sequence as two characters (RETURN and LINE FEED).
+/−nD	Delete n characters forward (+), including the CP, or delete n characters backward (−), not including the CP. If no n, delete only the character pointed to by CP.
E	End ED session normally. The E command saves the buffered text and the rest of the source file text in a temporary output file, then renames the output file to the name of the source file (while copying the source file into a backup ".BAK" file to preserve the original source file). ED then terminates, bringing back the system.
nFstring { ↑Z / ↵ }	Find the string of characters n times (if no *n* is specified, find it once). F searches after the CP in the buffer and moves CP to the end of the found string. Follow string with Z terminator if you will add more ED commands; otherwise, use RETURN to terminate string.
H	End ED session, perform an E command, then execute ED again on the new source file (save your file updates and return to edit again).

NOTE: you can substitute a "#" character for *n* in any of the ED commands; it gives n the highest value it can have –65535.

*CP is the character pointer.

I↲	Insert a new line of text after the CP, moving CP to the end of last line inserted. In CP/M 2.2: — If upper case I is used in the command, all text inserted will be in upper case only. — If lower case i is used, then the text will be inserted in upper and lower case.
Itext ↑Z	Insert characters after the CP, moving CP to the end of last character inserted.
nJstring1 ↑Zstring2 ↑Zstring3 {↑Z ↲}	Juxtapose strings of text by finding string1, inserting string2 at the end of string1, and delete all characters up to but no including string3 (juxtapose all three strings of text). CP is moved to the beginning of string3.
+/−nK	"Kill" (delete) the fillowing (+) n lines, including the CP and characters following it on the current line, or delete the previous (−) n lines including the characters behind the CP on the current line.
+/−nL	Move CP to the beginning of the current line if n is zero; otherwise, move CP to the beginning of the current line *and* move it forward (+) n lines or backward (−) n lines.
nMstring {↑Z ↲}	Repeat execution of the string of ED commands n times, if n is greater than 1. If n is zero or one, M will execute the string of commands repeatedly until an error occurs.
nNtext {↑Z ↲}	Search for the *n*th occurrence of text throughout the buffer and source file (terminate text with RETURN or Z to add more commands). N moves the CP to the end of the found text. N will append source lines until it finds text.
O	Omit ED session and return to original source file.

Command	Description
+/−nP	Move CP, display and print *pages* of existing text in buffer. The n is the number of pages (24 lines per page) printed, where +n prints n pages following the CP, and −n prints n pages prior to the CP. 0P (zero for n) will print the current line and page (first 23 lines following the current line). CP is moved to beginning of the printed page.
Q	Quit with *no* file alterations (leave the temporary file, source file and buffer file intact). Q returns you to the system. The ".BAK" backup file for the source file is *not* created, but if there was a previous ".BAK"file of the same name, it is *deleted*. (Watch out for this!)
R	Read from the file X$$$$$$.LIB and insert the lines following the CP, moving the CP to the end of the inserted lines (does not empty the ".LIB" file).
Rfilename	Read from the filename .LIB and insert the lines following the CP, moving the CP to the end of the inserted lines (does not empty the ".LIB" file).
nSoldtext ↑Znewtext { ↑Z / ↵ }	Find oldtext in the buffer following CP and substitute newtext for it; repeat the sequence n times if n is greater than one.
+/−nT	If n is not specified, or if n is 1, type (display) the characters following the CP to the end of the line. If n is zero, type (display) the characters on the current line up to but not including the CP. If n is positive (+), display the following n lines including the current line. If n is negative (−), display the previous n lines not including the current line, and display the characters on the current line up to but not including the CP. The command sequence "B#T" will display the entire buffer.
+/−U	Translate all lower case characters input (typed in or inserted) to UPPER CASE if +U, or turn off translation by executing −U.
V	Turn on line number display (line numbers are not actually in the file) for lines in the buffer.
*CP is the character pointer.	

0V	Display the number of free bytes left in the buffer and the total memory size of the buffer (in decimal numbers). For example, in the display "27648/28832", "27648" are the number of bytes free, and "28832" are the number of bytes, total, in the current buffer.
nW	Write out to the temporary output file with the ".$$$" extension the following n lines from the CP (including the current line). If no n, write out only the current line.
nX	Copies the following n lines of text to the file X$$$$$$$.LIB (does not delete original lines). Retrieve lines using R command. If n is zero, this command will *delete* the file X$$$$$$$.LIB.
**nZ	Suspend the ED program for n clock ticks (approximately *n* seconds).
+/−n	Perform a "+/−nLT" command sequence.
n:	Move CP to beginning of line number n.
n1::n2	Specify a range of line numbers beginning with n1 and ending with n2. If either n1 or n2 is missing, substitute for it "the current line."
*CP is the character pointer.	

APPENDIX F

PIP DEVICE NAMES

LOGICAL DEVICES

CON:	for "console" or terminal, including keyboard and display (Input/Output)
RDR:	for paper tape or card reader (input only)
PUN:	for paper tape or card punch (output only)
LST:	for "listing" device like a line printer (output only).

PHYSICAL DEVICES

TTY:	for a console or terminal, a reader, a punch, or a list device. (teletype)
CRT:	for a console or terminal, or list device (Cathode Ray Tube).
PTR:	for a paper tape or card reader device.
PTP:	for a paper tape or card punch device.
LPT:	for a list device (line printer).
UC1:	for a user-defined console or terminal.
UR1:	for a user-defined reader.
UR2:	for a second user-defined reader.
UP1:	for a user-defined output (punch) device.
UP2:	for a second user-defined output (punch) device.
UL1:	for a user-defined listing device.
NOTE:	BAT: is not included, since it only re-assigns the values for RDR: and LST: (see "Assigning Devices").

APPENDIX G

PIP KEYWORDS

NUL:	send 40 "nulls" (ASCII code 0) to the device, usually a punch device for output. Example, where PROG.HEX is sent to the punch: *PUN:=PROG.HEX,NULL: ↵
EOF:	send an end-of-file (ASCII ↑Z) to the device (sent automatically by PIP during ASCII text file transfers, and only needed for special cases). Example: *PUN:=NUL:,X.ASM,EOF:,NULL: ↵ This example sends 40 nulls to the punch device, followed by a copy of the file X.ASM, followed by the end-of-file character (↑Z and 40 more nulls.
PRN:	same as LST: (Send to the printer), except that tabs are expanded every eighth character, lines are numbered (as in the ED program), and page ejects (form feeds) are inserted every 60 lines (to advance the printer paper to the next page), with an initial page eject. Example: *PRN:=SAMPLE.TXT ↵
INP:	special input device code which can be "patched" into the PIP program itself (you must write the patch in assembly language and add it to PIP). PIP receives the input character by character by calling a location in memory (103H) and storing the data starting at location 109H (parity bit must be zero—use the Z parameter).
OUT:	special output device code which can be "patched" into the PIP program itself, like INP: described above. PIP calls location 106H and sends the data in register C (each character). Note to assembly language programmers: locations 109H through 1FFH of PIP memory image are not used and can be replaced with code for special-purpose device drivers (use DDT—the CP/M Debugger supplied by Digital Research with CP/M or MP/M). Examples: *GIZMO.CLK=INP: ↵ *(input from special device is stored in file GIZMO.CLK)* *OUT:=GIZMO.CLK ↵ *(copy of GIZMO.CLK is sent to the special device)*

APPENDIX H

PIP PARAMETERS

B	Block mode transfer. PIP puts data in a buffer until it reads an ASCII "x-off" character (↑S) from the device. PIP then clears the disk buffer and returns for more data. The size of the buffer depends on the size of your system (see the documentation provided with your system). Use this parameter to transfer data from a continuously reading device like a cassette player or reader. Example: *ENUFF.TXT=RDR: [B] ↵
Dn	PIP will delete characters which extend past column n (vertical columns on your terminal) while copying text files. Use this to truncate long lines if you are sending a file to a narrow device. Example: *PRN:=LONG.TXT[D52] ↵
E	Echo (redisplay) all copy operations on the terminal screen as they are being performed. Example: *COPY.TXT=SOURCE.TXT,S2.TXT,S3.TXT,S4.TXT[E] ↵
F	PIP will filter form feeds from the file (i.e., remove them). You can also use the P parameter to insert new form feeds.
Gn	Get file from user area n (CP/M version 2.2 and MP/M).
H	Hexadecimal data transfer: PIP checks all data for proper Intel hexadecimal format (see "Notes About Copying Into Machine-Code (HEX) Files").
I	Ignore ":00" records in the transfer of Intel hex format files (automatically sets the H parameter).
L	Translate all upper-case characters to lower-case.

N	Add line numbers to each line copied into new file (starting at line 1). Each line number is followed by a colon. Leading zeros (e.g., 003) are deleted, unless you specify the "N2" parameter. "N2" leaves the leading zeroes and inserts a tab space after the numbers. You can expand tab spaces using the T parameter.
O	Object file transfer (for non-ASCII files): PIP ingores the physical end of the file during concatenation (see "Concatenating Files" in Chapter 2).
Pn	PIP will include page ejects at every n line (with an initial page eject). If n is 1 (or if you don't specify n), page ejects occur every 60 lines. If you also use the F parameter, PIP removes the form feeds before inserting page ejects.
Qstring ↑Z	PIP will quit copying from the device or file when it finds the string of characters you specify (a string is a group of characters; e.g., STRING105%). You end your string with a ↑Z (CTRL and Z simultaneously). See "Copying Portions of Files" in Chapter 2.
R	Read (copy) system ($SYS) files; also performs a "W" parameter operation (CP/M version 2.2 and MP/M).
Sstring ↑Z	PIP will start copying from the device or file when it finds the string of characters you specify. End your string with a ↑Z. See "Copying Portions of Files" in Chapter 2.
Tn	Expand the tab space to every nth column during the transfer of text files. You create a tab space in a text file using ↑I; this parameter will expand the tab space from its usually fixed column amount.
U	Translate all lower-case characters to upper-case during the copying of the text files.
V	PIP will verify that data has been copied correctly by rereading the new copy file afterwards (copy file cannot be a device) and displaying a message if the copy was successful.
W	Overwrite (delete) read-only files (ignores the $R/O attribute). (CP/M version 2.2 and MP/M only.)
Z	Turn the parity bit to zero on inputs of ASCII characters. Use this parameter especially if you are inputting from the INP: patch device.

Here are examples of PIP expressions with parameters:

```
*LST:=SAMPLE.TXT[NT8P60]
```

This expression sends the file SAMPLE.TXT to the list device (LST:), with line numbers, tabs expanded to every eighth character column, and page ejects at every 60 lines.
NOTE: the PRN: device assumes these parameters; if the listing device were assigned to PRN:, the above example could be rewritten:

```
*PRN:=SAMPLE.TXT
```

APPENDIX I

CP/M (AND MP/M) COMMAND SUMMARY

COMMAND	CP/M VERSION 1.4	CP/M VERSION 2.2	MP/M VERSION 1
ABORT			X
ASM	X	X	X
ATTACH			X
CONSOLE			X
DDT	X	X	X
DIR	X	X	X
DSKRESET			X
DUMP	X	X	X
ED	X	X	X
ERA	X	X	X
ERAQ			X
GENHEX			X
GENMOD			X
GENSYS	X	X	X
LOAD	X	X	X
MOVCPM	X	X	X
MPMLDR			X
MPMSTAT			X
PIP	X	X	X

COMMAND	CP/M VERSION 1.4	CP/M VERSION 2.2	MP/M VERSION 1
PRLCOM			X
REN	X	X	X
SAVE	X	X	X
SCHED			X
SPOOL			X
STAT	X	X	X
STOPSPLR			X
SUBMIT	X	X	X
SYSGEN	X	X	X
TOD			X
TYPE	X	X	X
USER			X
XSUB		X	X

APPENDIX J

COMMAND EDITING CONTROLS

COMMON CONTROLS

rubout/delete	delete and echo last character
CTRL-U or CTRL-X	delete line
CTRL-R	retype line
CTRL-E	continue on next line
CTRL-C	reboot CP/M

OTHERS

CTRL-D	detach console (MP/M)
CTRL-H	backspace
CTRL-J (line feed)	terminate input
CTRL-M (carriage return)	terminate command
CTRL-P	printer on-off
CTRL-Q	secure the printer (MP/M)
CTRL-S	stop/restart console output

APPENDIX K

EXTENSION TYPES

Extension	Type	Example
COM	Required Command file of a transient command (program).	PIP.COM LOAD.COM
ASM	Required for assembly language source (text) files used with ASM command.	PROG1.ASM PATCH.ASM
PRN	Required for the listing file of the assembly language program.	PROG1.PRN PATCH.PRN
PRL	Required for MP/M relocatable programs.	RDT.PRL
HEX	Required for program file in "hex" format (machine language), which is ready to be LOADed.	PROG1.HEX PATCH.HEX
RSP	Required for MP/M "resident system programs."	SPOOL.RSP
BAS	Required for BASIC program source (text) files.	PROGBAS.BAS
INT	Required for BASIC program intermediate file for execution (already compiled).	PROGBAS.INT
BAK	Created by ED (text editor) as a backup copy of file before it is altered.	LETTER.BAK
$$$	Temporary (scratch) files created and normally erased by ED and other programs.	LETTER.$$$
SUB	Text file with CP/M built-in or transient commands or programs; to be executed batch style by the SUBMIT program.	TRANSFORM.SUB

APPENDIX L

SUPPLIES (CHECKLIST)

- ☐ Blank diskettes
- ☐ Printwheel
- ☐ Ribbons
- ☐ Printer paper
- ☐ Computer manual
- ☐ Printer manual
- ☐ CRT terminal manual
- ☐ CP/M documentation
- ☐ Application programs documentation
- ☐ System diskette
- ☐ Application programs diskettes

APPENDIX M

COMPUTER ROOM ORGANIZATION (CHECKLIST)

☐ Sufficient ventilation

☐ No object on computer ventilation outlets

☐ Non-metallic file holders for diskettes

☐ Sufficient computer supplies (see separate checklist)

☐ All required manuals

☐ Record of correct CRT terminal settings

☐ Record of correct printer settings

☐ Maintenance record

☐ Phone numbers for maintenance and assistance

☐ No telephone close to work area
(a phone ringing on top of a diskette or a disk drive wipes the diskette out)

☐ No screwdrivers close to work area (magnetic)

☐ No liquids in computer room unless you are well insured

☐ No smoking in close proximity to disk drives

☐ No moving or shaking of disk drives

☐ Posted turn-on procedure

☐ No static-prone carpeting

APPENDIX N

FAILURE CHECKLIST

NOTHING WORKS

- ☐ Check mechanical connections:
  - ☐ Power cords
  - ☐ Cables
  - ☐ Switches "on"
  - ☐ Fuses

PRINTER OUT

- ☐ Try the printer in "local"
- ☐ Execute CTRL P from the console
- ☐ Check all settings
- ☐ Re-insert paper properly
- ☐ Check fuse

PRINTER DOES NOT STOP

- ☐ Hit CTRL P
- ☐ Hit CTRL C
- ☐ Turn printer off

SYSTEM OUT

- ☐ Reboot (CTRL C)
- ☐ Stop the system and execute complete restart

DISK DRIVE ON CONTINUOUSLY

- ☐ No diskette in. Insert one.
- ☐ Remove diskette, restart procedure

GROSSLY ANOMALOUS BEHAVIOR

- ☐ Suspect operator error. Try again. Check for correct system diskette and correct settings on printer.
- ☐ Suspect damaged system diskette. Replace with fresh copy.
- ☐ Suspect damaged application program. Replace with fresh copy.
- ☐ Turn everything off. Try again.
- ☐ Suspect hardware failure.

APPENDIX O

BASIC TROUBLESHOOTING RULES

- In this order:
  1. Suspect operator error
  2. Suspect damaged diskette
  3. Suspect software
  4. Suspect hardware
- Keep detailed documentation about the failure.
- Try again from scratch. Use fresh diskettes. Check all mechanical settings and connections.

Index

SYBEX LIBRARY

AUDIO COURSES

REF. #	TITLE	
S1	Introduction to Microprocessors	(2½ hours)
S2	Programming Microprocessors	(2½ hours)
S3	Designing a Microprocessor	(2½ hours)
SB1	Microprocessors	(12 hours)
SB2	Programming Microprocessors	(10 hours)
SB3	Military Microprocessor Systems	(6 hours)
SB5	Bit-Slice	(6 hours)
SB6	Industrial Microprocessor Systems	(4½ hours)
SB7	Microprocessor Interfacing Techniques	(6 hours)
SB10	Introduction to Personal Computing	(2½ hours)

BOOKS

C200A	Your First Computer
C201	Microprocessors: From Chips to Systems
C207	Microprocessor Interfacing Techniques
C280	Programming the Z80
C281	Programming the Z8000
C300	The CP/M Handbook with MP/M
X1	Microprocessor Lexicon
Z10	Microprogrammed APL Implementation

The 6502 Series

C202	Programming the 6502
D302	6502 Applications Book
G402	6502 Games

PASCAL

P310	Introduction to PASCAL
P320	The PASCAL Handbook

BASIC

B245	Inside BASIC Games
B250	Fifty BASIC Exercises

SOFTWARE

BAS 65	BAS 65™ Cross Assembler in Basic
S402	6502 Games Cassette
S302	6502 Application Program Cassette
S6580-APL(T)	8080 Simulator for Apple II Cassette
S6580-APL(D)	8080 Simulator for Apple II Diskette
S6580-KIM	8080 Simulator for KIM I Cassette

SELF-STUDY SYSTEMS

CPT	Computeacher™
CPTG	Games Board™

FOR A COMPLETE CATALOGUE OF OUR PUBLICATIONS

U.S.A.
2344 Sixth Street
Berkeley, California 94710
Tel: (415) 848-8233
Telex: 336311

EUROPE
18 rue Planchat
75020 Paris, France
Tel: (1) 3703275
Telex: 211801